REWARDING STRIVERS

REWARDING STRIVERS

HELPING LOW-INCOME STUDENTS
SUCCEED IN COLLEGE

Richard D. Kahlenberg, editor

A CENTURY FOUNDATION BOOK

THE CENTURY FOUNDATION PRESS • NEW YORK

The Century Foundation sponsors and supervises timely analyses of economic policy, foreign affairs, and domestic political issues. Not-for-profit and nonpartisan, it was founded in 1919 and endowed by Edward A. Filene.

LIBRARY OF CONGRESS CATALOGUING-IN-PUBLICATION DATA

Rewarding strivers : helping low-income students succeed in college / Richard D. Kahlenberg, editor.
   p. cm.
Includes bibliographical references and index.
ISBN 978-0-87078-516-0
1. Low-income college students--Services for--United States. 2. Education, Higher--Economic aspects--United States. 3. College students--United States-- Economic conditions. 4. College dropouts--United States--Prevention. 5. Social classes--United States. I. Kahlenberg, Richard D. II. Title.
  LC4069.6.R48 2010
  378.1'9826240973--dc22
           2010006569
Manufactured in the United States of America
Cover design and art: Claude Goodwin

FOREWORD

For two centuries, Americans have enjoyed increasing access to education. In fact, the vast expansion in postsecondary education in the decades since World War II was built upon a foundation of universal schooling for children. It is hard to overstate the positive impact these developments have had on the nation's economic progress, scientific leadership, cultural evolution, and political life.

The expansion of higher education has not only been understood as being good for the nation as a whole, but also recognized as a critical factor in achieving individual prosperity and satisfaction. The spread of these benefits has played an important role in reducing the deep inequalities of previous eras. Access to higher education has expanded from a privilege largely enjoyed by elites to one available to many of the offspring of middle-class citizens. The GI Bill, enacted near the end of World War II, opened up college for eight million veterans. The mushrooming land grant institutions and other state college systems added tens of thousands of places for new students. By the late-twentieth century, California offered postsecondary educational opportunities to just about all who wanted them

Over these decades of booming college growth, one of the great disappointments was that not enough Americans of color were moving through the system and achieving the economic and social rewards that come with higher degrees. In response, affirmative action programs at the college level became common as many schools attempted to diversify their student body. These programs inevitably came under attack and have been curtailed as a result of a series of court decisions, referenda, and political actions by state government. At the same time, some have been questioning whether affirmative action based on race or ethnic background was the appropriate way to broaden educational access. Fresh research became available indicating that students from lower-income groups, whatever their race or social standing, had little chance of achieving college enrollment, especially in the more selective institutions. A growing number of education leaders thus began to raise questions about how to change the criteria for expanding opportunities and diversifying schools based on the economic backgrounds of prospective students.

In the new century, a substantial group of leaders from the higher education community, drawing on the seminal work of Anthony Carnevale and Stephen Rose, began to explore these issues and seek to redress the inherent inequities that become apparent when one looks closely at the evidence. According to Carnevale and Rose's 2004 Century Foundation study, for example, just 10 percent of students at the most selective 146 institutions come from families in the bottom socioeconomic half of the population. Likewise, Thomas Mortenson of the Pell Institute has found that roughly one in two students from families making more than $90,000 obtains a bachelor's degree by age twenty-four, compared with one in seventeen students from families making less than $35,000. The Jeffersonian ideal of cultivating the natural aristocracy of talent from students of all backgrounds largely has been forgotten.

The statistics offer a challenge to the prevailing system of admissions—a challenge that is especially sharp at the most selective institutions. The premium value of a degree from these colleges and universities is widely recognized. The career paths open to college graduates—and the socioeconomic stratification that they engender—are partially a reflection of the tracking that is embedded in the admissions policy of different groups of postsecondary institutions. The impact of this system on careers and income prospects is even more severe for the large number of students who graduate in the top half of their high school class, but do not go on to college.

As part of our continuing work in this area, The Century Foundation sponsored this volume, reflecting the latest contribution by three of the outstanding voices in this field: Edward B. Fiske, the former education editor and writer for the *New York Times*, and Anthony Carnevale and Jeff Strohl of the Georgetown University Center on Education and the Workforce.

This research is part of a longstanding effort at The Century Foundation to put social mobility at the center of education efforts. In recent years, we have published several books on education, including Richard Rothstein's *The Way We Were? Myths and Realities of America's Student Achievement* (1998); Richard Kahlenberg's *All Together Now: Creating Middle-Class Schools through Public School Choice* (2001); Joan Lombardi's *Time to Care: Redesigning Child Care to Promote Education, Support Families, and Build Communities* (2002); Jeffrey Henig's *Spin Cycle: How Research Is Used in Policy Debates—The Case of Charter Schools* (2008); and Gordon MacInnes's *In Plain Sight: Simple, Difficult Lessons from New Jersey's Expensive Effort to Close the Achievement Gap* (2009).

In addition, we have supported several volumes of essays on education edited by Kahlenberg, including *A Notion at Risk: Preserving Public Education as an Engine for Social Mobility* (2000); *Public School Choice vs. Private School Vouchers* (2003); *America's Untapped Resource: Low-Income Students in Higher Education* (2004); and *Improving on No Child Left Behind: Getting Education Reform Back on Track* (2008). The Century Foundation also sponsored a task force, chaired by former Connecticut governor Lowell Weicker, Jr., that issued a report, *Divided We Fail: Coming Together through Public School Choice* (2002).

In the near future, we will be publishing an edited volume on the use of legacy preferences in college admissions.

Rewarding Strivers takes up and expands upon this body of work. The authors conclude, after assessing all the evidence, that "upward mobility in the United States has slowed to European levels, in large part due to differences in postsecondary opportunity"—a startling and deeply troubling conclusion. The contributions to this volume outline two ways—one already in place, the second aspirational—for universities to renew their commitment to serving the public interest by promoting social mobility. In the first, Ted Fiske describes and evaluates the "Carolina Covenant," which provides substantial financial aid and support programs for low-income students attending the University of North Carolina at Chapel Hill. In the second, Anthony Carnevale and Jeff Strohl articulate a coherent and concrete way for universities to provide a leg up to economically disadvantaged students in selective college admissions.

On behalf of the Trustees of The Century Foundation, I thank the authors for this important contribution to our understanding of these issues—issues that go to the heart of our notions about opportunity in America. I also offer special thanks to the Nellie Mae Education Foundation, which provided a grant to make the research by Carnevale and Strohl possible.

Richard C. Leone, PRESIDENT
THE CENTURY FOUNDATION

Contents

1

INTRODUCTION

Richard D. Kahlenberg

In January 2004, The Century Foundation published *America's Untapped Resource: Low-Income Students in Higher Education*, which included a statistic that struck a chord with the public and some key leaders in American higher education. At the most selective 146 colleges and universities, according to the volume's chapter by Anthony Carnevale and Stephen Rose, 74 percent of students came from the top socioeconomic quarter of the population, and just 3 percent from the poorest.[1] In other words, one was twenty-five times as likely to run into a rich kid as a poor kid on the nation's selective campuses.

Coming on the heels of the University of Michigan's victory defending race-based affirmative action in the U.S. Supreme Court, Carnevale and Rose's finding helped move discussions of diversity to consider not just race, but also larger issues of socioeconomic status. Their findings indicated that it might be time to move beyond the narrow question of "what color skin the rich kids should have," as critic Walter Benn Michaels acidly observed.[2]

In the national conversation that followed, the voices of a trio of higher education leaders proved particularly important. In February 2004, then-Harvard University president Lawrence Summers, citing Carnevale and Rose's research, announced an economic diversity

1

initiative that would eliminate the family financial contribution for students from families making less than $40,000 a year, increase recruiting and admission of low-income students, and assist in creating a larger pipeline of highly qualified low-income students.[3] In April 2004, in a series of lectures at the University of Virginia, William Bowen, the former president of Princeton University, called for selective universities to provide a thumb on the admissions scale for socioeconomically disadvantaged students as well as under-represented minorities.[4] (The support for class-based affirmative action was a stunning reversal for Bowen, who had dismissed the idea six years earlier as impractical.)[5] And in May 2004, Anthony Marx, the president of Amherst College, delivered a stirring commencement address laying out the case for increasing the salience of economic diversity, something Amherst now explicitly factors into admissions decisions.[6] In June 2004, The Century Foundation assembled a small group of university and college presidents and researchers, including Summers, Bowen, Marx, and Carnevale, to discuss the growing push for economic diversity in higher education. Now, several years later, the book you are holding is an indirect product of that meeting.

In the intervening years, the issue of class inequality in higher education has gained increasing salience. A slew of newspaper and magazine articles and books focused sharp attention on the gaping economic inequalities on campuses, including *Equity and Excellence in American Higher Education*, William Bowen, Martin Kurzweil, and Eugene Tobin's book-length explication of Bowen's University of Virginia lectures; Jerome Karabel's *The Chosen: The Hidden History of Exclusion at Harvard, Yale and Princeton*; Daniel Golden's *The Price of Admission: How America's Ruling Class Buys Its Way into Elite Colleges—and Who Gets Left Outside the Gates*; Walter Benn Michaels's *The Trouble with Diversity: How We Learned to Love Identity and Ignore Inequality*; *College Access: Opportunity or Privilege?* edited by Michael S. McPherson and Morton Owen Schapiro; Peter Schmidt's *Color and Money: How Rich White Kids are Winning the War Over College Affirmative Action*; Peter Sacks's *Tearing Down the Gates: Confronting the Class Divide in American Education*; and William Bowen, Matthew Chingos, and Michael McPherson's *Crossing the Finish Line: Completing College at America's Public Universities*.[7]

It was not merely journalists and academics who wrote about these economic inequities; the commitments by Harvard and Amherst to greater socioeconomic diversity were part of a tidal wave of new, more generous financial aid programs. Among the leaders was the University of North Carolina (UNC) at Chapel Hill, which announced in October 2003 the Carolina Covenant—a free financial ride (no loans) for high-achieving, low-income students.[8] So committed to the issue was UNC's chancellor, James Moeser, and financial aid officer, Shirley Ort, that the two organized a national conference, held in Chapel Hill in September 2006, that identified 24 schools with new financial aid initiatives. A year later, the number had risen to 44.[9] Today, it stands at nearly 100.[10]

With all this flurry of activity, hopes were high that serious progress was being made to open up access to higher education for low-income students, just as a generation before, higher education affirmatively had increased racial and ethnic diversity on campus. So it was deeply discouraging, then, that the early reports suggest that progress is slow, and that indeed most selective institutions actually are headed in the wrong direction regarding economic diversity.

In May 2008, the *Chronicle of Higher Education* published a study finding that the percentage of students receiving Pell Grants declined at the wealthiest 75 private and 39 public colleges and universities between the 2004–05 and 2006–07 academic years. In the 75 private institutions with the largest endowments, 13.1 percent of undergraduates in 2006–07 received Pell Grants, which typically go to students from families earning less than $40,000 a year, down from 14.3 percent two years earlier. In 39 public institutions with endowments of $500 million or more, 18 percent were Pell Grant recipients in 2006–07, compared with 19.6 percent two years earlier. Amherst was one exception, as Pell Grant recipients increased from 13.8 percent to 17.1 percent during that time period. Harvard also has demonstrated recent progress, with the percentage of its undergraduates receiving Pell Grants increasing from 9.4 percent in 2003 to 15 percent in 2008.[11]

The economic downturn has put pressure on colleges and universities to reduce financial aid packages. As Morton Schapiro, then president of Williams College, noted in the spring of 2009, "You've always been in an advantaged position to be rich and smart. Now you're at an even greater advantage."[12] Compounding the lack of economic diversity in the freshman class are high attrition rates among low-income students, a problem spotlighted by the Gates Foundation and the Obama administration. Of those who enroll in a four-year college, 78 percent of affluent children of educated parents graduate by age 26, compared with just 36 percent of low-income students whose parents are not college graduates.[13] Taking the problems of access and attrition together, 68 percent of students from affluent educated families receive a bachelor's degree, compared with just 9 percent of students from low-income, less-educated families. This socioeconomic gap—in which advantaged children are seven times as likely to get bachelor's degrees as disadvantaged children—is even larger than the black/white attainment gap of two-to-one.[14]

Meanwhile, new clouds have appeared on the horizon, threatening the future of race-based affirmative action programs at leading colleges and universities. When *America's Untapped Resource* was published in 2004, shortly after the 2003 U.S. Supreme Court decision upholding affirmative action at the University of Michigan, proponents of race-based programs were triumphant. But then, in 2006, rank-and-file voters in Michigan overwhelmingly voted to reverse the decision in the state, barring racial preferences at the University of Michigan and other public colleges and universities in Michigan. In 2008, another anti-affirmative action initiative passed in Nebraska (and one was narrowly defeated in Colorado). In so voting, Michigan and Nebraska joined California (1996), Washington (1998), and Florida (1999) in banning racial preferences in university admissions (Florida's ban was by executive order). Ward Connerly, the architect of these initiatives, has plans to bring anti-affirmative action initiatives to the states of Arizona and Missouri in November 2010.[15] Already, a quarter of the U.S. population now live in states where affirmative action is banned at public universities.

Perhaps more significantly, changes in the makeup of the U.S. Supreme Court may jeopardize the breadth of the 5–4 ruling in *Grutter* v. *Bollinger,* sustaining affirmative action at the University of Michigan Law School. The justice who cast the swing vote in that case, Sandra Day O'Connor, has been replaced with the much more conservative Samuel Alito. The court's new pivotal vote is Justice

Anthony Kennedy, who dissented in *Grutter*. Indeed, in 2007, the newly constituted court ruled 5–4 against using race in K–12 education in *Parents Involved in Community Schools (PICS) v. Seattle School Board No. 1*, a worrisome harbinger for those supportive of race-based affirmative action in higher education.

Although the *PICS* decision did favorably cite the *Grutter* decision, it is important to note that Seattle and Louisville school officials had a more sympathetic case than did the University of Michigan to the extent that there was no issue of "merit," no argument that a given student "deserved" to go to a particular nonselective elementary or secondary school because she worked hard and "earned" it.[16] The "non-merit-based" nature of the K–12 decisions, Justice Stephen Breyer argued, was part of what made the Seattle and Louisville plans "more narrowly tailored than the race-conscious admissions plans that this Court approved in *Grutter*."[17] The fact that five justices struck down the fairly mild use of race when the fundamental issue of merit was not involved does not bode well for the next occasion when the Supreme Court revisits affirmative action in higher education.

Although there is good reason to believe that the Supreme Court will not overturn *Grutter* directly—out of respect for precedent and given its reaffirmation of *Grutter* in *PICS*—the court could severely limit the ability of colleges and universities to use race by exploiting a provision in Justice O'Connor's holding for the court in *Grutter*. In that decision, the court declared that universities must engage in "periodic reviews to determine whether racial preferences are still necessary to achieve student body diversity." The opinion then pointed to universities in California, Florida, and Washington, which were "engaged in experimenting with a wide variety of alternative approaches."[18]

For many years, the courts have required that government explore alternative means before using race—but there is considerable disagreement over how aggressively race-neutral alternatives must be pursued. In *Grutter*, O'Connor applied a very relaxed standard, declaring: "We take the Law School at its word that it would 'like nothing better than to find a race-neutral admissions formula' and will terminate its race-conscious admissions program as soon as practicable."[19] The new swing vote on the court—Justice

Anthony Kennedy—by contrast, used a much tougher standard in both *Grutter* and the Louisville and Seattle cases. In *Grutter*, Kennedy joined with Justices William Rehnquist, Antonin Scalia, and Clarence Thomas in arguing that "Although the Court recites the language of strict scrutiny analysis, its application of that review is unprecedented in its deference."[20] Then, Kennedy wrote separately, emphasizing "Were the courts to apply a searching standard to race-based admissions schemes, that would force educational institutions to seriously explore race-neutral alternatives. The Court, by contrast, is willing to be satisfied by the Law School's profession of its own good faith."[21]

Likewise, the court's rulings invalidated Seattle and Louisville's integration plans because, in Kennedy's words, "the schools could have achieved their stated ends through different means."[22] Before categorizing individuals by race, other methods must first be explored, he said. The court opinion, joined by Kennedy, found that in Seattle, several race-neutral alternatives had been rejected "with little or no consideration" and that Jefferson County had "failed to present any evidence that it considered alternatives."[23] In his dissent, Justice Breyer appeared to detect a heightened form of strict scrutiny, arguing that in fact there were no viable race-neutral alternatives, making the court's requirement one "that in practice would never be met."[24]

Conservative opponents of affirmative action are fully aware of this feature of the *Grutter* decision, and their latest challenge to affirmative action targets this particular vulnerability. In the case of *Fisher v. Texas*, conservative organizations have pressed *Grutter*'s requirement that schools must pursue "a "serious, good faith consideration of workable race-neutral alternatives that will achieve the diversity [it] seeks." They note that after the Fifth Circuit struck down the use of race in the 1996 *Hopwood* decision, Texas adopted a class-based affirmative action plan, combined with a program to admit automatically students in the top 10 percent of every high school, which together produced a net increase in racial diversity compared with the pre-*Hopwood* race-based plan. (African-American and Latino representation grew from 18.8 percent in 1996 to 21.4 percent in 2004.) Given the viability of this program, they say, Texas's decision after *Grutter* to reintroduce racial preferences, as a supplement of the socioeconomic and top 10 percent plan, is unconstitutional. A lower court judge rejected the plaintiff's suit, but in September 2009 the case was appealed to the Fifth Circuit, where it currently resides.[25]

It will be fascinating to watch how Barack Obama, America's first African-American president, handles the question of racial preferences. Whether fair or not, Obama's election to the ultimate office in American society may well undercut already limited public support for the continued use of racial affirmative action. According to a January 2009 *Washington Post*-ABC News poll, the percentage of Americans saying that racism is a "big problem" stands at just 26 percent, down an astounding 28 percentage points from 1996.[26] Obama's election does not usher in a "post-racial" nirvana, as Jabari Asim has written, "but it exposes the fallacy of referring to all black Americans as particularly oppressed."[27] Interestingly, Obama has hinted that he is ready to begin moving in the direction of a class-based affirmative action, famously observing that his own privileged daughters do not deserve a preference in college admissions, and the poor kids of all races do. In emphasizing the primacy of socioeconomic status, Obama's approach parallels that of Dr. Martin Luther King, Jr., who argued for a Bill of Rights for the disadvantaged rather than a Bill of Rights for blacks.[28] (While it is commonly argued that white women are the chief beneficiaries of affirmative action, that is demonstrably false in the context of selective college admissions, where women are over-represented among applicants and are generally held to a higher standard in admissions.)[29]

With race-based affirmative action under attack, and the number of low-income students declining at leading colleges and universities, this volume seeks to advance the discussion by examining two possible promising remedies: an innovative and aggressive new financial aid and support program at the University of North Carolina; and an idea to reward low-income "strivers" through the college admissions process.

FINANCIAL AID AND ACADEMIC SUPPORT
THE CAROLINA COVENANT

In his chapter in this volume, Edward B. Fiske, the former *New York Times* education reporter and editor, provides a fascinating overview of the Carolina Covenant. Begun in the fall of 2004, the Carolina Covenant provides low-income students at the University of North Carolina at Chapel Hill the ability to graduate debt-free through a combination of grants, scholarships, and work-study opportunities. The brainchild of Shirley Ort, director of student aid, and former chancellor James Moeser, the covenant provides guaranteed financial aid to students who come from families earning less than 200 percent of the poverty line (about $44,000 for a family of four). UNC, the nation's first public university, became in 2004 the first public institution of higher education to provide loan-free financial aid—and helped set off a string of new financial aid programs at almost one hundred other universities.[30]

The Carolina Covenant was designed to do three things: provide adequate financial aid to students who need it; send a powerful message that UNC is open to all students, regardless of economic background; and help students succeed and graduate once on campus.[31]

As Fiske notes, a key component of the program is a series of academic and social supports. Rather than simply letting Covenant Scholars sink or swim on their own, the program provides faculty and staff mentoring of first-year students; peer mentoring by experienced Covenant Scholars; special development opportunities such as etiquette dinners and career workshops; and social events for Covenant Scholars. Scholars often participate in ten to twelve hours of weekly work study, but generally do not put in the much more extensive number of job hours that low-income students typically engage in.[32] Faculty support has been strong; more than eighty offered to serve as mentors the first year, even though only fifteen were needed.[33] Funding has been provided in part by an annual dinner co-chaired by UNC basketball coach, Roy Williams, whose own background would have qualified him to be a Covenant Scholar, Fiske says.[34]

Fiske finds that the preliminary outcomes of the financial aid and support programs are quite positive. For one thing, applications from low-income students (those requesting application fee waivers) more than doubled from the introduction of the covenant idea in 2003 through 2009.[35] Moreover, persistence rates among low-income students have increased. In the past, low-income students dropped out at almost four times the rate of wealthy students. In the UNC classes entering in 1997 and 1998, 21 percent of students with family incomes of $30,000 or less neither graduated nor transferred, according to a 2004 study. By comparison, among those from families making more than $100,000, the rate was 5.3 percent.[36] The low-income dropout rate was blamed in part on aversion to taking on debt and having to work long hours at on- and off-campus jobs, which undermined academic success.[37]

Compared with a control group (students entering in 2003 who would have been eligible to be Covenant Scholars had the program existed), Covenant Scholars entering in 2004 were 24 percent less likely to take a term off.[38] Covenant Scholars were also 17 percent less likely to become academically ineligible than the 2003 control group.[39] By year four, 89.6 percent of Covenant Scholars were still in school, compared with 84.3 percent of the 2003 control group and 90.5 percent of all students.[40] Most importantly, 61.9 percent of the 2004 Covenant Scholars graduated within eight semesters, compared with 56.7 percent of the 2003 control group, a 5.2 percentage point increase.[41] Put differently, eight-semester graduation rates increased 9.2 percent.

Still, there is one significant limitation to the program: UNC's insistence that admissions be "need-blind." The term is considered a sign of progressive attitudes in admissions circles, even though to be "color-blind" in admissions would be considered reactionary. One UNC dean, Harold Woodard, told Fiske, "there is no doubt that these students are Carolina material. . . . There has been no lowering of standards. They have not been given a break because of their circumstances." Ort concurred that this is not an "affirmative action" program, and that students are accepted through the normal admissions process. "These scholarships are given to students who are admitted to Chapel Hill on their merits," she told Fiske.[42]

The decision not to provide a leg up in admissions to low-income students, comparable to what is provided for under-represented racial minorities, makes the program less controversial in the eyes of administrators, but it also helps explain the extreme and persistent tilt of UNC's student population toward the wealthy. According to Fiske, 72 percent of freshmen come from families making more than $75,000 a year (usually requiring no financial aid whatsoever) and 54 percent from families making $100,000 or more (compared with 12 percent making that amount statewide).[43] Moreover, according to the *Journal of Blacks in Higher Education*, the proportion of students at UNC who were eligible for Pell Grants remained flat between 2003–04 (14.4 percent) and 2008–09 (14.4 percent).[44] In a 2010 Education Trust report, UNC ranked 43rd out of 50 state flagship universities in percentage of Pell Grant recipients. In Education Trust's "Low-Income Student Access Radio," which considers Pell Grant rates in the context of state demographics, UNC tied for 43rd.[45]

For all its strengths—and there are many—the Carolina Covenant has not significantly increased socioeconomic diversity because it does not take up the critical issue addressed in this volume's second chapter: admissions.

SELECTIVE COLLEGE ADMISSIONS: IDENTIFYING STRIVERS

In their chapter in this volume, Anthony P. Carnevale and Jeff Strohl, of Georgetown University's Center on Education and the Workforce, make a powerful case that if college admissions officers want to be fair—truly meritocratic—they need to consider not only a student's raw academic credentials, but also what obstacles she had to overcome to achieve them. Carnevale, in particular, has been at the task of identifying strivers—students who overcome the odds to do quite well despite various disadvantages—for more than a decade.

In 1999, the *Wall Street Journal* reported that Carnevale, then a high-ranking official at the Educational Testing Service (ETS), was devising a program to identify strivers who scored 200 points above their predicted standardized test score based on fourteen factors, including parents' income, education, and occupation; whether the student speaks English as a second language; and her high school's academic strength and income level. The article caused an enormous stir. The program came under immediate attack from colleges, which did not want to fall under pressure to admit low-income students.[46] And it also came under attack from some civil rights groups, whose leaders worried that an effort to provide affirmative action for low-income students would displace affirmative action for students of color.[47]

At the time, Carnevale noted, a class-based affirmative action program could supplement, rather than replace, race-based affirmative action—an argument that he and Strohl advance in the current iteration of strivers. Nevertheless, ETS quietly abandoned the strivers project. Carnevale and Strohl, by contrast, never gave up on the idea, and their new research outlining how strivers would work is outlined in their chapter.

The chapter begins by noting a disturbing trend: while increasing numbers of low-income students attend college in America, there is heightened stratification within higher education. Just as public elementary and secondary schools saw affluent white flight to suburban schools in the 1970s and 1980s, so higher education is seeing wealthy white flight to selective institutions. Between 1994 and 2006, white student representation declined from 79 percent to 58 percent at less-selective and noncompetitive institutions, while black student representation soared from 11 percent to 28 percent, twice their share of the high school class. Meanwhile, the over-representation of whites at highly selective institutions increased during this time period, as did the under-representation of blacks and Hispanics.[48]

This stratification matters, the authors note, because selective colleges, on average, provide many advantages. Colleges with low selectivity spend about $12,000 per student, compared with $92,000 per student at the most selective institutions.[49] Moreover, per-pupil subsidies at selective universities are eight times greater than at nonselective institutions.[50] In the wealthiest 10 percent of institutions, for example, students pay $0.20 for each $1 spent on them, compared with poorest 10 percent of colleges, where students pay $0.78 cents for each $1 spent on them.[51]

Carnevale and Strohl also find that selective colleges and universities graduate equally qualified students at much higher levels—a finding reinforced by William Bowen's new study.[52] (At the extreme, only 10 percent of those who start community college end up with a bachelor's degree.)[53] Moreover, extensive empirical data support Justice Sandra Day O'Connor's view that America's leadership class derives disproportionately from the ranks of top colleges and universities. As Thomas Dye's research has found, 54 percent of America's corporate leaders and 42 percent of government leaders are graduates of just twelve institutions—Harvard, Yale, the University of Chicago, Stanford, Columbia, MIT, Cornell, Northwestern, Princeton, Johns Hopkins, the University of Pennsylvania, and Dartmouth.[54]

In light of these various findings, the Obama administration's effort to pour additional funds into the community college system, while surely a welcome development, can be seen as analogous to the effort to make "separate" primary and secondary schools "equal." In addition to strengthening community colleges, which Carnevale and Strohl advocate, they say attempts must be made to integrate socio-economically the selective institutions themselves.

In a chapter replete with interesting findings, one stands out above all others: on the verbal and math sections of the SAT, where scores range from a low of 400 combined points to a high of 1600, all other things being equal, the least-advantaged student is predicted to score 544 while the most advantaged student will score 1328.[55] The gap is an astonishing 784 points, accounting for 65.3 percent of the 1200-point range of possible scores. It is as if, in a hundred-yard dash, rich kids start sixty-five yards ahead of poor kids when the gun goes off. The difference between the least-advantaged student and the average student (scoring 1054) is 544 points, while the disparity between the average student and the most-advantged student is 274 points.[56]

Of course, admissions officers have long known that test score results do not reflect the full potential of students who have faced economic and racial obstacles. As Amherst admissions officer Tom Parker said of one low-income African-American first generation college student who scored 1200 on the verbal and math portions of the SAT, "Tony Jack with his pure intelligence—had he been raised in Greenwich, he would have been a 1500 kid."[57] But what Carnevale and Stroh do, for the first time, is to quantify the predicted SAT gap between the least and most advantaged and break out for colleges and university administrators the rough weights of various disadvantages. For example, having a father who is a laborer as opposed to a physician costs an applicant 48 SAT points, on average. Attending a school where 90 percent of classmates are eligible for free and reduced-price lunch predicts an SAT 38 points lower than one where no peers receive subsidized lunch. Being black (as opposed to white) costs 56 points, on average.[58]

In outlining these data, Carnevale and Strohl make clear they do not believe institutions should mechanically add points to the SAT

scores of disadvantaged students; rather, the authors wish to provide general guidance on the depth of the obstacles faced by disadvantaged applicants. Moreover, the authors note, there is a distinc-
tion between readiness and deservedness. A very deserving student
who scores 700 on the combined verbal and math SAT—and would
have scored 1484 if she had had all the advantages—nevertheless
is unlikely to survive at a selective college. The authors note that
universities would want to set their own individual cutoffs for how
deep in the SAT pool they are able to go and still have students
succeed and graduate.

Having said that, Carnevale and Strohl note, for selective colleges and universities nationally, there are many talented students
who could do the work and succeed. As Carnevale found in an
earlier study, a pure class-based affirmative action model could
increase the representation of students from the bottom socioeconomic half from 10 percent currently to 38 percent at the most
selective 146 colleges and universities, and graduation rates would
be similar to those found under the existing system, which provides
preferences for legacies, underrepresented minorities, and athletes.[59]
These findings are buttressed by others who observe that many low-
income students significantly "undermatch," attending institutions
that are less selective than ones to which they could be admitted.[60]
Likewise, Carnevale and Stroh's findings track with research from
the Jack Kent Cooke Foundation and Civic Enterprises, which
identified 3.4 million high-achieving, low-income K–12 students,
defined as those coming from families below the national median
income and scoring in the top academic quartile.[61] Astoundingly,
Carnevale and Strohl find, only 44 percent of high-performing (top
quartile), low-income students go on to a four-year college at all.
The authors note, "our lowest-performing affluent students go to
college at a higher rate than the highest performing youth from the
least-advantaged families."[62]

Although race per se accounts for just 56 of the 784-point gap
between the most- and least–advantaged students, Carnevale and
Strohl make clear that they do not believe class preferences should
replace racial preferences, noting that racial discrimination continues to stunt the lives of African-American students. As a legal matter,
however, courts have never recognized ongoing societal discrimination as a justification for racial preferences. In the 1978 *Regents of*

the University of California v. *Bakke* case, where the Supreme Court upheld the use of race as a factor to promote diversity in education, the court flatly rejected the idea of racial preferences as a remedy for generalized discrimination in society—a rejection reaffirmed in the 2003 *Grutter* case.[63]

Still, in the event that the U.S. Supreme Court significantly curtails the use of racial preferences in college and university admissions, Carnevale and Strohl leave open a tantalizing possibility for preserving racial diversity: using family wealth. On the merits, research finds that having low net worth has an independent effect on one's educational chances, net of income, because it affects whether one can afford to buy a home in a good neighborhood with good schools, and whether a student has the confidence that if she works hard she can afford to attend college.[64] And while black median income is 62 percent of white income, black median net worth is just 12 percent of white net worth.[65] On some outcomes—such as college completion rates—comparing students from families of similar net wealth completely eliminates the black/white gap.[66]

While Carnevale and Strohl's analysis does incorporate wealth— and still finds a 56 SAT point "penalty" for being black—the measure of wealth employed (self-reported savings for college) is weak.[67] As Carnevale has noted, using a sophisticated and robust wealth factor in admissions very well could maintain levels of racial diversity currently achieved by employing race-based affirmative action.[68]

How can we reconcile the finding that discrimination continues to affect the life chances of African Americans negatively with the idea that economic affirmative action—including a strong wealth variable—could produce substantial levels of racial diversity? The answer is that the right set of economic criteria may be able to capture past and current instances of racial discrimination. Racial discrimination in the employment sector is reflected in lower earnings for black families. Likewise, ongoing discrimination in the housing market is reflected in the fact that black and Latino students are much more likely to live in neighborhoods with concentrated poverty than whites of similar income.[69] In fact, one recent study found that black families with incomes in excess of $60,000 live in neighborhoods with higher poverty rates than white families earning less than

$30,000.[70] Counting whether a student lives in concentrated poverty when deciding college admissions will benefit students of color disproportionately. Most powerful of all, because wealth is accumulated over generations, it reflects in some important measure the legacy of slavery and segregation as well as ongoing discrimination in the housing market.[71]

The larger question is, what will it take for universities to add Carnevale and Strohl's concern about class diversity to their strong commitment to racial diversity? Carnevale's earlier research found that race-based affirmative action triples the representation of blacks and Hispanics at the most selective 146 institutions, but that universities do virtually nothing to boost socioeconomic representation per se.[72] Their finding was confirmed by Bowen and colleagues in a study of nineteen selective institutions.[73] A new analysis by Thomas Espenshade and Alexandria Walton Radford likewise finds that, at highly selective private institutions, the boost provided to African-American applicants is worth 310 SAT points (on a 1600 scale), compared with 130 points for poor students.[74] This practice—a little affirmative action for the poor, and a lot for African-American students—is the mirror opposite of what would be needed to counteract the various disadvantages weighed by Carnevale and Strohl (56 points for African Americans and 399 points for various socioeconomic disadvantages).[75]

The authors want universities to "do both": pay attention to race and class, and for a brief period—with the leadership of Summers, Bowen, and Marx—it appeared they might try to do so. But the early returns are sobering, and the evidence suggests that the universities pay the closest attention to socioeconomic diversity when they are unable to promote racial diversity directly through the use of race.[76]

It may be that higher education will take on profound class inequality aggressively on campuses only if there is a push—simultaneously—from two very different forces: a conservative U.S. Supreme Court, which curtails the use of race, spurring liberals to look to class; and a liberal U.S. president, who pushes for a strong class-based alternative, and the funding to make it a reality. If we are to address the twenty-five-to-one ratio of wealthy to poor students on selective campuses forcefully, we will need to attack the problem from all angles:

inequality at the K–12 level, admissions, financial aid, and support once students are enrolled. Expanding upon the idea of the Carolina Covenant on the one hand, and the strivers admissions policy on the other, provides an excellent starting place.

2

THE CAROLINA COVENANT

Edward B. Fiske

On October 1, 2003, as part of his annual State of the University address, James Moeser, then the chancellor of the University of North Carolina at Chapel Hill (UNC), announced a dramatic new approach to financial aid. Under a plan known as the "Carolina Covenant®," dependent students from low-income families who had demonstrated their academic ability by gaining admittance to the state's flagship university would no longer be obliged to take out loans to complete their studies. Instead, the financial need of these high-ability, low-income students would be covered entirely by a combination of grants, scholarships, and a federal Work-Study job.

The goal of the Carolina Covenant was to send a message to young people harboring aspirations of attending UNC that, if they worked hard in high school and gained admission, lack of money would not be an obstacle to becoming a "Tar Heel." "College should be possible for everyone who can make the grade, regardless of family income," Chancellor Moeser asserted. "With the Carolina Covenant, we are telling students that college is affordable—no matter how little their family makes."

Although Princeton already had begun offering loan-free financial aid packages to students from low-income families, UNC was the first public university to do so, and its actions did not go unnoticed. Virginia followed suit the following year, and nearly one hundred other public and private universities have adopted related policies, many of them consciously modeled on the UNC plan.[1] UNC has become a leader in the current movement to assure that talented low-income students have access to higher education.

The first cohort of 224 Carolina Covenant Scholars entered UNC in the fall of 2004, and many graduated in 2008. Additional cohorts of 352, 413, 391, 409, and 533 Covenant Scholars, respectively, including both freshman and transfer students, entered in the five years that followed. Now that the program has reached its "cruising speed," it involves approximately 1,800 Scholars, who constitute about 10 percent of all undergraduates at the university

While the loan-free financial aid is the most visible feature of the Carolina Covenant, it may not be the most important one. Moeser and his colleagues realized early on—and national and institutional data confirm—that low-income students at academically challenging institutions face special problems, including lack of informed guidance from parents unfamiliar with the ways of higher education. Thus, shortly after the arrival of the first cohort of Covenant Scholars, officials began establishing a comprehensive system of support services that includes:

- mentoring by faculty and professional staff for first-year students;

- peer mentoring by continuing Covenant Scholars;

- monitoring of Covenant Scholars' academic performance and linking them to support services when needed;

- career and personal development opportunities, such as etiquette dinners, financial literacy instruction, and career workshops; and

- social events to encourage students to make connections with faculty, administrators, and other Covenant Scholars.

A plan for research on the academic and other impacts of the Carolina Covenant was built into the program from the outset. A rich set of data has been accumulated on each of the first several cohorts, as well as on a control group from low-income families who would have qualified for the program had it existed when they enrolled as freshmen in the fall of 2003. Initial findings suggest that the program has enhanced

UNC's ability to attract high-ability, low-income students, and that it has had a positive impact on the persistence and graduation rates of such students over a three-year period. Data from the UNC Office of Scholarships and Student Aid and the Office of Institutional Research and Assessment show that the graduation rate in June 2008 for the first cohort of Covenant Scholars was 5.2 percentage points higher than that of the control group.[2] What follows is a report on the initial years of the Carolina Covenant.

"The University of the People"

It is no coincidence that UNC has taken a leadership role in efforts to increase access to high-ability, low-income students. Chartered in 1789, UNC was nation's first public university to open its doors, and North Carolinians take pride in the university's identity as, in the words of prominent alumnus Charles Kuralt, "the university of the people." It is the flagship university of a state that has a more progressive tradition than do its neighbors. North Carolina was the last state to secede from the Union, and, lacking the plantation-driven wealth and aristocratic traditions of South Carolina and Virginia, North Carolinians could not afford to send their children north to Princeton or other prestigious colleges. "So we had to create our own 'university of the people,'" said Chancellor Moeser in an interview.[3]

Chancellor Moeser noted that, while all great public universities embrace populist ideals to some extent, "at Carolina they are part of our DNA." Twentieth-century administrators took this identity seriously. In his inaugural address as president in 1914, Edward Kidder Graham famously declared that "the boundaries of the campus should be co-terminus with those of the state," and set out to extend the university's service mission. In the 1920s and 1930s the pioneering sociologist Howard Odum made the carrying out of serious research on poverty and racism academically respectable. Robert Shelton, who as provost at the time was instrumental in establishing the Carolina Covenant, observed that such a vision is not only "self-perpetuating among faculty and students," but also extends throughout the state. "When polls ask what is the most important institution in the state, something like 85 percent of respondents say UNC," he said. Linda LaMar, a consultant who helped implement the Carolina Covenant, commented on the unusual "institutional commitment" that she found to the idea at Carolina. "At no point did I ever need to twist anyone's arm," she said. "The answer was always 'How can I help?'"

The article of the North Carolina Constitution that addresses education charges the General Assembly with assuring that "the benefits of The University of North Carolina and other public institutions of higher education, as far as practicable, be extended to the people of the State free of expense." Consistent with this mandate, which has been conscientiously honored by the state legislature, UNC has honored a longstanding tradition of relatively low tuition levels.

CHALLENGES TO ACCESS

In the late 1990s, however, several factors threatened the state's tradition of access to higher education for low-income students.

FINANCIAL PROBLEMS

As a consequence of fiscal problems faced by the state legislature, the entire University of North Carolina system was facing budget shortfalls that had to be met by increases in tuition. The costs for room and board, books, transportation, and other costs borne directly by students also were increasing.

CHANGING STUDENT POPULATION

The demographic profile of North Carolina residents has been changing rapidly. North Carolina's population is one of the fastest growing in the nation, and it is projected to become the seventh most populous state by 2030 (up from eleventh in 2000). The state's white population is aging, with fertility rates below replacement. Much of the state's population growth will occur among less-affluent populations. North Carolina currently ranks eleventh (tied with Georgia) in the nation in the percentage of its population living below the federal poverty level (14.3 percent), and between 2007 and 2017, the proportion of students of Hispanic origin graduating from North Carolina high schools is projected to increase by 489 percent.

The number of entering Carolina Scholars (freshmen and transfer dependent students) coming from homes with incomes at or below 200 percent of the federal poverty level has risen substantially, from 352 in 2005 to more than 500 in 2009. A large increase, from 409 students in 2008 to 533 in 2009, may be attributable to the downturn in the economy and to the success of recruitment efforts. In all, over 11 percent of the entering freshman class in 2009 came from families at or below the 200 percent of poverty threshold. Approximately 33 percent of all undergraduates qualify for need-based aid (see Table 2.1), and 14.5 percent are Pell Grant–eligible—percentages that have remained fairly constant despite the fact that the size of the entering class has been growing in recent years.

Table 2.1 Trends in Percentage of Needy Undergraduate Students at UNC

	Size of Undergraduate Class	Percent Qualifying for Aid
1999–2000	4,155	27
2000–01	4,344	28
2001–02	4,543	29
2002–03	4,911	31
2003–04	5,301	33
2004–05	5,563	34
2005–06	5,458	32
2006–07	5,585	33
2007–08	5,836	33
2008–09	5,817	33

Note: "Needy" is defined as having documented need as determined by the Free Application for Federal Student Aid (FAFSA) methodology.

Source: UNC Office of Scholarships and Student Aid, November 2009.

Major changes also are under way in the likely future makeup of North Carolina's workforce and citizenry. The state's economy is moving away from its traditional manufacturing and agricultural base to one that is increasingly dependent on knowledge-intensive economic sectors such as finance, government, biotechnology, and information technology. As the flagship public university in the state, UNC thus faces the challenge of preparing an increasingly diverse group of students—many from socio-economic, racial, and ethnic groups that have not been served well by higher education in the past—for a workforce that requires increasingly sophisticated skills.

It must be noted, however, that while both the number and proportion of low-income students at UNC has grown, they have not done so at a rate that is likely to change the widespread perception of the university as a bastion of privilege. Institutional data show that more than two-thirds (72 percent) of UNC freshmen come from families with yearly incomes of $75,000 or more, and more than half (54 percent) come from families with incomes of at least $100,000. The comparable proportion of such families in the state as a whole is roughly 12 percent.[4]

University officials are quick to point out that the university has little control over the nature of its applicant pool. As a highly selective academic institution, it must limit its acceptances to students who have done well in a secondary education system in which academic success and socioeconomic status have shown to be closely linked. As Stephen Farmer, associate provost and director of undergraduate admissions, put it in an interview, "The hard truth is that educational advantage at the K–12 level accrues to affluent students." In a letter to UNC president Erskine Bowles, Chancellor Moeser also cited "the increasing interest of affluent students in public higher education" and commented, "Nationwide, families who ten years ago would have gravitated toward elite private universities are now more inclined to consider public universities, and especially flagship publics, as an acceptable or even desirable alternative."[5]

Enrollment Disincentives

As Carolina administrators grappled with this challenge of serving substantial numbers of low-income students, they were aware of a number of major obstacles. National studies have shown that high achievers from low-income families enroll and persist in four-year colleges at much lower rates than their peers, and this pattern was confirmed by UNC's own internal research, including a 2004 longitudinal study of the entering classes of 1997 and 1998. According to the study, 21 percent of students from families with annual incomes of $30,000 or less had neither graduated nor transferred from the university. The comparable figures were 12.1 percent for students in families in the $30,001 to $75,000 range, 9.7 percent for those in the $75,001 to $100,000 range, and only 5.3 percent for students whose family income was above $100,000.

A growing body of national research has also shown that the primary obstacles to enrollment of high–ability, low-income students are financial. Although UNC tuition rates remain low in comparison with other flagship public universities, many poor families assume that the cost of college is beyond their reach. Part of this judgment reflects hard economic realities, but research has also shown that some of the disincentives are psychological and related to inadequate information. Researchers have shown that low-income students and family members tend both to overestimate college costs and to underestimate the extent to which they qualify for student assistance. Perhaps most important, they are reluctant to assume loans to pay for college. Fearful as they are of indebtedness, students from low-income families may choose to take on- and off-campus jobs to an extent that undermines their academic progress.[6]

Thus, the challenge facing UNC administrators as they thought about such issues was to design a financial aid policy that would accomplish three purposes:

1. provide the necessary financial assistance to the low-income students who were becoming an increasing part of the university's constituency;

2. send out a powerful message to these students that, contrary to what these students and their families may have been assuming, a UNC education was within their reach; and

3. help these students to persist and graduate once on UNC's campus.

Origins of the Carolina Covenant

The administrator whom Chancellor Moeser and others are quick to describe as the "architect" of the Carolina Covenant is Shirley Ort, the associate provost and director of scholarships and student aid. Ort is a personable administrator who grew up on a farm in rural Michigan. Neither of her parents was a high school graduate, and she headed for the workforce as soon as she graduated from her small high school. When her former principal noticed that she was not going to college, he stopped by her house for a talk with the family. "He encouraged me to apply to a small college and told me, 'If you get in, the college will help you stay there,'" Ort recalled. "I owed money on my bill every single year, and they let me go back. They made me a residence hall counselor so I'd get free room and board, and they worked with me so I could make it. For two years, I worked full-time and went to school full-time."

She went on to earn a master's degree in ancient and medieval history from Western Michigan and a law degree from Seattle University. Throughout her career in the areas of student services and student financial aid, Ort has focused on issues of equal educational opportunity. "It's probably not a coincidence that I spent my career in an area I know is so important," she reflected. "I myself would have been a Covenant kid."

Ort recalls that the idea for the Carolina Covenant was planted in January 2002 during a conversation she had with Provost Robert Shelton, now president of the University of Arizona. The two officials were lamenting the likely negative impact of tuition increases on low-income students. "Robert was frustrated at the fact that people did not understand that there was adequate financial aid to protect this group of students," she recalled.

Ort was aware of research over four decades by Alexander Astin, Edward St. John, Jacqueline E. King, and others showing that, as measured by student persistence, the most effective financial aid packages are those with a small amount of loan, modest amounts of work, and the balance in grants.[7] She was also acutely conscious of how wary low-income families are of taking on debt. She suggested to Shelton that UNC needed to "get away from student aid-speak and send a clear message to low-income families that college was affordable." The way to do this, she suggested, was to scrap the loan component in the interests of simplifying the message. "If we could talk about a 'no-loans' policy," she told him, "everyone would know what we meant."

Shelton liked the notion and invited Ort to cost out what was formally designated as the Low-Income Student Initiative. Ort asked Lynn Williford, assistant provost for institutional research and assessment, to perform the essential financial analyses, but her numbers showed that the university could not afford the program at that time. "We calculated that the recurring cost of replacing the loan component would be $2.1 million a year, which was more than the university could afford given the grant resources that were available at the time," she recalls. So the proposal went onto a shelf, literally and figuratively, in Ort's office.

The following year, in the spring of 2003, Ort attended a meeting of the National Association of State Scholarship, Grant and Aid Programs at Jury's Hotel in Washington, D.C. She was struck by a presentation by Stephen Heyman of Sallie Mae in which he offered data showing that a major reason that students from low-income families do not enroll in higher education is that they have "no idea" how they would ever pay for it. "After listening to Stephen I realized that we had been right on the money the previous year and that we had to go back and do it," she said. Ort wrote "I have a dream" on a yellow pad and started making notes on how to conceptualize what would soon become the Carolina Covenant. "I still have that piece of paper," she says proudly.

Ort went back to Williford and asked her to run the numbers again over the summer, and she also spoke with Jerry Lucido, the university's director of enrollment management. By late July they determined that, with an infusion of $1.4 million in new funds annually, it would be possible to eliminate all loans from the financial aid packages of high-ability, low-income students for a full complement of four classes.

The financial picture looked much brighter in the spring of 2003 than it had the previous year, Ort explained, because in the meantime the state legislature had approved a significant increase in the amount of need-based grants available to low-income students at UNC-Chapel Hill and at other UNC system institutions. The initial projections performed in January 2002 were based on $1.6 million in state grants. This amount increased to $2.5 million in the fall of 2003, jumped to $4.5 million by the fall of 2004 when the Carolina Covenant was rolled out, and today amounts to over $10.7 million. In addition, the legislature authorized a supplemental grant program targeted to the state's neediest students (with eligibility that coincided with the covenant) in 2007, which added another $900,000 to Carolina's available covenant funding for two years, 2008–09 and 2009–10. Unfortunately, the supplemental grant program was repealed because of cost during the 2009 legislative session and will not exist going forward, unless reauthorized. "Without the infusion of new state need-based grant dollars, funding for the Carolina Covenant would have been a stretch—even for Carolina," Ort commented.

Other assumptions built into the plan were that there would continue to be modest increases in federal Pell Grants, in need-based aid intended to offset campus tuition increases, and in private giving for need-based scholarships. In fall 2004, the maximum Pell Grant was $4,050 and for 2009–10 it was $5,350. In 2004–05, Chapel Hill received $6.1 million in Pell Grants, and today is approaching $9 million. "Thus all of our earlier predictions came true, and actually exceeded our expectations," Ort commented recently.

On August 29, 2003, Ort drafted a two-page briefing paper with the new numbers and, accompanied by Williford and with the support of Lucido, presented it later that morning to Provost Shelton, who signed off on the idea immediately. That same day, Lucido was flying to Charlotte with Chancellor Moeser on a small plane, so Ort encouraged him to run it past Moeser. "I shared the briefing memo with the Chancellor," Lucido recalled. "He looked at it and said that this was a great idea and that we should go for it." Ort comments: "It's a rare day indeed when two senior administrators both sign off on a bold new plan on the same day. This time we were quite sure of ourselves."

In an interview, the chancellor recalled the reason that he approved the idea on the spot. "Although we were already meeting 100 percent of demonstrated financial need, we were aware that we were not getting as many applications as we should have been getting from low-income families," he said. "Our research showed that people perceived our tuition as higher than it really was. The Carolina Covenant sends the message that there are no financial barriers to a UNC education."

Underlying Principles of the Carolina Covenant

As already noted, the Carolina Covenant was designed not only to provide financial assistance to the target group of high–ability, low-income students, but also to communicate to high school students in this category that attending Carolina is within their reach. As such, the program is organized and promoted around several clear-cut principles.

First of all, the Carolina Covenant describes itself as a *promise*. It represents a pledge to eligible low-income students throughout North Carolina and beyond that if they are admitted, they will be able to graduate from UNC debt-free. It represents a pledge that the university will meet the full need of eligible students and that it will do so through a combination of federal, state, university, and privately funded grants and scholarships and a reasonable amount of Work-Study (ten to twelve hours per week) during the academic year—with no need for loans. This is seen as a promise that extends beyond the tenure of one chancellor—an institutional commitment that is expected to endure for generations. This promise to the public is perhaps the most distinguishing characteristic of the Carolina Covenant: it is more than a financial aid "packaging" policy implemented for a certain period of time. Access and persistence will not be compromised by increases in tuition or other costs.

During the planning stage, the program was referred to as the "Carolina Compact," nomenclature that would not seem to suggest any sense of obligation on the part of the university. At the suggestion of a member of the university Board of Governors, however, Moeser upped the ante and substituted "Covenant" for "Compact." "A covenant," he explained, "is a promise."

Second, the Carolina Covenant functions as an *entitlement* for admitted qualifying students. There is no quota or limit on the number of students who can qualify for the program each year, nor is there any special application process. Entering freshmen and transfer students who meet basic eligibility criteria are automatically considered for the Carolina Covenant based on the information they submit on standard financial aid application forms. The admissions process at UNC remains need-blind. Students from all states are eligible for consideration. To be eligible, students must meet the following criteria:

ACADEMIC

- admitted or enrolled in good standing at UNC

- pursuing a first undergraduate degree

- enrolled full-time during the regular academic year

FINANCIAL NEED

- dependent on parents for support[8]

- parents' adjusted gross income at or below 200 percent of federal poverty guidelines (the threshold was 150 percent for first cohort entering in fall 2004)

- documented financial need, based on federal and institutional methodology

- in compliance with federal financial aid eligibility criteria

Consistent with standard financial aid procedures, the financial threshold for eligibility for the Carolina Covenant program varies by the size of the student's family. For a family of four, for example, the current cutoff is $42,400. The average family income of Covenant Scholars today is now $26,179. Fifty-five percent are first generation (neither parent had a postsecondary degree), and 60 percent are students of color.

Students' eligibility for the program is reevaluated each year, and Covenant Scholars may continue to be eligible for the program until they have completed the requirements for a baccalaureate degree, up to a maximum of nine semesters (by appeal, for the ninth semester). If a student becomes ineligible because family income increases beyond the loan-free threshold, he or she still may continue to participate in all covenant-sponsored mentoring and other support services.

Finally, eligibility for the Carolina Covenant is *predictable*. By design, the covenant is easy for families to understand, and eligibility is transparent. As Ort put it, "Our intent is to communicate a simple message of predictability of financial aid for admitted low-income students, particularly in the face of rising tuition and other college costs."

A Phased Implementation

The Carolina Covenant has been implemented in stages. The first cohort of 224 Covenant Scholars entered in the fall of 2004. They represented the contingent of freshmen who came from families with incomes at 150 percent of the poverty level or below; they constituted just over 6 percent of the entering freshman class. Today, at 200 percent, Covenant Scholars comprise 11 percent of the entering freshman class. Since the 2004 cohort of students did not know they were Covenant Scholars until after they had been accepted, the program did not play a role in their decision to apply to UNC. However, designation as a Covenant Scholar did affect the decisions of some to attend UNC rather than another institution where they had also been accepted.

The second cohort of 352 Covenant Scholars entered in the fall of 2005 and differed from the first cohort in two respects. First, the income cutoff for eligibility was raised to 200 percent of the poverty level, a standard that Ort explained was consistent with general consensus among researchers and policy makers as to what constitutes an appropriate definition of significant financial need, or "low-income." Secondly, the existence of the Carolina Covenant played a role in their decisions to apply to and enroll at UNC. Some of this cohort transferred to UNC as sophomores.

The subsequent cohorts entered each fall, and by the fall of 2007 the program had reached its "cruising speed" of about 1,700 scholars. Today, it is around 1,800 and rising.

PROFILE OF CAROLINA COVENANT SCHOLARS

An important operational characteristic of the Carolina Covenant is that the university does not explicitly recruit students to be Covenant Scholars. Rather, the admissions office assembles the best class that it can muster based on standard criteria and then looks to see how many of the admitted students qualify as Covenant Scholars by virtue of family income and other criteria. "We are not looking to burnish our image by having more Covenant kids in the class," said Steve Farmer, associate provost and director of undergraduate admissions. "We do not know the financial circumstances of applicants when we make admissions decisions, and we do not want to know. They become Carolina Scholars only after they are admitted." Nevertheless, he readily concedes that the ability to tell high-ability, low-income students that they would be able to graduate from Carolina debt-free is an important tool for recruiting such students.

Farmer described UNC's recruiting policy as "consciously inclusive" with regard to socioeconomic, racial, ethnic, and other forms of diversity. "We work hard to foster access," he said, "but we also have an obligation to foster excellence and to recruit

students who will take advantage of Carolina." Farmer said that
there is no simple formula that is used in evaluating the applications of all students and that students' backgrounds are taken
into account when evaluating their grades and admissions test
scores. "We go out looking for great students with an eye to the
circumstances they have faced," he said.

Given such admissions criteria, the profiles of the first six
cohorts of Covenant Scholars contain no surprises. Consistent
with what would be expected given the fact that, by definition, they come from low-income backgrounds, the cohort of
Covenant Scholars entering in fall 2009 includes more students
of color than the general student population (27.17 percent are
black versus 11.29 percent of all students), and a slightly higher
percentage of them are female than the general population (61.19
percent versus 59.47 percent). They also have somewhat lower
high school grade point averages (4.39 versus 4.47) and SAT
scores (1230 versus 1302). Notably, the average SAT scores of
Covenant Scholars are within the range of the middle-half of
students—those in the twenty-fifth to seventy-fifth percentiles—
that has become the standard criterion for comparing SAT scores
across institutions. (See Table 2.2, page 32.)

Lynn Williford pointed out that there have been some shifts
across the years in the categorical variables of sex, race, and
parent education. For example, the proportion of males among
Covenant Scholars rose from 31 to 39 percent—still slightly less
than the student body as a whole. She added, however, that "these
are still fairly small groups, and shifts in just a few students can
appear to make a lot of difference." One difference, however, is
significant. "I do think you can say that, in general for the 2005
and 2006 cohorts, the 200 percent group contains significantly
fewer minorities and first generation college graduates than the
150 percent group," she commented. This difference presum-
ably reflects the more expansive selection criteria. This pattern
was sustained up through 2008, but in 2009 the proportion of
students of color in the 200 percent group slightly exceeded the
proportion in the 150 percent group.

Table 2.2 Profile of First–Year Covenant Scholars and All First–Year Students

	2003 Control		2004		2005		2006		2007		2008		2009	
	All	Covenant	All	Cov.	All	Cov.	All	Cov.	All	Cov.	All	Cov.	All	Cov.
Male	41.1	31.25	41.5	31.25	39.47	36.5	40	36.58	39.72	35.05	41.1	39.48	40.53	38.8
Female	58.9	68.75	58.5	68.75	60.53	63.5	60	63.42	60.28	64.95	58.9	60.52	59.47	61.2
Asian	6.49	11.61	7.75	16.52	6.8	13.5	7.65	13.86	7.99	10.27	8.8	12.39	9.02	15.3
Black	11.7	37.5	11.1	33.48	11.06	33.74	12.3	37.46	11.02	34.14	10.8	36.6	11.29	27.2
Hispanic	3.53	7.14	3.6	6.7	4.56	8.28	5.44	7.08	5.52	9.06	5.64	10.09	5.91	12.1
Native American	0.83	2.23	0.95	1.79	1.04	2.76	0.87	2.65	0.9	3.02	0.85	1.44	1.14	0.91
White	73.9	38.84	73.4	37.5	73.59	39.26	70	34.51	69.84	38.37	68.8	35.45	67.42	38.1
Other	3.56	2.68	3.18	4.02	2.96	2.45	3.81	4.42	4.73	5.14	5.1	4.03	5.23	6.39
Average SAT	1282	1196	1287	1209	1299	1225	1293	1212	1301	1216	1301	1215	1302	1230
HS GPA	4.23	4.09	4.29	4.21	4.4	4.28	4.37	4.29	4.42	4.35	4.44	4.36	4.47	4.39

Source: UNC Office of Scholarships and Student Aid, November 2009.

COVENANT SCHOLAR SUPPORT SERVICES

As already noted, abundant research has shown that low-income students encounter academic and personal obstacles not faced by other students. Many, if not most, are first-generation college students who are entering a world unknown to their parents. They lack the support system of relatives able to offer advice on how to handle problems ranging from dealing with difficult roommates to the choice of a major. Many worked in high school and missed out on some of the cultural experiences that help prepare more privileged peers for academic life. Some shoulder an obligation to send money back to their families.

"These students are often disturbed by what is going on back home, such as how a younger sibling is doing in middle school or family financial crises," said Harold Woodard, associate dean of the office for student academic counseling. "These are distractions that other students don't have." They also face fundamental academic issues. "We know they are smart," he continued. "What they need is an atmosphere that will help them perform at their best. They need help in adjusting both to academics and to their new social world. They need to learn how to skim documents, how to manage time, how to deal with the volume of college level reading, how to take notes and figure out what is important. And they need help on who to hang out with."

Woodard made an important contribution to the Carolina Covenant during the early planning stages in the summer of 2004 by proposing that beneficiaries of the covenant should be identified as "scholars." "Such a designation shaped how they saw themselves," he explained. "These were students who became part of the Covenant only after they were admitted. They ran a longer and harder race than others. They *are* scholars. They should be identified and treated as such."

Given these issues, Ort and her colleagues understood from the outset that eliminating loans from financial aid packages for Covenant Scholars was only the starting point. If the goal was to increase the percentage of low-income students who not only enroll but who also meet academic demands, persist, and eventually complete their undergraduate degrees, they would have to supplement the monetary aid with a network of academic and personal support services. She compares the program to "invisible fencing" that we are able to "wrap around them and make a difference in terms of graduation." Indeed, James H. Johnson Jr., a professor and demographer at the Kenan-Flagler Business School who is an expert on college access, suggested that this idea—embedding students from low-income backgrounds in a network of personal and institutional resources—is the covenant's most important innovation.

Ort turned for assistance to Linda LaMar, a longstanding colleague and financial aid expert who had just retired from the Washington State Higher Education Coordinating Board. Over the summer of 2004, LaMar met with representatives from offices providing various aspects of academic and other support services at UNC. Under the guidance of Professor Fred M. Clark, associate dean for academic services within the College of Arts and Sciences, she recommended a set of strategies aimed at providing Covenant Scholars with the support they would need to be successful. Support services—all of which are strictly voluntary—have continued to expand and now take multiple forms.

Faculty/Staff Mentoring for First-Year Students

A major objective of the support system is to provide quality interaction between Covenant Scholars and members of the faculty. Although a faculty mentoring system was built into the plan from the beginning, the flurry of activities required to mount the program meant that it did not actually become functional until midway through the first cohort's freshman year. In the fall of 2004, Chancellor Moeser sent an e-mail message to the university faculty asking for volunteers who would be willing to serve as mentors to small groups of Covenant Scholars. More than eighty faculty members offered to serve, and fifteen were selected that first year. As the program has expanded so has the number of mentors, which now total twenty-six.

Mentors meet at least twice a semester with groups of about fifteen to seventeen scholars, sometimes over a meal at a local restaurant. They also work with individual students as issues arise. "Every mentor is different," said Ann E. Trollinger, senior assistant director of the Office of Scholarships and Student Aid who serves as a mentor herself and manages the program within the office. "We deal with roommate issues and housing. I do a lot of budgeting. Some have done team-building activities. I know one who takes scholars to Playmakers [the on-campus repertory theater] and a jazz festival." Trollinger sees her mentoring role as being there to "give students the advice that their parents can't give." She helped one student locate a specialized tutor to help her with her biology course and assisted another in obtaining an emergency loan for books. She recalls taking one of her scholars to the Top of the Hill restaurant on Franklin Street and realizing that it was "the first time that he had ever been to a nice restaurant." Sometimes the relationship extends beyond the freshman year. "Students will come back and tell me about their summer and share their successes with me," she said. "That's very rewarding."

Another faculty mentor, Beth Black, an assistant professor in the School of Nursing, noted that she herself would have been a Covenant Scholar. "I came from a low-income family and know what it is like to come here and listen to students talking about cruises on spring vacation and having a sense of not having as much," she said. Black was mentor to fourteen students, eight of whom she saw on a regular basis. "Many of them feel over their heads because their classmates are so smart," she said. "Some come from small high schools and question their ability to do the work. So I look at their study habits and ask if they are using the resources of the learning center. I try to give them practical ways to succeed. Nursing is good for low-income kids because you know you are going to have a job when you graduate." Black said that her students e-mail her with academic or personal issues. She takes them out to dinner and asks if they would like to attend concerts or even a basketball game. Occasionally she has to put her foot down. "One student seemed to think of me as an ATM machine," she recalled. "I felt she was abusing the system a bit."

The mentoring program was envisioned and is coordinated by Professor Fred Clark, who now serves as the faculty academic coordinator of the Carolina Covenant. Clark reviews the grades of each Covenant Scholar every semester and intervenes if it looks as if one of them is struggling. Clark is a human face of the Carolina Covenant. He exchanges dozens of e-mail messages with scholars every week and becomes a part of the lives of many of them. His colleagues teasingly call him "The Covenant Dude," and he hosts students for lunch daily at the Top of the Hill, the restaurant on Franklin Street. As Clark told the alumni magazine, "I think it makes a difference to have somebody to talk with. I'm booked for lunch for the foreseeable future. The students love the attention. Some say they enjoy spending time with a grownup. It's a marvelous experience for me. They become family." He is proud of one e-mail that he received that ran as follows:

> Hi Mr. Clark—I always receive your e-mails and I read all of them but I've never replied before. I just wanted to tell you that throughout the school year, I've been very moved by your devotion and for you putting yourself out there for us! I mean, you're even giving us your home phone number! Thanks for always encouraging us, and checking up on us. We really appreciate your kindness! You're awesome!

Conversations with Covenant Scholars suggest that, at least for many of them, these relationships with faculty members are important. Kristin Boykin is a native South Carolinian whose goal is to become a cell biologist and find a cure for leukemia, the disease that took the life of her grandfather. Although she had done well academically in high school, she found the academics at Carolina intimidating. "Carolina is very draining," she said. "The course loads are hectic. I came in thinking I was smart, but that changed at orientation." Boykin went through a period of depression and for a time was on academic probation. "The support system made me get help," she recalled. "Dean Clark vouched for me. He told them what I had been going through. He did not prod and make me uncomfortable. His impact alone on my emotional and mental well-being in one semester let me know that I will be okay for the next four years."

Boykin said that she also received helpful academic advice. "My mentor told me outright not to take a course that I was signed up for, translating Greek epic poems," she said. "Then she helped me get into a different one." She added, "Our mentors will ask questions we would not ask. Why do you want to be a doctor? Is that the only way to help people? The mentors and faculty members help mold us into the people we want to be by caring for us. We can walk into an advising office and not be afraid. We have enough stress; they don't have to add to it. All we need now is a secret handshake." In what might be a poster quote for the program, Boykin observed, "We're poor, but we have the potential not to be poor. We appreciate our education. We are starting off at a certain level, but know we will not finish there."

Not all Covenant Scholars make use of the mentoring services available. Amour Wolfe, for example, said that "I only saw my mentor twice." Matt Richmond said, "I did not use the services that much. I'm not that kind of person," but he added that "it was nice to have someone to email with a question." He recalled that his mentor organized an excursion to watch Saturn on the university telescope. "This sparked an interest in astronomy," he said. "It also helps you become part of the university."

Each mentor receives $1,000 per semester, or $2,000 per year, plus an annual hospitality allowance of $1,500 per year, on an expense reimbursable basis. "No one does it for the money," Ort explained, "but we think that it is important for accountability purposes that we have some sort of contractual arrangement."

Peer Mentoring

The faculty mentoring program operates only during the students' first year at UNC, in part for financial reasons but also because, as Ort put it, "For those entering as freshmen, we assume that by sophomore and junior year students will have found their niche." Nevertheless, Ort and Clark were reluctant to leave Covenant Scholars without any formal support system, so they looked for some way to continue to offer support for scholars during the rest of their time at UNC.

They found it in the form of a peer mentoring program that had been developed primarily for African-American and Native-American freshmen by the office of Dean Woodard over thirty years ago. Now available to all freshmen, this program provided the ideal template for establishing a new peer mentoring initiative for Covenant Scholars. Under this new program, Woodard recruits older Covenant Scholars to work as unpaid volunteers to meet with groups of up to five younger counterparts. The peer mentoring program is available to freshmen not already enrolled in a peer mentoring program as well as to Covenant Scholars in their first year as sophomore or junior transfer students.

In the fall of 2006, Woodard put out a call for volunteers to work with the third cohort of entering Covenant Scholars, offered training, and began tracking the results. Woodard found that about 15 to 20 percent of Covenant Scholars had "intense" experiences with peer mentoring, meaning that they had face to face or other contact with a mentor at least twice a month. Woodard said that one of the biggest concerns that emerged on the part of Covenant Scholars was the amount of time that they had to spend studying and doing homework assignments. The peer mentors helped guide their younger colleagues to support services such as a self-paced reading program available to all students.

Woodard said that an important accomplishment of the peer mentors had to do with social adjustment. "They provided the reassurance of knowing that there was at least one person at this large school who knew their name," he said. "They let them feel that they are part of a community." Although he believes strongly that any such support service must be voluntary rather than mandatory, Woodard said that his office is going to be more "proactive" in encouraging participation in the peer mentoring program.

Interviews with Covenant Scholars from the first cohort of peer mentors suggest that many welcomed the opportunity to give something back to the university. "I was a mentor to three freshmen," said Ashley Heilprin. "I appreciated how helpful my own faculty mentors had been. I wanted to do something for someone else." Katie Phillips, another junior, agreed: "It was important to give back something."

Career Guidance and Personal Development

Another important component of the support services built into the Carolina Covenant was long-term career advising. Marcia Harris, the university's director of career services, was enlisted to create a Step by Step Career Planning Program modeled on her regular work but tailored to the particular needs of Covenant Scholars.

As freshmen, Scholars are invited to sign up for the four-year program, which begins with sessions focusing on career exploration and on basic topics such as how to write a resume or find an internship. As the students progress through their education the program takes up increasingly sophisticated topics such as career planning and how to select an appropriate major. When they reach their junior and senior years, they are offered help with job searching, business communication, public speaking and self-presentation and, eventually, how to make the transition into the job market or graduate school. "All of these services are available to any Carolina student," said Ort, "but they are structured for Covenant Scholars in way that gives them that little bit of extra edge early on. Again, these are students who are not getting this extra push from home. They don't have anyone hounding them to get that resume done."

One noteworthy activity is the annual "etiquette dinner" hosted by University Career Services at the on-campus hotel, the Carolina Inn. For many years, Career Services had been offering such dinners about a dozen times a year under the sponsorship of the General Alumni Association's Career Services program. These were targeted either at the general student population or to particular groups of students, such as Women in Business. The purpose was to help students develop social skills ranging from proper table manners to making small talk at a reception.

During the first year, several of the Covenant Scholars who had been called upon to give presentations about the program to alumni and other groups confided to staff that they were not always sure how to handle themselves at receptions and dinners. "They wanted to represent the university well, but found it a little intimidating," said Ort, who asked Career Services if they could organize an etiquette dinner for the Carolina Scholars. Rekita Moody, a member of the initial cohort, described her experience to the alumni magazine as follows: "It was nice. We all dressed up. They showed us proper techniques, how to use your napkin, how to do everything. How to butter rolls, how to eat a salad. Most of us don't know that. In my home, we don't eat at a table. We eat in front of the TV unless it's Thanksgiving or something. The workshop really helped me out. I was recently in a professional setting, and I used those techniques."

SOCIAL EVENTS

As a way of maintaining communication, building a sense of community, and providing opportunities for building connections with faculty and administrators, the university also holds a number of special events for Covenant Scholars, including receptions at the beginning of each pre-exam reading period. Clark understands that undergraduates, like armies, run on their stomachs "We have pizza and other food that students like, and we provide plastic bags so that they can carry home some food to sustain them while they are studying," said Clark. Dean Woodard observed that Covenant Scholars and their peer mentors often get together over food.

Attendance at such functions is strictly optional. "We realize that there are some students who are reluctant to identify themselves as Covenant Scholars," he said. Students who do attend often remark that they are frequently—and pleasantly—surprised to run into a classmate who they did not realize was a fellow Covenant Scholar.

Taneisha Livingston, a member of the first cohort, viewed attending the social gatherings as "a way to affirm how proud you are to be a Covenant Scholar and to meet others just like you." Still, she added, "you can never be sure how people will react." Versall Nourani said that he will sometimes be asked what the Carolina Covenant is all about and why he is getting a free ride. "It's because I'm poor," Nourani explained. "I don't feel bad about saying that. But it is weird when people judge you."

ADDITIONAL SUPPORT

Summer School. Once the Carolina Covenant was under way, administrators realized that some of the students in the first cohort would need to attend summer school—something that was not built into the program and for which no funds had been budgeted. Administrators have adopted a policy that the program would cover the expenses of Covenant Scholars who are required by the university to attend summer school in order to remain in good academic standing. Other scholars electing to study over the summer must rely on loan funds through the university or find the funds themselves.

Students have the choice of staying with the regular academic years and getting all grants and work study, or going to school during the summer and borrowing. Ashley Heilprin, for example, borrowed $7,000 so that she could take three economics courses over the summer.

During the summers of 2008 and 2009, Clark and his full-time assistant, Michael Highland, experimented with some alternative approaches. Although the covenant usually provides grant funding only during regular semesters, students who were on the brink of losing academic eligibility were given summer aid awards comprised of loans, but with the agreement that, if students entered into a contract and made a good faith effort to fulfill the terms of that contract, the loans would be converted automatically to grants at the conclusion of the summer term. The contract thus created a financial incentive, but more importantly provided a mutually agreed upon structure for academic interventions. Students were advised on which classes to take and encouraged to use supplemental services. The results were very positive, and will soon be reported by RTI, International—a research entity that has just concluded an evaluation of the initiative.

Study Abroad. Given that the university is now encouraging undergraduates to have some sort of international experience, study abroad poses another policy issue. Covenant Scholars may use their regular student assistance during regular semesters to participate in study abroad programs, and, in the one conspicuous exception to the "no loan" principle, scholars are permitted to borrow any amount that exceeds the cost of a semester in Chapel Hill in order to have an international experience. Fifty-nine Covenant Scholars from the first two cohorts opted to study abroad, and twenty-eight of them took out loans totaling $114,486. Versall Nourani, for example, planned on traveling to Uganda to pursue development studies. He opted for a high-quality and relatively expensive program, one run by the School for International Training in Vermont, and said that he is willing to "rely on loans for now" to finance this experience. Another 133 scholars engaged in study abroad in the following three years of the program.

Although no Carolina Covenant funds have been allocated for summer study abroad programs, Barbara Lee, former chair of the UNC board of visitors, and her husband, Alston Gardner, have endowed two spots in the Southeast Asia Summer Program specifically for Covenant Scholars.

Athletes. Students who receive full athletic scholarships and come from families whose income is below the 200 percent poverty threshold for designation are eligible for designation as Covenant Scholars. The handful of students who fall into this category do not receive additional funding from the covenant but are still eligible to participate in the mentoring and other support services.

IMPACT OF SUPPORT SERVICES

Although the program is still young, Carolina Covenant administrators have attempted to gauge the impact of the mentoring and related programs. The first and second cohorts of Covenant Scholars were surveyed by the Office of Institutional Research and Assessment in the spring of 2006 concerning their use of academic support services. Approximately 60 percent of respondents reported taking advantage of the services offered by at least one of the academic support offices, such as the Writing Center and the Learning Center. These students reported a high degree of satisfaction with the assistance they received from staff in those centers.

The survey results also revealed that nearly half of the Covenant Scholars had met at least once with the faculty or staff mentor assigned to them during their first year at UNC. Over 95 percent of these respondents described their faculty mentors as available, extremely helpful, and sincerely concerned about their welfare. Other important aspects of the mentoring relationship were explored in more detail in focus group sessions held with the first-year Covenant Scholars. Students who had had a mentor with professional ties to their chosen major or career were especially enthusiastic about the value of this relationship. They indicated that they had been able to ask questions about what majors were most likely to help them achieve their career goals and what types of courses and internships would best prepare them for graduate or professional study. In addition, the informal conversations with these mentors had provided many opportunities for students to learn "the inside scoop" (as one student put it) about what it was like to be a practicing professional in a certain field.

Although the participation rate of 50 percent might seem low, Dean Woodard finds it encouraging. "This is a lot more contact with faculty members than the normal first year student would have," he said. "And you have to remember what a huge step it can be for these students given the power that is associated with anyone on the faculty. Many were not sure that the faculty really meant it when they offered to help." He added that Covenant Scholars, having by definition beaten the odds associated with coming from low-income homes and making it to UNC, are used to relying on their own devices to solve personal and academic problems.

ECONOMICS OF THE CAROLINA COVENANT

At its core, the Carolina Covenant is a financial aid program aimed at reducing the monetary obstacles to a UNC education for low-income students while supporting student success. From the outset, university leaders resolved that, if it were to be initiated, the program would have to be built on a solid financial footing that would assure its existence for the foreseeable future. "Our fear was that we would start something that we cannot sustain," recalled Chancellor Moeser. As it sought to place the Carolina Covenant on a solid fiscal footing, the university had several factors working in its favor.

First, the population of low-income students expected to be eligible for the covenant was modest and manageable. Like other major flagship public universities, UNC is highly selective in its admissions policies and, given the well-documented correlation between wealth and academic achievement as measured by criteria such as test scores, it draws a high proportion of its students from affluent families. As shown in Table 2.3 (page 44), 72 percent of UNC freshmen have come from families with yearly incomes of $75,000 and 54 percent from families with incomes of at least $100,000. No members of the first cohort of Covenant Scholars came from families in these income ranges. Indeed, only 2 percent came from homes with more than $50,000 annual income.

Table 2.3 Family Income of Covenant Scholars and Other Freshmen (percent of total)

	Covenant Scholars	All Other Freshmen
$25,000 or less	61.0	2.6
$25,001–$50,000	37.6	10.1
$50,001–$75,000	1.6	15.6
$75,000–$100,000	0.0	17.7
$100,000 and up	0.0	53.9

Note: Cohort includes all new entering freshman students from 2004 to 2008 who provided their family income information through student financial aid or other surveys.

Source: UNC Student Financial Aid Data, GA Freshman Survey, Cooperative Institutional Research Program (CIRP) Survey.

While the number of students from low-income homes has been increasing steadily, such students still represent a small proportion of the overall undergraduate body. This observation raises the broader question of whether UNC—the virtues of the Carolina Covenant notwithstanding—is doing as much as it should to serve the needs of high-ability, low-income students in North Carolina. Steve Farmer, associate provost and director of undergraduate admissions, describes this as "a reasonable question," but points out that UNC has recently launched two new programs aimed at increasing college-going rates among low- and moderate-income students in the state.

The first is the Carolina College Advising Corps, which places recent UNC graduates in North Carolina high schools serving low-income students. Corps members supplement the work of guidance counselors by giving advice on admissions and financial aid to students and their families. Since its inception in 2007, the Carolina Corps has placed forty-four advisers in forty North Carolina schools. The program, funded by the Jack Kent Cooke Foundation, is one of twelve such programs at selective universities run by the National College Advising Corps, which also is headquartered at the undergraduate admissions office at UNC.

The second program is the Carolina Student Transfer Excellence Program (C-STEP), which seeks to increase the number of low- to moderate-income community college transfer students entering and graduating from UNC. Talented students are identified while they are still in high school or early in their community college careers, offered advising and special events, and given guarantees of eventual transfer admission to UNC if they earn an appropriate associate degree.

Farmer emphasizes that the Carolina Covenant is not an "end in itself." "The point of practicing affirmative action is not to have more Covenant Scholars in a class," he said. "The goal is to get the word out that Carolina is a place that is accessible to everyone and to make sure that they succeed."

Second, the Carolina Covenant is premised on the assumption that the federal student assistance program will continue to operate in more or less its current forms and at current levels. Specifically, said Chancellor Moeser, "We are assuming that the Federal government will keep its commitment to Pell Grants for low-income students."

Finally, making the numbers work for the Carolina Covenant was facilitated by the fact that the program was providing only one piece—loan relief—of financial aid packages that were already relatively generous. Both the North Carolina General Assembly and the Board of Governors of the University of North Carolina system historically have favored low tuition. In 1999, the General Assembly established a Need-Based Grant Program that targeted low-income students in the sixteen institutions that make up the UNC system. Since 2000, each time the Board of Governors has imposed a tuition increase throughout the system, it has added funding to this program. Even in the face of fiscal realities in recent years, the General Assembly and Board of Governors have authorized institutions to raise tuition only with the provision that they protect access.

At the institutional level, UNC has long had a need-blind admissions policy, meaning that admissions decisions are made without regard to whether an applicant will require financial aid. Following the first campus-initiated tuition increase in 1995, UNC has dedicated up to 40 percent (but no less than 35 percent) of new tuition revenue generated each year for grant assistance for needy students, in order to hold such students "harmless" from the increases. In 2010–11, the share will become 50 percent, as directed by the Board of Governors. These funds have allowed the university to improve aid packages to all students and reduce student indebtedness across the board.

Figure 2.1 Financial Aid Awarded to Covenant Scholars, by Type, 2007–08

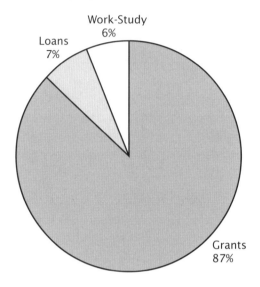

Source: UNC Office of Scholarships and Student Aid.

Moreover, the university has followed a policy of minimizing the loan components of financial aid packages that predates the covenant. During the 1990s, financial aid packages tended to be equally divided between grants and scholarships on the one hand, and loans and Work-Study on the other, but this commitment to reducing the loan component of financial aid packages has improved significantly in recent years. In 2007–08, the composition of the average financial package for an aid-eligible undergraduate student reached 70 percent grant, 2 percent Work-Study, and 28 percent loan. This is about the inverse of the national financial aid-packaging norm of approximately 40 percent in grants and scholarships and 60 percent in loans and Work-Study. As shown in Figures 2.1 and 2.2, the comparable proportions for Covenant Scholars were 87 percent grants and 13 percent in loans and work study, and the biggest share is funded through institutional and private sources.

UNC also has had a longstanding policy of not funding merit aid at the expense of need-based aid. Expenditures for merit scholarships at UNC have more than doubled over the past seven years, and such scholarships now comprise 10 percent of total student aid program

Figure 2.2 Financial Aid Awarded to Covenant Scholars, by Source, 2007–08

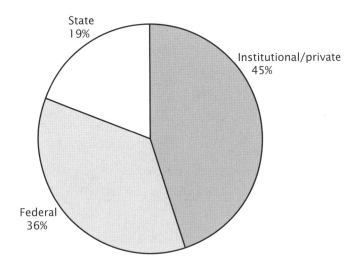

Source: UNC Office of Scholarships and Student Aid.

disbursements of $235 million. But merit scholarships are funded from different revenue streams than need-based aid. For example, the $600,000 needed each year to support UNC's 110 National Merit Scholars comes from interest from a private bequest, and in 2005 the Board of Trustees authorized the creation of sixty new merit scholarships to be funded through trademark licensing revenue. In 2006, the university launched a separate $60 million campaign to raise an endowment for merit scholarships that remains under way.

The cumulative effect of these financial aid policies has been that both the proportion of seniors graduating with debt and the average amount of their indebtedness has remained remarkably constant in recent years in spite of rising college costs. The 23 percent of seniors who graduated in 2000 with debt, both subsidized and unsubsidized, emerged with an average indebtedness of $13,687. The comparable figures for those who graduated in 2007 were 34 percent and $14,912. By 2008–09, borrowing actually had declined, with 28.8 percent of May 2009 graduates having borrowed a cumulative average amount of $14,262. Shirley Ort suggested that the decline resulted from "the increase in Covenant students as well as the growth in state grant program funding."

The all-important bottom line was thus that the university was already funding needy students at relatively high levels and, as it sought to enhance this support by eliminating loans, the additional investment was not all that high. "We were already meeting 100 percent of demonstrated need, so the Carolina Covenant did not cost us that much more," recalled Provost Robert Shelton. "We had a shorter distance to go than most other universities."

FINANCING THE CAROLINA COVENANT

Despite the fact that UNC had "a shorter distance to go" than peer institutions, designers of the Carolina Covenant still had to find a way to finance even this relatively modest amount of additional student aid.

The estimates that Shirley Ort and Jerry Lucido presented to Provost Shelton and Chancellor Moeser indicated that the initial cost of running the Carolina Covenant would be approximately $1.4 million more over a four-year period than what would be spent normally under existing packaging policies ($210 million for all students at that time). This analysis was based on cost estimates at the time of the program's creation, with assumptions built in about how much tuition and room and board charges would increase.

Administrative costs for the Carolina Covenant have been minimal. Although their workloads have increased appreciably, most of the staff members involved in running it have been current personnel already on the payroll. Offices across the university that have provided in-kind contributions include the Office of Minority Affairs, Admissions, College of Arts and Sciences, Academic Advising, Academic Services, and Student Affairs. The Office of Student Affairs and the Office of Scholarships and Student Aid have collaborated to waive charges for freshman orientation and to allow each Covenant Scholar and a parent to stay in residence halls without charge.

Mounting the program required considerable manipulation of old computer systems in order to carry out tasks such as tracking recipients and maintaining academic and other records. About $60,000 was invested over eighteen months in contracts for developing the Carolina Covenant's policy manual, administrative guidelines, design of the faculty mentoring program and training module, and preparation of promotional materials. Other administrative expenses for the current year include $30,000 for the faculty academic coordinator for the program, $2,000 for twenty-six mentors, and entertainment and hospitality allowances for mentors of $1,500 each. The $10,000 cost of the etiquette dinner and other social functions was covered by a number of smaller private gifts for these purposes.

As already discussed, the cost for the additional grant assistance is limited by the fact that Covenant Scholars by definition qualify for a full financial aid award, and Work-Study replaces some of what would have been awarded as loans had the students not been eligible for the covenant.

The four-year costs of $1.4 million in recurring operating costs and additional grant aid is still a substantial amount of money. Because the university remains committed to meeting the full need of all students with need, not just Covenant Scholars, it was agreed that no financial resources were to be shifted from other aid programs to fund the Carolina Covenant unless absolutely necessary—which has not been the case even in the most recent, difficult year. This meant that additional funds would have to be raised from multiple sources. Some of the additional gift assistance will be provided through increases in financial aid that kick in when tuition rises, some from additional state-funded grant funds, and some through donor gifts. The university also has raised $9.3 million toward a $10 million fund drive to create an endowment and expendable funds that will assure the future stability of the program. Major gifts included $1.5 million from Pepsi Bottling Ventures and $1.0 million from the Bank of America Charitable Foundation.

The honorary chairs of the drive are Roy Williams, the UNC basketball coach, and his wife Wanda, who host an annual fund raising dinner in behalf of the covenant. Their participation was announced just before the tip-off of the February 2006 UNC-Duke basketball game. Williams, whose two children also are lending their support, appears in a thirty-second institutional television spot that promotes the Covenant in broadcasts of UNC athletic events. "The Carolina

Covenant is special because it opens the doors of Carolina to young people, regardless of one's financial status," said Williams, whose own background would have qualified him to be a Covenant Scholar. "It makes UNC accessible to many students for whom getting an education at Carolina will be a life-changing experience." The fundraising goal was recently increased to $20 million.

One sign of the way that the Carolina Covenant is viewed on campus is that the 2007 graduating class voted to make a donation to the covenant as its senior class gift. "I think it's doing a lot more for the University than a sign would do," said Meg Petersen, the senior class president. "It's making the University a better place."

Former chancellor Moeser and other senior administrators have taken seriously the need to spread word about the covenant as a means of encouraging more low-income students to aspire to attend UNC. "When I travel around the state it is rare that I don't go into a high school and talk about it," Moeser said in an interview. At some point, the chancellor paid a visit to Peck Elementary School in Greensboro, where he had been invited by Francine Mallory, the principal, who was eager to use the program to raise the aspirations of students in her school, 82 percent of whom qualify for free or reduced-price lunch.

In his talk to the Peck faculty, Moeser spoke about the importance of raising student expectations. "Your students don't come to school with the same dreams of going to college as middle class children," he said. "You are planting dreams in these kids that they would not have if you did not plant them. We created the Carolina Covenant to show that the path to college, while difficult, is not impossible. Your job is to take them step by step. When you pass them on to middle school, we need to keep the dreams alive."

The program is heavily promoted by the admissions office, and the university operates a traveling science laboratory that tours the state and, in the process, advertises the covenant.

IMPACT OF THE CAROLINA COVENANT

Just as the decision to go ahead with the Carolina Covenant was made only after careful analysis had shown that it was financially viable, so designers of the program were careful to build evaluation of the impact of the covenant into the project from the very beginning. The study design, developed by Linda LaMar and Lynn Williford, who heads the Office of Institutional Research and Assessment, included both quantitative data on the overall demographics of the program and qualitative data on how the program affects individual students. The evaluation activities are intended to answer the following set of questions:

- *Aspirations.* Does knowledge of the existence of the Carolina Covenant impact educational aspirations and academic preparation of students from low-income families?

- *Applications.* Does the Carolina Covenant increase applications from qualified students of low-income families?

- *Enrollment.* How does the offer of the Carolina Covenant award influence students' enrollment decisions?

- *Achievement.* What is the impact of the Carolina Covenant award and accompanying institutional resources and support services on student achievement?

- *Persistence and graduation.* How does the existence of the Carolina Covenant impact persistence and graduation rates of Carolina Scholars?

- *Policy.* What are the policy implications of the Carolina Covenant experience for improving access, affordability, and completion rates for low income students?

The evaluation design involves both longitudinal and comparative data. The progress of members of each cohort of Covenant Scholars is being followed from admissions through graduation and up to five years after graduation. In addition, the outcomes of each cohort of Covenant Scholars will be compared to three sets of undergraduates: (1) first-year students without financial need, (2) first-year students who received need-based aid but did not qualify for covenant status, and (3) a control group consisting of members of the class that entered in the fall of 2003 who would have been eligible for the covenant had it existed when they enrolled. The control group was constructed by matching 224 students entering in the fall of 2003 with the 224 students in the first cohort of Covenant Scholars according to criteria such as sex, family income, and parental education.

All of the evaluation activities are conducted and coordinated by Williford's office, supplemented by the assistance of RTI, International. Internal sources of the data, both quantitative and qualitative, include the UNC student information system, records from the Office of Scholarships and Student Aid, student responses to national surveys by the Cooperative Institutional Research Program (CIRP) and National Survey of Student Engagement (NSSE) and locally developed questionnaires, focus groups conducted with students, surveys of faculty and staff members, and individual interviews with samples of enrolling and non-enrolling students receiving covenant awards. External sources include U.S. Census data and information from the North Carolina Department of Public Instruction on characteristics of the high schools and school systems that Covenant Scholars attended.

While the program is still young, some initial conclusions are beginning to emerge around two broad topics: (1) the impact of the covenant on enrollment decisions of high-ability, low-income students, and (2) the effect of the covenant award and accompanying support services on student achievement and persistence.

Impact of the Covenant on Recruitment and Enrollment

An important goal of the Carolina Covenant has been to increase the number of high-ability, low-income students who apply to UNC and who accept offers of admission. In thinking about this objective, it is important to recall that students do not apply for a covenant award. Rather, Covenant Scholars are selected from the pool of students who already have been accepted to the university through the regular competitive admissions process. "They have earned their space here fair and square," said Steve Farmer, associate provost and director of undergraduate admissions. "They may not have all the numbers of other applicants, but they have competed for admission and won." Thus, in important respects, they mirror the academic and

personal characteristics of the broader student body. It is also fair to
assume that, like other members of their entering first-year class, they
were recruited by other prestigious institutions and had a variety of
admission offers from which to choose.

Data on the application patterns of first-year students in the fall
of 2004 show strikingly similar patterns among Covenant Scholars
and other UNC freshmen. Both groups applied to similar numbers of
schools, and four of the six top schools for the two groups overlap
(North Carolina State, Duke, Appalachian State, and Wake Forest).
Covenant Scholars also were attracted to UNC-Greensboro and
UNC-Charlotte, while other students were drawn to the University
of Virginia and UNC-Wilmington. (See Table 2.4.)

Data on where Covenant Scholars and other UNC students were
accepted show similar parallels. (See Table 2.5, page 54.) Students in
each group were accepted at an average of four institutions, and the
top seven schools for both groups included North Carolina State,
UNC-Wilmington, Appalachian State, and Wake Forest. Substantial
numbers of non-covenant students were also accepted at Duke and
Elon—suggesting that Covenant Scholars were not as attractive to
these private institutions.

Table 2.4 College Applications of First-Year UNC Students

Covenant Scholars	Other UNC Students
Applied to 2–18 schools (average of 4)	**Applied to 2–15 schools (average of 4)**
Top Schools:	**Top Schools:**
NC State	NC State
Duke University	Duke University
UNC-Greensboro	Wake Forest
Appalachian State	University of Virginia
UNC-Charlotte	Appalachian State
Wake Forest	UNC-Wilmington

Source: UNC Office of Undergraduate Admissions.

Table 2.5 College Acceptances of First-Year UNC Students

Covenant Scholars	Other UNC Students
Accepted at 2–9 schools (average of 4)	Accepted at 2–20 schools (average of 4)
Top Schools:	Top Schools:
NC State	NC State
UNC-Greensboro	Wake Forest
UNC-Charlotte	Appalachian State
UNC-Wilmington	UNC-Wilmington
Appalachian State	Elon University
East Carolina University	Other
Wake Forest	Duke University

Source: UNC Office of Undergraduate Admissions.

Has the Carolina Covenant encouraged more low-income students to apply to UNC-Chapel Hill? This question is tricky to answer given that most of the first cohort of Covenant Scholars, who entered in the fall of 2004, did not know about the program when they applied to UNC. Some students in subsequent cohorts have indicated that the existence of the covenant was a spur to apply to UNC.

Farmer suggested that, since admissions is need-blind and his office has no access to information on the financial need of applicants, the best way of assessing whether the covenant has encouraged more low-income students to apply is to track the number of freshman candidates who have requested and received waivers of their application fees over the past five years. Such waivers are available only to low-income students.

"Since the introduction of the Covenant, we have seen big increases in the number of students requesting waivers," he said. Specifically, the numbers of waivers rose consistently, from 727 in the fall of 2003 and 772 in the fall of 2004, the year that the first cohort of scholars entered, to 1,527 in the fall of 2009. "This is much higher than the overall increase for all applications during that period," he said. The proportion of total application fees waived rose from 4.1 percent in the fall of 2004 to 6.6 percent in the fall of 2009. Farmer conceded that a spike in waiver applications in 2009 may have had "less to do with the Covenant than with the economy." Nevertheless, he continued, "We have continued to enhance our outreach to and recruitment of first-generation-college students and students who attend low-income high schools. I don't think there's any doubt that the Covenant has contributed to the increase in the number of low-income students applying for admission."

Some forces independent of the Carolina Covenant may have contributed to this increase in applications for fee waivers. Farmer noted that in 2009 the university saw a record number of applicants, low-income and otherwise, and that special efforts were made to bring low-income students to the campus, including travel scholarships to 100 such students.

IMPACT OF THE COVENANT ON YIELD RATES

Data on what admissions officers describe as "yield"—the proportion of applicants who accept an offer of admission—suggest that the offer of Covenant Scholar status is a strong incentive to enroll at UNC rather than in prestigious institutions that had offered them admission. The average yield rate at UNC during the three years from 2004 to 2006 was 55 percent for all entering freshmen and 67 percent for transfers. For students receiving Covenant Scholar offers during these years, the average was slightly over 90 percent for both types of student.

Data from a 2006 survey of Carolina Covenant Students reinforce the suggestion that the loan-free financial aid package encouraged students to accept an offer of admission from UNC. Five out of six (83 percent) of responding Covenant Scholars from the first and second cohorts reported that being given Covenant Scholar status influenced their final decision to enroll at Carolina. Two-thirds (66 percent) said they probably would not have been able to afford to attend UNC without the covenant, while nearly all (95 percent) said that it was important to them to avoid borrowing to pay for college.

Jessica Petrini, a junior, said that the offer of a covenant scholarship definitely affected her decision to come to UNC. "My mom is a single mom who took a second job in preparation for me going to college," she said. "I applied to all in-state schools. My mom said that she would figure out a way to pay for wherever I chose. I probably would have come here and struggled and would have had to take out loans in both our names. Then I found out about the Covenant and realized I did not have to do this." Petrini, who comes from a large Italian family, said that she wants to get an MBA and then go to culinary school and open her own restaurant.

Although members of the first cohort of Covenant Scholars were not aware of the program until after they had applied to UNC, for some the designation was decisive in their decision to enroll. "I was accepted early at Wellesley, Bryn Mawr and Carolina, and Bryn Mawr was my first choice," recalled Ashley Heilprin. "But I was disappointed with their financial aid offer, so the Carolina Covenant was the deciding factor. I didn't like the idea of $100,000 in debt. I have younger siblings, and it is not fair for me to monopolize the financial resources." Taneisha Livingston was hoping to attend the University of Tulsa, which was close to home. "But it was really expensive," she said. "I got the letter from Carolina in March, and there was no other option."

Farmer predicted that the yield rate for low-income students could decline somewhat in the future as more universities, both public and private, follow UNC's lead and enact programs aimed at enrolling low-income students. Noting that nearby Davidson recently initiated a no loan/no debt financial aid policy," Farmer said, "We hate to lose students to other universities, but we also want such students to have the opportunity to get into a quality school."

Impact of the Carolina Covenant on Socioeconomic Diversity

The premise of the Carolina Covenant is that it will increase economic diversity on campus by attracting high-ability, low-income students who otherwise would not enroll at UNC. An important sign that this goal is being achieved, according to Ort, is that the number of entering covenant-eligible students (at or below 200 percent of the poverty line) has risen from 352 in 2005 to 533 in 2009.

A major objective of the covenant in general and the counseling and other support services in particular is to bolster the academic performance of low-income students at Carolina. Initial evidence (Table 2.6, page 58) suggests that this objective is being realized.

Academic eligibility. The most basic measure of academic performance is the proportion of freshmen who are eligible to return to UNC for their sophomore year. Ort reports that about 4 percent of all freshmen are typically ineligible for academic reasons to return. Of the first cohort of 224 Covenant Scholars all but five, or 2 percent, achieved the required grade-point average to return for their sophomore year. One student found Carolina too big, and five others left the university for unknown reasons, albeit in good academic standing.

Data through their senior year show that 94.7 percent of the first cohort of Covenant Scholars remained academically eligible, which is slightly higher than the proportion of 94.5 percent registered by the 2003 control group. Based on data from the previous year, Ort estimated that 8.2 percent of Covenant Scholars would have to attend summer school in order to retain their academic eligibility. The actual number turned out to be 14, or 6.3 percent. Put another way, the number of 2004 Covenant Scholars who became academically *in*eligible was 17 percent lower than the 2003 control group.

Grade point averages. Consistent with overall patterns for low-income students, the grade-point averages for Covenant Scholars as a group were lower than those for the undergraduate body as a whole. Data for the first semester of the 2004 cohort show that 13.9 percent of Covenant Scholars registered grade point averages under 2.0—double the proportion of 6.4 percent for all freshmen. At the high end of the performance chart, 37.7 percent of Covenant Scholars achieved a GPA above 3.0 in comparison with 57.0 percent of all freshmen. By the end of their senior year the first-year cohort of Covenant Scholars had a mean GPA of 2.97. This compares favorably with the mean GPA of 2.89 for the 2003 control group. Significantly, the average GPA for Covenant Scholars at graduation is within 0.2 points of the average for all students.

Table 2.6 Impact of the Carolina Covenant on Student Achievement and Persistence

Cohort/Poverty Status	Year 1 Fall	Year 1 Spring	Year 2 Fall	Year 2 Spring	Year 3 Fall	Year 3 Spring	Year 4 Fall	Year 4 Spring
Enrollment								
2003 150% (Control)	100.0%	99.1%	94.2%	89.7%	86.6%	84.8%	84.8%	81.3%
2004 150%	100.0%	99.1%	95.1%	91.1%	90.2%	87.9%	89.3%	84.4%
2005 150%	100.0%	97.8%	94.3%	91.7%	88.6%	85.5%	86.0%	83.8%
2005 200%	100.0%	99.0%	95.9%	92.9%	93.9%	92.9%	87.8%	82.7%
2006 150%	100.0%	100.0%	97.9%	94.6%	94.6%	91.7%	90.9%	.
2006 200%	100.0%	98.0%	94.9%	93.9%	91.8%	89.8%	87.8%	.
2007 150%	100.0%	97.3%	93.3%	92.0%	92.9%	.	.	.
2007 200%	100.0%	99.1%	91.6%	88.8%	86.9%	.	.	.
2008 150%	100.0%	96.9%	94.9%	.	.	.	.	.
2008 200%	100.0%	98.9%	95.6%	.	.	.	.	.
2009 150%	100.0%	.	.	.	.	.	.	.
2009 200%	100.0%	.	.	.	.	.	.	.
Mean Credit Hours Earned								
2003 150% (Control)	13.5	13.8	12.9	13.0	13.5	13.8	13.2	12.6
2004 150%	13.9	13.8	13.4	13.5	13.6	13.3	13.2	12.3
2005 150%	13.3	13.6	12.9	13.0	13.7	13.5	13.3	13.2
2005 200%	13.2	13.6	13.5	13.2	13.9	13.5	13.1	13.0

2006 150%	13.6	13.5	13.2	13.1	13.3	13.6	.	.
2006 200%	13.7	13.6	13.4	13.1	13.6	13.6	.	.
2007 150%	13.3	13.9	13.4	13.3	.	.	.	.
2007 200%	13.5	13.9	13.1	13.6	.	.	.	.
2008 150%	13.4	13.9	.	.	.	.	.	.
2008 200%	13.7	13.7	.	.	.	.	.	.
2009 150%	.	.	.	.	.	.	.	.
2009 200%	.	.	.	.	.	.	.	.

Mean Cumulative GPA

2003 150% (Control)	2.68	2.69	2.69	2.76	2.81	2.85	2.85	2.89
2004 150%	2.78	2.80	2.81	2.86	2.89	2.92	2.92	2.97
2005 150%	2.66	2.72	2.73	2.76	2.82	2.86	2.89	2.93
2005 200%	2.78	2.84	2.88	2.90	2.93	2.97	3.04	3.08
2006 150%	2.83	2.79	2.80	2.81	2.83	2.86	2.85	.
2006 200%	2.87	2.85	2.85	2.86	2.91	2.93	2.96	.
2007 150%	2.79	2.83	2.87	2.88	2.89	.	.	.
2007 200%	2.98	2.97	2.96	2.97	3.00	.	.	.
2008 150%	2.81	2.89	2.93	.	.	.	.	.
2008 200%	2.96	2.97	2.99	.	.	.	.	.
2009 150%	.	.	.	.	.	.	.	.
2009 200%	.	.	.	.	.	.	.	.

Continued on next page

Cohort/Poverty Status	Year 1 Fall	Year 1 Spring	Year 2 Fall	Year 2 Spring	Year 3 Fall	Year 3 Spring	Year 4 Fall	Year 4 Spring
				End of Term Eligibility				
2003 150% (Control)	99.6%	90.1%	96.2%	92.0%	97.9%	96.3%	97.9%	94.5%
2004 150%	99.6%	93.2%	98.1%	93.6%	98.5%	95.4%	96.0%	94.7%
2005 150%	99.1%	93.3%	98.1%	92.3%	97.0%	94.4%	98.0%	97.4%
2005 200%	100.0%	92.8%	97.9%	95.6%	97.8%	94.5%	95.3%	97.5%
2006 150%	100.0%	93.4%	98.3%	90.4%	97.4%	94.1%	.	.
2006 200%	99.0%	95.8%	97.8%	94.6%	98.9%	97.7%	.	.
2007 150%	97.8%	95.0%	97.1%	97.6%	.	.	.	.
2007 200%	100.0%	93.4%	98.0%	96.8%	.	.	.	.
2008 150%	96.1%	95.6%	.	.	.	.	.	.
2008 200%	98.9%	97.8%	.	.	.	.	.	.
2009 150%	.	.	.	.	.	.	.	.
2009 200%	.	.	.	.	.	.	.	.

Note: Cohort includes all the new entering freshman Carolina Covenant students from 2004 to 2009, and 2003 control group.

Source: UNC Office of Institutional Research and Assessment, October 2009.

Credit hours. Another measure of academic success is the number of credit hours that a student accumulates. Data for the 2004 first-year cohort show that, by the end of their senior year, Covenant Scholars had accumulated a mean total of 106.0 credit hours, which is virtually identical to the 106.3 hours for the 2003 control group.

By and large these patterns continued to be seen with subsequent cohorts of Covenant Scholars. By the spring of their senior year, the 2006 cohort of Covenant Scholars showed slightly higher performance than the 2003 control group in the categories of enrollment, credit hours earned, cumulative GPS, and end-of-term eligibility. The only exceptions were that Covenant Scholars in the 150 percent part of the 2006 cohort registered the same GPA as members of the control group and were slightly lower in eligibility.

Retention. A major objective of the Carolina Covenant is to increase the rate at which low-income students persist and eventually graduate from the university. As seen in Table 2.7, data show that, by their fourth year, Covenant Scholars in the first cohort had persisted at a considerably higher rate—by a margin of 5.3 percentage points—than members of the 2003 control group. Moreover, the 2004 Covenant Scholars closed much of the persistence gap observed between themselves and the student body as a whole. Data also show that the number of 2004 Covenant Scholars who temporarily stepped out for at least one fall or spring term was about 20 percent lower than the number of their counterparts in the 2003 control group. Likewise, the number of 2004 Covenant Scholars who stepped enrolling at some point during their first three years was about 24 percent lower than for members of the control group.

Table 2.7 Retention Rates for Covenant Scholars and Other Students

Group	Percentage Enrolled in Year 4		
	2003 Control Group	2004 Cohort	Improvement
Covenant	84.3	89.6	5.3
Other Needy	87.6	88.2	0.6
No Need	90.5	91.6	1.1
All Students	89.3	90.5	1.2

Source: UNC Office of Scholarships and Student Aid.

Graduation. The most fundamental question surrounding the Carolina Covenant is, of course, whether the program has succeeded in increasing the graduation rate of participating students. Initial evidence suggests that the answer is yes. As shown in Table 2.8, 61.9 percent of the first cohort of Covenant Scholars graduated within eight semesters (in June 2008)—a proportion that is 5.2 percentage points higher than members of the 2003 control group. The gap drops to 3.1 percentage points for graduation within nine semesters—72.7 percent for Covenant Scholars versus 69.3 percent for the control group.

These data are particularly significant when viewed in relation to other groups of students. The gap between the graduation rates of Covenant Scholars and all students was 13.7 percentage points for eight semesters and 9.2 percent age points for nine semesters—in both cases smaller than the gap for the control group. It is also note-

Table 2.8 Graduation Rates for Covenant Scholars and Other Students

Group	Percentage Graduated within Eight Semesters		
	2003 Control Group	2004 Cohort	Improvement
Covenant	56.7	61.9	5.2
Other needy	71.8	71.2	−0.6
No need	77.0	78.9	1.9
All students	74.3	75.6	1.3

Group	Percentage Graduated within Nine Semesters		
	2003 Control Group	2004 Cohort	Improvement
Covenant	69.6	72.7	3.1
Other needy	78.3	77.4	−0.9
No need	83.9	84.7	0.8
All students	81.5	81.9	0.4

Source: UNC Office of Scholarship and Student Aid.

worthy that the graduation rates for other needy students declined slightly in both time periods.

Commenting on these preliminary data as a whole, Lynn Williford observed that "none of these differences were significant at a level of probability that I would bother to report." She found it encouraging, though, that "the 2004 cohort has so far outperformed the 2003 control group consistently in terms of GPA and retention, even though the differences at any one point of comparison are not very large." She added, "There is still much that we don't know about the individual experiences and choices of these students that we will continue to study."

ISSUES RAISED BY THE CAROLINA COVENANT

ROLE OF WORK-STUDY

The economic model of the Carolina Covenant calls for the funds that otherwise would be raised by loans to be replaced by a combination of outright grants and ten to twelve hours of Work-Study. The work requirement was included for reasons that go beyond finances per se. Having worked her way through college herself, Shirley Ort is receptive to research showing that students are more likely to succeed in school when they work a reasonable number of hours. "Research shows that 10 to 12 hours of work has salutary effect on student engagement and persistence," she explained. "We see Work-Study as a critical element of the program."

Initial data for the first two cohorts showed that two-thirds (66 percent) of Covenant Scholars were awarded Work-Study and that roughly 80 percent of these awards were accepted. The other third either received state aid or externally funded scholarships, or athletic scholarships, which eliminated the Work-Study component for that year. Some, but few, students simply elected not to take a Work-Study position. In subsequent years, however, participation in Work-Study declined sharply to the point where in 2008–09 only 52 percent of Covenant Scholars were offered

Work-Study and only 68 percent accepted these awards. (See Table 2.9.) Ann E. Trollinger attributed the decline to an increase in the UNC need-based grant program in 2007 and an increase in state grants, notably the EARN scholarship that was implemented in 2008. The EARN scholarship has since been rescinded by the General Assembly for financial reasons, however, and Shirley Ort asserted, "I believe we will see a huge increase [in Work-Study participation] again in 2010–11 with the absence of EARN funding."

The university does not have reliable information on how many Covenant Scholars take on additional part-time jobs in addition to Work-Study. This practice is discouraged, but Ort acknowledges that it can be a problem. "We don't know how many of our Scholars work extra to help their families," she said. "We tell our advisers to try to discourage that as much as possible, but there's really no way we can control them or prevent that. We can coach them and explain how important it is that they study and not work too much. Research shows that if students work over 19 hours a week, they're very much at risk."

BORROWING BY COVENANT SCHOLARS

Some Covenant Scholars opted out of the Work-Study program either because they preferred to borrow the equivalent amount or because they brought other private scholarships with them.

Although the financial aid packages for low-income students cover full demonstrated need, Covenant Scholars are not prohibited from borrowing funds to cover needs beyond the standard student expense allowances built into a student's financial aid package. Ort reports that among the 2004 entering cohort, the university was aware of only four (less than 2 percent) who borrowed during their first year through the program.

One potentially significant statistic is that the 2 percent figure is dramatically less than the 51 percent figure for students in the 2003 control group. "That is what the Carolina Covenant is designed to do," commented Williford. Ort said that her office is tracking the borrowing patterns of Covenant Scholars. "We want to know who borrowed how much and why," she said.

Table 2.9 Participation in Work–Study

	2004–05	2005–06	2006–07	2007–08	2008–09	2009–10
Total entering cohort	224	352	417	398	413	533
Awarded Work-Study	148	222	271	235	215	NA
Percentage awarded Work-Study	66	63	65	59	52	NA
Filled a Work-Study position	123	177	204	167	146	NA
Percentage of awards accepted	83	80	75	71	68	NA
Percentage engaged in Work-Study	55	50	49	42	35	NA
Average hourly wage	$7.97	$8.33	$8.95	$9.29	$9.58	in progress

Source: UNC Office of Scholarship and Student Aid.

Colin Justice came to UNC as a Covenant Scholar with an academic scholarship that covered the amount of money that he would have had to earn through Work-Study. He has taken out a $2,000 loan for summer school. "I would never have come to Carolina except for the Covenant, but I am willing to take out some loans," he said. "I see it as an investment in my career."

STIGMA

One question that has received a good deal of discussion is whether there is any stigma attached to designation as a Covenant Scholar. This was one issue in the mind of Dean Woodard when he argued for designating participants in the program as "scholars."

Obviously, different students will respond differently. Covenant policy has been to be protective of students' privacy and to give them the choice of whether or not to participate in group activities that would identify them as having come from a low-income family. Some have stayed away; others have joined in with no qualms. Ort recalls leading a class where former U.S. senator and vice presidential candidate John Edwards was talking about the problem of poverty. "Someone asked whether there were any Carolina Scholars in the audience, and two of them came forward," she recalls. "They were greeted by spontaneous applause."

The issue of stigma is one that students sometimes discuss among themselves. Beth Black of the School of Nursing recalls a group session in which those she mentored talked about how they should deal with fellow students who confront them with "I wish someone would pay *my* way through college." The riposte that they settled on was: "I'm glad for you that you don't *have* to have someone pay your way through college." "I just sat and listened as they talked," said Black. "They kept their own integrity intact without criticizing others."

However, there is no research to confirm whether and to what extent students feel some sort of stigma. But as Ort says, "happily, such conversations are noticeably absent on campus."

CRITICISM OF THE CAROLINA COVENANT

The Carolina Covenant has generated remarkably little criticism. In the early days of the program George Leef, director of the conservative Pope Center for Higher Education Policy, wrote a column declaring that he was "skeptical about the need for the covenant" because the university already has one of the lowest tuitions anywhere and students can easily meet the rest of their needs through borrowing and a campus job. He cited the fact that 8 percent of entering freshmen come from families with incomes low enough to qualify as Covenant Scholars as proof that "a large number of poor families are currently able to afford UNC," and he asked, "Why give them a free ride in hopes of attracting a few more students who might have been deterred from applying?" Leef concluded that "there are certainly better uses for the funds than a program that treats the poor as though they're so helpless that government must relieve them of the last small burden of sending a child to college."[9]

But such voices have been rare. "One of the remarkable things about the Carolina Covenant is that there has been no serious opposition to it," observed Dean Woodard. "That's because there is no doubt that these students are Carolina material. They come in as extraordinary students, diamonds in the rough who have achieved and excelled in spite of their backgrounds. There has been no lowering of standards. They have not been given a break because of their circumstances."

The work component also serves to drive home the message that, in Ort's words, "the Covenant is not a give-away program." Nor is it an "affirmative action" program as this term as usually defined because students are not designated Covenant Scholars until they have applied and been accepted at the university though normal admissions procedures. "These scholarships go to students who are admitted to Chapel Hill on their merits and whose only roadblock is lack of funds," she said. Steve Farmer, the undergraduate admissions director, emphasized this point as well. "I'm concerned that over time there will be a backlash against low-income students," he said. "We may be hearing the same thing about low-income kids that we heard about minority kids, especially if people think they are getting a break in admissions."

Policy Issues

One question that inevitably arises is whether the university might seek to broaden eligibility for the Carolina Covenant, perhaps by raising the income threshold above 200 percent of the federal poverty level—a pattern that can be seen at Princeton and other selective private schools. Ort takes the view that such a move would be a mistake. "We're already beginning to get some national pushback, and this would invite more middle income unrest," she said. "We are comfortable with our definition of low-income. The 200 percent figure is one that is typical of many programs and thus has currency in the broader policy context. Besides, other needy students are already getting 65 percent of their aid in the form of grants."

UNC's tradition of low tuition and generous financial assistance raises the basic philosophical question of why, if tuition is low, the university should be spending money on converting loans to grants? The university's answer to this question relates to the fact that low-income students are not so much *price-sensitive* as they are *aid-sensitive*. Linda LaMar, the consultant who helped design the Carolina Covenant, makes the point that low-income students appear to base their decisions about where to enroll more on the financial aid offered to them than on the published price of attendance. Grants, as a source of aid, are particularly important to such students, so they cannot be asked to increase their borrowing in order to offset tuition increases. "With good packaging, these students will be less price-sensitive," she said.

Conclusion

Shirley Ort is encouraged by the results shown by study of the first five cohorts of Carolina Covenant Scholars, as indicated through retention rates, grade-point averages, and graduation rates. Currently, RTI, International is conducting a major study of the program, with results to be released in early 2011. It is clear, however, that the university remains pleased by the growth in the number of Covenant Scholars enrolled, and in their academic performance.

University officials are concerned about one issue relating to academic eligibility. Ort said that examination of academic transcripts has revealed a pattern of some Covenant Scholars failing the same course two or even three times—possibly a reflection of the fact that, although these students may have had near-perfect grades in high school, the standards of their high school may have been modest. Many of these students are those who are hoping to attend medical school or who do well in courses other than math and science. She observed that, while university officials are eager to support students in their aspirations—"No one wants to convey bad news"—they might be better advised to take a quite different approach. "We need to develop a bridge program between freshman and sophomore years that will move beyond helping students hold on to their original dreams and redirect them to majors or programs where they can do well," she said. "We might offer summer school to students only if they agree to be part of the bridge program."

Dean Woodard said that the issue of how to offer mentoring and other support in helpful ways has special nuances at UNC and other flagship public universities. "A lot of our students are dealing with the 'Chosen One' syndrome," he said. "They were stars in high school and arrive at Carolina with high expectations for their success on the part of their families and communities. For them the stakes of failure are high. They can't go home and tell their parents that 'your future doctor just flunked introductory chemistry.' So they dig in and try to tough it out in courses where they have not done well even though they would be much better off looking at different options. These students in general—not just Covenant Scholars—are the most difficult students to redirect."

Woodard said that, from a policy point of view, it is important to allow high-ability, low-income students to hear "multiple voices" offering guidance to Covenant Scholars as they face the challenges of four years at a flagship university. "They need to hear from more than one person that it is okay to have a Plan B and choose a major for which they are better prepared. The counseling cannot be mandatory, because it is important that these students discover this for themselves. But they are used to doing this. I've been here long enough to see students re-tool and move on to law school or whatever."

The Carolina Covenant has also taken on national significance. Since it began a number of public universities have initiated their own programs aimed at increasing the number of low-income students in their undergraduate bodies. The University of Virginia has explicitly developed its Access UVA on the Carolina Covenant model. In September 2006, UNC held a conference, "The Politics of Inclusion," during which representatives of about two dozen institutions described what they were doing in this area. Recent studies suggest that the number of institutions employing similar approaches has now grown to nearly one hundred.[10]

Professor James Johnson of the Kenan-Flagler School of Business views the Carolina Covenant as a means of promoting diversity. The Carolina Covenant, he said, "puts Carolina where it has always been: at the leading edge of innovation. You don't just fold tent with challenges to affirmative action. You think outside the box. It's the classic entrepreneurial spirit: one door closes, so you cut another one. And it's politically smart because it's based on class, not on race. You can, if you do it right, still achieve racial gains."

Steve Farmer echoed a sentiment that is frequently heard on campus regarding the extent to which the Carolina Covenant has "reinforced the way in which we think about ourselves as a university." "It has given us a concrete way to live out the ideals to which we aspire," he said. For her part, Shirley Ort says that the Carolina Covenant has "exceeded my expectations" not only because it has attracted highly qualified students to Carolina who otherwise would have gone elsewhere but also because of the way it has been received.

"I never appreciated the extent to which it would resonate with the public," she said. "The program has reinforced and reinterpreted what it means to be a People's University. It has simplified a complex subject and let us talk about it in a way that makes sense to the public. It has given us a way to think about first generation, low-income students in our midst. It has added mindfulness of who is among us and what their challenges are and how we can intervene to help them. I think we all wanted to push the 'refresh' button on these historic values. The Covenant helped us do that."

How Increasing College Access Is Increasing Inequality, and What to Do about It

Anthony P. Carnevale and Jeff Strohl

Introduction

In the postindustrial economy, educational attainment, especially post-secondary educational attainment, has replaced the industrial concept of class as the primary marker for social stratification. In particular, in the post–World War II era, access to postsecondary education has become the salient mechanism driving access to middle-class earnings and status.[1]

Our own analysis of data from the Current Population Survey (CPS)[2] shows that high school dropouts and high school graduates who do not attain postsecondary education are losing their middle-class status.

- In 1967, only half of the nation's high school dropouts were concentrated in families within the bottom two deciles of family income. By 2004, more than 60 percent of high school dropouts lived in such families.

- In 1967, 25 percent of the nation's high school graduates who did not attain postsecondary education were concentrated in families in the bottom two deciles of family income, and almost 69 percent were in families in the middle five deciles in family income. By 2004, more than 37 perecent of high school graduates were in families in the bottom two deciles of family income, and the amount in the middle five had dropped to 52 percent.

People with some college or an associate degree have lost some ground, but they have done much better in holding on to their middle-class status than high school graduates and dropouts, and among those who left the middle-class, rougly equal shares have moved up or moved down.

- In 1967, 21 percent of people with an associate degree or some college were in the bottom two deciles of family income; this increased to 26 percent by 2004. But over the same period, the share in the upper three deciles of family income increased from 11 percent to 18 percent.

People with baccalaureates or graduate degrees either have stayed in the middle class or have moved up into the top three income deciles.

- In 1967, 66 percent of people with baccalaureates were in the middle five deciles of family income and 22 percent were in the top three deciles. By 2004, 50 percent of baccalaureates were still in the middle five family income deciles and more than 36 percent were in the top three income deciles.

- In 1967, 57 percent of people with graduate education were in families with incomes in the middle five deciles and 32 percent were in the upper three deciles. By 2004, 37 percent of people with graduate education still had incomes in the middle five deciles and 57 percent were in the upper three deciles of family income.

Because of its growing strength as the arbiter of economic opportunity, postsecondary education has become the preferred and the most effective economic leveler, serving as an engine for mobility. For example, almost 20 percent of adults with a college degree who are the children of a parent in the bottom 20 percent of the income distribution end up in the top 20 percent of the income distribution, and there is a 62 percent chance they will be middle class or higher.[3]

As is often the case, regarding the equalizing effects of education, the public was the first to know. Experts still contest the notion that everyone needs at least some college in order to make it in today's economy,[4] but the train has already left the station with the general public on board. The belief that access to postsecondary education is indispensable to success, like high school used to be, is widespread among the public, and the notion that there are alternatives is in rapid decline.[5] The vast majority of Americans believe that access to post-secondary education is crucial for successful careers, and that no one should be denied access to college because of cost. And despite rising costs, more than three-quarters of high school graduates now give college a try, increasing college enrollments more than fourfold since the 1950s.

But our nation's progress on postsecondary access has been bit-tersweet. Postsecondary enrollments are increasing, but the rate of increase has slowed significantly since the 1980s. Graduation rates have declined. Moreover, access to a college education and the completion of it have become more stratified by race, ethnicity, and socioeconomic status (SES). Americans can tolerate a lot of inequality compared with people of other nations, but only if everyone has a chance at upward mobility. But both economic mobility and educational mobility seem to be slowing with each generation.[6] More than 30 percent of whites and nearly 50 percent of Asians have earned baccalaureate degrees, compared with only 18 percent of African Americans and 12 percent of Hispanics. Our own analysis of the National Educational Longitudinal Survey (NELS) shows that only 7 percent of high school youth from the bottom quartile of SES, as measured by parental income, education, and occupational status, get baccalaureate degrees.[7]

Our mixed performance suggests that we have been underinvest-ing in postsecondary education and training since the early 1980s, and virtually all the underinvestment has come in the less-selective tiers of four-year colleges and among community colleges.[8] Moreover, there is substantial evidence that we have been disinvesting in public postsecondary institutions relative to private institutions.[9]

Our postsecondary system expanded dramatically in the post–World War II era, but at the same time it became less productive, less fair, and less competitive in the global race for human capital development. The rate of increase in postsecondary enrollments lost momentum in the 1980s and completion rates declined from 50 percent to 45 percent. Virtually all the decline in completion came in the less-selective four-year and community colleges where most students enroll and the spending per student is lowest. In addition, it seems clear that no more than a third of declining completions are due to student preparedness. At least two-thirds of the decline can be explained by lack of institutional resources in the lower-tier four-year colleges and community colleges.[10]

Ever since the 1980s, postsecondary access, persistence, and completion in the United States have fallen further and further behind the demand for postsecondary educated workers.[11] As a result, earnings inequality between those with at least some college and those with a high school diploma or less has spiked, and we increasingly have become a nation of "postsecondary haves" and "postsecondary have-nots."[12]

The growing inequality in opportunity between postsecondary haves and have-nots has been accompanied by a simultaneous stratification within the college-going population itself. The increasing stratification is due, in part, to the rationalization of the domestic postsecondary selection system and its ability to sort students nationwide.[13] Following World War II, students with high test scores—a group that previously had gone to schools locally—increasingly attended schools all over the country. Throughout the post–World War II era, growth in postsecondary enrollments has become more integrated into a nationwide sorting system, differentiated by a hierarchy of test-based admissions requirements. With students no longer tied to their local area, there has been a growing divide among postsecondary students by years of instruction, the mix of general education and occupation-specific training, and per-student spending.

In addition, postsecondary growth in the United States is no longer keeping up with the postsecondary expansion in other advanced economies. America still leads the world with an average of 12.5 years of schooling for its population.[14] The United States is still number one in baccalaureate production among the Organisation for Economic Co-operation and Development (OECD) nations,[15] but the United

States has fallen to seventh in high school graduation rates, the crucial preparation for postsecondary access and success. In addition, America's postsecondary performance has not improved in decades, and the United States is quickly losing ground due to rapidly accelerating increases in postsecondary attainment in virtually all the other OECD nations. The United States is twenty-second in attainment below the baccalaureate level. As a result of its poor performance below the baccalaureate level, the United States ranks seventh in total postsecondary performance.

Most disturbing is the fact that America is dead last in the rate of increase in both postsecondary attainment at the sub-baccalaureate level and in baccalaureate attainment. And it is last by a lot. Only the United States and Germany have postsecondary attainment increases in the single digits. And the Germans are hampered in their OECD ranking because their apprenticeship programs are not fully counted as part of the postsecondary system. The other twenty-nine OECD nations have been increasing baccalaureate attainment and overall postsecondary attainment at double- or triple-digit rates.[16]

Moreover, the steady drumbeat of bad news for the United States on international achievement tests shows that American students are still behind in terms of what U.S. students actually know and can do. America consistently is ranked low in all the international tests of educational achievement in reading, math, and science, as well as in work-based skills and literacy.

It is news to most Americans that other advanced economies have surpassed them in sub-baccalaureate attainment, are running faster and catching up at the baccalaureate level, and have overtaken and surpassed American students in tested achievement. Until recently, the United States led the world in the democratization of educational attainment and achievement. The U.S. education system grew faster than anywhere else because of its fragmentation, its flexibility, and its forgiving entry standards. Over the past two centuries, America's market-driven education system encouraged innovation and flexibility in response to new challenges. It allowed growth from the bottom up, drawing on a wide variety of public and private funding sources. It also discouraged the dangers of central government control over the education of American youth. Education in America grew by the accretion of a diverse array of public and private investments and an equally diverse array of public and private purposes. Religion, for example, played an early role in prompting basic literacy in order to read Bibles, Torahs, and catechisms so as to ward off false prophets. In the Jacksonian era, literacy became necessary in order to read the news and participate in a populist democracy and the opportunities that came from a booming frontier moving west. Governments chipped in for particular purposes along the way by providing educational land grants as part of the westward expansion. In the post–World War II era, when we moved toward a mass postsecondary system, the federal government continued the laissez-faire system of expansion and funding by empowering students with grants and loans for college with very few strings attached in choosing providers.

The flexible, fragmented, and forgiving American education system made the United States the global leader in democratizing education: first in elementary education, then in secondary, and more recently in postsecondary education. But the postsecondary expansion began to slow in the 1980s. The fragmentation of the American system that once encouraged growth and access may have matured to the point where it now discourages growth and access. The highly fragmented PreK–12 system led to wide differences in resources and quality throughout the PreK–16 system. The wide differences in resources, for example, results in lower student-teacher ratios, less counseling, and fewer student support services, all of which affect access to postsecondary education. Many of those less advantaged students who do run the PreK–12 gauntlet fail to complete college because they face an even more unequal distribution of resources in the two-year and four-year college system than they faced in the PreK–12 system. In the end, fragmentation leads to an inefficient use of resources because it does not match resources to marginal increases in quality and completion. Fragmentation also encourages a very high correlation between educational spending and student family income, resulting in a high concentration of students who are least prepared for college work and who do not enroll in college or who become enrolled in institutions with the least resources to help them.

By way of contrast, centralized governments shaped the education systems in many of the other OECD nations. The centrally funded, governed, and administered higher education systems limited postsecondary growth and access, but invested heavily in all students, including those in non-college apprenticeship tracks. As a result, when these more-centralized regimes finally decided in the 1970s that they needed to build a mass postsecondary education system, they had the benefits of central funding, governance, and accountability systems that allowed them to expand rapidly and deliberately in a cost-effective manner.

As a result, America is falling behind in the global race for human capital development.[17] Postsecondary enrollments and completions in the other advanced nations are growing much faster than in the United States; at their current pace, those nations likely will expand their lead at the sub-baccalaureate level and eventually overtake the United States in baccalaureate attainment.

To be clear, we are not arguing for a centralized, European-style system. Centralizing educational authority is tempting for efficiency's sake, but rigid at best and dangerous at worst. Centrally controlled systems tend to be inflexible, unresponsive to diverse missions, and downright dangerous if central authority gets captured by the authoritarian visions of either the left or right. But it does seem apparent that we have moved into a period when the historical advantages of our market-driven system have become a mixed blessing. Our laissez-faire system has inspired overall growth in postsecondary access, institutional innovation, and quality. But the rising costs in the most selective tiers has helped drive up prices for high-quality four-year postsecondary education overall. The rising per student costs of selective, high-quality postsecondary education has limited growth by absorbing resources that could have been spent to expand the overall number of students served in the less selective postsecondary education institutions, especially community colleges. We are building a postsecondary system polarized by race, ethnicity, and class and a mismatch between resources and need. The rising tuitions charged in selective colleges have pushed once-affordable quality education beyond the reach of the vast majority of Americans, including hundreds of thousands of high school graduates who are qualified for selective colleges but cannot afford them. Our forgiving PreK–12 standards have left many other students unprepared for college or learning on the job. In addition to the problems of skyrocketing costs and uneven quality, our postsecondary education system has become increasingly stratified even as access grows. The fragmentation of financing and governance in the postsecondary system into thousands of relatively independent public and private institutions makes it difficult to control costs or to promote consistent quality.

The American postsecondary system more and more resembles a dual system, with half of the annual enrollments concentrated in what the Barron's rankings[18] call the "competitive" four-year colleges and the other half of annual enrollments concentrated in community colleges and other sub-baccalaureate institutions at the bottom of the distribution of selectivity. This bi-modal distribution of enrollments is connected in the middle by declining enrollments in the group of schools that Barron's calls "Less" and "Non-Selective" four-year colleges (see Figure 3.1). This polarization of the postsecondary system is doubly concerning, because it mirrors the parallel concentration of white students and students from affluent families at the top and a concentration of African Americans, Hispanics, and students from low-SES families at the bottom.[19]

Figure 3.1 Postsecondary Enrollments, by Type, 1994 and 2006

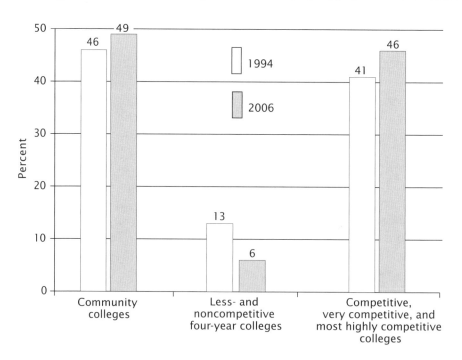

Source: National Education Longitudinal Study: Base Year through Fourth Follow-Up, 1988–2000 (Washington, D.C.: U.S. Dept. of Education, National Center for Education Statistics, 2000); The Education Longitudinal Study of 2002: Base Year through Second Follow-Up, 2002–2006 (Washington, D.C.: U.S. Department of Education, National Center for Education Statistics, 2006).

Students in selective colleges get more for less. Advantaged students attend higher-quality institutions and pay a smaller share of the costs of their education relative to less-advantaged students in community colleges and in the less-prestigious four-year colleges. Students in the wealthiest 10 percent of institutions pay 20 cents for each dollar spent on them. Students in the poorest 10 percent of colleges pay 78 cents for each dollar spent on them.[20]

The U-shaped postsecondary system in Figure 3.1 produces an equally polarized pattern in career opportunities and individual empowerment after the college years. Those students in the more-selective four-year institutions are tracked into professional and private sector managerial careers that bring high earnings, as well as greater autonomy on the job and in society. Students in the less-selective four-year colleges are tracked into the rank and file professions such as K–12 teaching, health care technician jobs, and state and local public administration. Students tracked into the two-year college system become more narrowly skilled workers in technical roles in the middle-range of earnings and autonomy on the job.

This growing stratification is not just about money—it is also about what money buys. The best education that money can buy is still one that combines general preparation at the baccalaureate level with postgraduate professional training. Those at the top of the postsecondary system get the most general preparation and are on the professional track. Those at the bottom are tracked into narrower job training that diverts them into good but less secure mid-level jobs.

The economy now rewards the richest mixes of general cognitive competencies such as problem-solving and critical thinking as well as soft competencies such as teamwork and communications. The highest returns come to those who mix these general competencies with solid occupational preparation. High-octane combinations of general- and occupation-specific competencies maximize learning and adaptability at work as well as access to flexible technology on the job. The effects are cumulative and build enormous differences in earnings momentum over careers.[21]

The growing importance of general education and general cognitive and behavioral competencies such as problem-solving, critical thinking, communication, and teamwork is at the heart of the switch from the industrial to the postindustrial service economy. In the postindustrial economy, repetitive, job-specific tasks increasingly are embodied in computer technology or shipped offshore, while more and more of the higher wage and more secure career jobs are made up of non-repetitive tasks that require sharpened general cognitive and behavioral competencies. As a result, general skills have more direct value in the short term and increase adaptability over the long haul.[22]

POSTSECONDARY EDUCATION AND THE AMERICAN SOCIAL CONTRACT

Increasing postsecondary stratification and the growing divide between students pursuing general education and those pursuing job training are troubling because they threaten the grand bargain in the American social contract. The bargain struck early on in the industrial era was necessary to reconcile the conflicting values implicit in the institutions of democratic citizenship and economic markets. During the eighteenth and nineteenth centuries, the ideas that animated democratic citizenship and economic markets grew together in the same British and European neighborhoods. At the time, the idea of democratic citizenship and the emergence of industrial capitalism were allied in their revolt against feudalism, but they were also natural antagonists.

Democratic citizenship and markets are driven by irreconcilable principles. Democratic citizenship presumes equality, but market economies are driven by inequality. This inequality is necessary to motivate work effort, entrepreneurship, and the inherently lopsided accumulation of wealth necessary to generate investment capital.

Publicly supported education, along with expansion in government protections and social services, became the key elements in reconciling the inherent conflict between democratic citizenship and market economies. The seminal statement on the role of education and the welfare state in sealing the social contract was formulated in a speech by Alfred Marshall to the Cambridge Reform Club in 1873. Marshall squared the equality implicit in citizenship with the inequalities inherent in markets by arguing that markets would become the paymaster for a constant expansion in publicly funded education and social services. Market economies would generate taxable wealth necessary to fund enough publicly provided education and social services to guarantee citizens full membership in society while preserving free markets. "The question," he said, "is not whether all men will ultimately be equal—that they certainly will not—but whether progress may not go on steadily, if slowly, till, by occupation at least, every man is a gentleman" who values education and leisure more than the "mere increase in wages and material comfort."[23]

In 1873, Alfred Marshall was referring to the intrinsic, cultural, and civic values of learning, not its direct economic value. He viewed public education as a mechanism that would lead the populace to "steadily accept the private and public duties of citizenship."[24] He assumed that education would be a universal common experience rather than a sorting device. In Marshall's day, most people learned their occupations on the job, not in universities. He did not foresee that education would eventually confer market power and wealth through access to the most highly leveraged occupations and knowledge.

In 1949, T. H. Marshall (no relation to Alfred) updated the original concept in a speech commemorating Alfred Marshall's classic formulation of the Western social contract.[25] T. H. Marshall asserted that the equality implicit in citizenship implied "a modicum of economic welfare and security" sufficient "to share to the full in the social heritage and to live the life of a civilized being according to the standards prevailing in the society." He went on to explain that the institutions most closely connected with this notion of citizen equality "are the education system and the social services."[26] T. H. Marshall's speech was seminal because it became the widely recognized summation of the argument for the massive expansion in both public education and the welfare state after World War II.

In his 1949 speech, T. H. Marshall updated Alfred Marshall's original vision on the role of education as a democratizing force. T. H. Marshall worried that the democratizing role of education increasingly was compromised by the growing strength of the relationship between education and the unequal access it provided to the growing economic, social, and political value of knowledge. Up to a point, access to education made everyone equal as citizens, but those with the most education were, as is often said, more equal than others.

Marshall begins by noting that industrial society "has been accused of regarding elementary education solely as a means of providing capitalist employers with more valuable workers, and higher education merely as an instrument to increase the power of the nation to compete with its industrial rivals. . . . As we all know, education today is closely linked with occupation" and that "(T)hrough education in its relations with occupational structure, citizenship operates as an instrument of social stratification."[27]

T. H. Marshall's ambiguity on the subject of education as a democratizing force is still germane and is amplified by the increasing stratification of the education system. In the knowledge economy, postsecondary education has become the principal arbiter of access to elite careers, as well as a powerful marker for social stratification. At the same time, the increasing economic value of postsecondary education (as well as research and development) also creates tensions between the intrinsic, cultural, and civic values of knowledge and its value as economic capital or human capital in its embodied form.

Of course, using education as the arbiter of wealth and power has the obvious virtue of its connection to meritocracy and individual responsibility. But as social science and cognitive science prove more and more, individual educational success is, in substantial part, a social construct. Ability is for the most part developed, not innate. Quality education develops ability, but access to quality education is stratified by race, ethnicity, and class.

It is hardly news that college education has been the preferred path to middle-class status and earnings in the United States. What is news, however, is that the strength of the relationship between education and social and economic status has increased dramatically, especially since the 1980s. With the disappearance of the blue-collar economy, college education became the only game in town. Postsecondary education is now not only the preferred path to middle-class status, it is also the most-traveled path.

The built-in tension between postsecondary selectivity and upward mobility is particularly acute in the United States. Americans rely on education as an economic arbiter more than do other modern nations. The American course since industrialization has been exceptional. The Europeans have relied more on the direct redistributive role of the welfare state to reconcile citizenship and markets. Americans always have preferred education over the welfare state as a means for balancing the equality implicit in citizenship and the inequality implicit in markets. The welfare state advances in the United States, but grudgingly, as the recent debate over health care demonstrates vividly.

In our individualistic culture, education is preferred over direct redistribution as the arbiter of economic outcomes because, in theory, education allocates opportunity without surrendering individual responsibility. The basic assumption is that we each have to do our homework and ace the tests that get us through the education pipeline and into good jobs. Using education to allocate opportunity also provides a uniquely American third way between the high risk that comes with doctrinaire market fundamentalism and the dependency that comes with an expanded welfare state. Consequently, access to education, especially high-quality postsecondary education, bears more and more of the political weight that comes with the nation's founding commitment to equal opportunity and upward mobility.

It is not surprising that postsecondary access and completion have become the consensus priority in response to both social and economic change. Access and completion goals have been bold. The Lumina Foundation has committed to the goal of doubling the share of Americans who receive a postsecondary credential. The Gates Foundation has committed to the goal of doubling the number of students who earn a postsecondary credential with labor market value by the age of twenty-six.

Successive national administrations have moved gradually toward the recognition that postsecondary education and training is a general requirement for economic success. The Clinton administration supported a two-pronged strategy that endorsed high-school-to-work programs in the first term, but shifted to a stronger emphasis on student aid for college funding in the campaign for the second term. Margaret Spellings, the secretary of education under George W. Bush, was the first to make a cabinet-level commitment to universal postsecondary education. According to the 2006 U.S. Secretary of Education's Commission on the Future of Higher Education: "We acknowledge that not everyone needs to go to college. But everyone needs a postsecondary education. Indeed we have seen ample evidence that access to postsecondary education is increasingly vital to an individual's economic security."[28]

In 2009, the Barack Obama administration began with the presumption of universal postsecondary access and affordability. President Obama challenged all Americans, both youth and adults, to complete an additional year of college, thereby shifting the focus away from traditional degrees and broadening the scope of postsecondary goals toward a more general notion of postsecondary education that included job-related learning and lifelong learning. In his first speech to a joint session of the Congress, the new president articulated a vision that included both education and training when he said: "I ask every American to commit to at least one year or more of higher education or career training. This can be community college or a four year school; vocational training or an apprenticeship."

Subsequently, in the American Graduation Initiative (AGI), President Obama turned the usual trickle-down funding approach upside-down by targeting spending toward community colleges at the bottom of the postsecondary hierarchy. As of this writing, the Obama initiatives open the door for efforts to move public resources for high-quality programs to the community colleges and less-selective four-year institutions where the mass of new and less-advantaged students are concentrated.

We agree with this expanding scope for postsecondary policy. It reflects a recognition of the crucial role that postsecondary education and training plays in expanding individual opportunity and increasing U.S. competitiveness. At the same time, we recognize that education, especially postsecondary education, has a wide variety of cultural, political, and economic roles. However, the increasing value of knowledge as human capital makes the economic role of postsecondary education pivotal in achieving the cultural and political goals of postsecondary institutions. Ours is a society based on work. Those unable to get or keep jobs for extended periods are excluded from full participation in American life. Those unable to get and keep good jobs disappear from the mainstream economy, culture, and political system. In the worst cases, those excluded from the mainstream economy may create alternative economies, cultures, and political movements that are a threat to the mainstream. Consequently, if postsecondary institutions do not empower their students with employability, their role of preparing students to thrive in the culture and political system of the nation will be severely undermined.

Successful Postsecondary Reform

How will we know when we are headed in the right direction in postsecondary reform? We believe that the first sign that we are headed toward a more effective and fair postsecondary system will come when college funding and program quality depend more on prospective graduation rates than the test scores of the students who attend. Completion is the most obvious and measurable goal within arm's reach in the short term. Completion goals, properly constructed, naturally encourage program reforms that tie program quality and resources to persistence and graduation. For example, we know that graduation rates among students from every race, ethnicity, and SES category increase as spending per student and selectivity increase. Moreover, the completion rates go up as spending and selectivity increase, even among equally qualified students in the top half of the test score distribution. As a result, it seems intuitively sound to suppose that some mix of increased spending and the program quality it buys will increase graduation rates in the entire postsecondary system. Pursuing the goal of increasing completion rates therefore must lead us to consider the relationships among spending, quality, and graduation rates. That line of inquiry and practice seems much more likely to yield cost-effective quality than the spiraling costs and stratification that come with our current reliance on selectivity alone as the singular standard for quality.

A focus on completion also seems to move us toward a more equitable standard for admissions. In our current system, for

individual students, small variances in SAT or ACT scores can make
the difference between getting into the school of your choice or being
rejected, and for colleges, they can result in being higher or lower in
the Barron's ranking. But among the upper-half of the SAT or ACT
test score distribution, these minor score variations do not matter
nearly as much in terms of predicting graduation rates—or, for that
matter, in terms of career success.

Focusing Only on Access and Completion Is Not Enough

In general, the current wave of postsecondary reform emphasizes improving access and completion as goals, but is silent on
questions of postsecondary tracking. We believe that the focus on
access and completion are ambitious and laudable, but the postsecondary challenges do not end there. As we will argue throughout this
chapter, expanding postsecondary education and training increases
opportunity, but also results in increasing stratification in degree
and non-degree attainment, spending per student, and the balance
between general education and narrower job training. And the ongoing stratification of the postsecondary system threatens to exacerbate
and reproduce inequality across generations of American families on
the basis of politically charged categories including race, ethnicity,
and socioeconomic status.

Adding the goals of improving upward mobility and the quality
of curriculums to access and completion as goals seems to be a step
in the right direction. There is a rich menu of fully developed policy
options to consider in this regard. More affirmative action based on
race, ethnicity, and socioeconomic status is an obvious and controversial strategy that brings at least a small number of less-advantaged
students into the highest quality postsecondary programs. There are
many less-controversial strategies that also need more emphasis in
the current dialogue, such as better K–12 preparation, K–16 alignment and transparency, effective remediation, counseling, more and
simpler need-based financial aid, and better information on postsecondary costs, program choices, and educational and career outcomes
for use by consumers, administrators, and policymakers.[29]

We are concerned that strengthening incentives for access and
completion alone may have unintended consequences that actually

exacerbate stratification. Successive rounds of budget and performance pressures driven by completion and "time to degree" metrics naturally will bias individual institutions toward enrolling more-advantaged students as well as narrowing, shortening, and watering down their curriculums. The same incremental pressures can result in a gradual movement toward system-wide policies that overemphasize access and completion in ways that squeeze out equity and quality. Access and completion improvements all by themselves cannot deliver on equally important equal opportunity and upward mobility goals. Access and completion beg the question: access to and completion of what, and by whom? Our current system is becoming more accessible, but it becomes so by tracking minorities and students from working-class families into lower-cost and lower-quality two-year programs and tracking high-income white students into high-cost four-year programs with a graduate school option included. In sum, absent explicit goals for equity in funding as well as racial, ethnic, and class diversity, reform can become an engine for inequality.

A similar pattern was obvious in the transition to the mass high school system in the twentieth century. The "comprehensive high school" created a college track, a vocational track, and a watered-down general track that conformed closely with hierarchies built along lines of race, gender, and SES.[30] Ironically, we have been laboring since 1983, when the report A Nation at Risk was released,[31] to undo the damage done by high school tracking, even as we are building a tracking system along the same lines in the postsecondary system.

Improving the quality of curriculums is the missing middle ground in reform efforts that focus on achieving higher rates of access and completion. Ultimately, access and completion are standards that can be met satisfactorily with quantitative metrics that have little to do with the quality of education programs. Quality is the proper standard for what happens between access and completion. In order to set quality standards, we need to decide what students need to know to succeed in a postindustrial and globalized economy, culture, and political system. The quality of the curriculum is the distinguishing characteristic of programs that train for a job using best practices that educate for professional careers in a broad range of job clusters. The quality of the curriculum also distinguishes between job training and broader liberal arts curriculums that prepare people for full inclusion in the culture and polity.[32]

The current reform focus (at the time of this writing) on access and completion also tends to accept the hierarchy of postsecondary curriculums as given. Even the thrust of policy proposals for increasing upward mobility, such as affirmative action, tend to focus on leveraging minorities and less-advantaged students into the existing hierarchy of spending and quality. But there are limits to available seats in high-quality four-year programs in the upper half of the current postsecondary hierarchy.

The radical notion that the United States can spread quality by redistributing postsecondary resources downward has its practical, political, and ethical limits as well. While the current system tends to ensure that the rich institutions get richer, the rich institutions are never going to be rich enough to fund quality in the bottom half of the postsecondary system. The idea of redistributing resources from rich to poor institutions would be politically difficult. Moreover, few would deny parents the opportunity to do the best they can for their children. And while competition for prestige for prestige's sake may be overdone, healthy competition among postsecondary institutions and among students can act as a source of innovation and high-end quality.

Strategies for improving access and completion are inextricably bound up with questions of fairness. If we do not pay attention to equity and quality, attempts to increase access and completion are likely to backfire. For example, the general acceptance of using our underfunded community colleges to absorb the brunt of the increases in postsecondary enrollment does increase access on the cheap, but ignores the implicit tracking of minorities and less-advantaged students as they crowd into the community colleges. The current argument for turning four-year degrees into three-year degrees, as has been proposed by former U.S. education secretary Lamar Alexander is another strategy that may do more harm than good. The notion of knocking off a year at Harvard and the other selective private colleges and the public flagships is a political non-starter but might gain some traction in the less-selective public four-year colleges where less-advantaged students and lower-spending programs are concentrated. It also seems a bad idea in general when we need more, not less, high-quality postsecondary education. If we turn to three-year baccalaureates by watering down curriculums for the sake of affordability, access, and completion, the three-year degree likely will be forced upon the revenue-starved, least-selective colleges, and only add another tier to the increasingly stratified postsecondary system.

Accelerating curriculums makes sense, especially for adults and working students with a specific career certificate in mind, but it is a baby and bathwater strategy if it closes off further education leading to degrees or reduces program quality. There are limits to the extent to which teaching and learning can be sped up if quality is to be preserved. Compressed or speeded-up programs that are not structured carefully are bound to take some of the meat and bone with the fat. Compressing curriculum can help, but the best way to speed up programs and to increase completions is to provide working students, who include most of our postsecondary students already, with stipends that will allow them to take time off work to devote to their studies.[33]

MOVING QUALITY WHERE IT IS NEEDED

If we cannot move large numbers of less-advantaged students into quality programs at the selective colleges, then we may need to move quality programs, and the money to pay for them, to the community colleges and less-selective four-year colleges where the least-advantaged half of American postsecondary students are currently enrolled. Improving quality from the bottom up is largely unexplored territory. For example, while eliminating a year at selective four-year colleges that already require five and six years for graduation is unlikely, adding a year onto two-year institutions would meet with little resistance and could improve college quality appreciably, once we understood what we mean by quality. Leavening sub-baccalaureate education, including vocational associate degrees, certificates, and certifications with more powerful curriculums would help close the quality gap and educate for job clusters rather than single jobs. For example, turning many of our two-year curriculums into three-year or four-year curriculums would improve program quality and meet with much less resistance. Adding more high-quality two-year programs with guaranteed access to four-year institutions would provide more access to quality education for those who cannot afford it now. Transfer strategies make sense in a system such as America's, where students already transfer frequently. Transfer strategies also make sense where four-year public institutions are overcrowded, postsecondary demand has already outstripped postsecondary capacity, and students are trying to piece together alternatives that are less costly and less crowded routes to baccalaureate and graduate education.[34]

If we do not pay very explicit attention to postsecondary tracking by race, ethnicity, and class and differences in program quality, postsecondary reform that emphasizes cost cutting may further limit access to high-quality education for the least advantaged. Public leaders have signed on to the notion that everyone needs at least some postsecondary education or training. But tight budgets make the costs of this widely agreed to goal financially prohibitive. As a result, the consensus strategy is to get there with "affordability" as the principle strategy. Ultimately, if history is any guide, that means cuts in public postsecondary programs, especially in community colleges where the least advantaged are concentrated.

There are inefficiencies in postsecondary budgets, no doubt, and sensible cost cutting and technology can give us more wiggle room to create more access. Once exposed, the inefficiencies can free up resources for improving access, quality, and completion rates in general, and the same outcomes by race, ethnicity and class, in particular. Every university does not need a graduate school in every department. There could be more teaching and less research done in four-year colleges. Forced choices between teaching, learning, and extracurricular activities should favor teaching and learning. Not every college has to be residential, and computer and communications technology can substitute for full-time, rigidly scheduled courses.

But cutting institutional costs and adding technology may not result in lower tuitions and may well result in less access and quality, especially for the least-advantaged students and students who do not fit the traditional college student profile of full-time residential education for eighteen-to-twenty-four-year olds. Tuition revenues are still well below the actual costs of educating students.[35] Except for profit-making proprietary schools, tuition never covers full costs. Tuition falls short of costs by thousands in public institutions, and sometimes tens of thousands in selective privates with big endowments. In the public institutions, rising tuitions reflect declining public aid as much as rising costs. The state and federal governments make up the difference between tuition revenue and total cost per student, especially in public institutions. As the government withdraws under growing fiscal pressure, all other things equal, tuitions will rise to cover a growing share of costs, but postsecondary institutions are likely to continue to take the rest of their cost cutting in the form of declining access and quality. Reform, in the guise of cost cutting, may get us some part of the way toward more access and completion, but only if we sacrifice access to more enriched curriculums, both general and applied, in the bottom tiers of the current system of selectivity. Marginal reforms also are risky in that they are most likely to erode spending in the most underfunded and overcrowded parts of the public system, and do so slowly enough so that they will not be noticed or mobilize resistance.

The notion that we can reach our access and completion goals just by cutting costs tends to rely on a view of postsecondary cost structures that does not square with the facts on the ground in the public and sub-baccalaureate institutions. It is generally presumed in most reform proposals that the cost of a new student should be cheaper because of economies of scale (marginal cost per student should be lower than average cost per student). This may be true in the final two years of the elite private schools, where class sizes are small, but there is very little excess capacity in much of the public system, where all the new students are crowding in and there are already quality deficits. In the public institutions, especially the community colleges, overcrowding, capacity shortages, and increases in enrollment in combination with declining per-student investments have resulted in declining quality.[36] In institutions that are already over capacity, new students reduce quality, not marginal costs.

When budgets are tight, reforms that emphasize accountability and standards-based quality may only exacerbate the negative unintended consequences of cost-cutting reforms. Absent specific goals for including minorities and low-income students, the combined effects of affordability and accountability goals can lead to a self-reinforcing spiral of inequality. For example, some schools may decide that the surest way to make up for declining government aid is to admit only students who can pay the full tuition; the best way to increase the speed and rate of graduation is to admit only full-time students with the highest test scores; and the best way to attract students who can and are willing to pay full tuition is to spend heavily on prestige-building, test-based admission standards, star faculties, impressive facilities, and other amenities that will attract well-heeled and well-prepared students (attracting the most prepared students will in turn increase prestige, which attracts even more affluent, well-prepared and full-time students).

Examining the Problem in Depth

With these perspectives in mind, the remainder of this chapter will look more closely at the growing racial, ethnic, and socioeconomic stratification in postsecondary education.

Part 1 provides an historical context. We discuss the current postsecondary regime and its evolution. We lay out the current pattern of stratification in postsecondary education, its alignment with racial, ethnic, and socioeconomic stratification, and the resulting funding stratification among postsecondary institutions. We conclude, as have many others, that the current stratification has more negative than positive effects and can be reversed only by shifting our emphasis toward an outcomes-based system of postsecondary governance that balances access, quality, and completion goals in general, as well as the achievement of the same goals with more attention to racial, ethnic, and class diversity.

Part 2 shows that stratification is increasing within higher education, as affluent and white Americans flee the lower echelons of college selectivity to more exclusive precincts. We find a hierarchy of selectivity and resources per student through five tiers of selectivity, with the great divide in resources, quality, and equity coming abruptly between the top three tiers of selectivity and a melding of the lowest two tiers of four-year colleges and community colleges.

Part 3 demonstrates that access to selective colleges matters, because resources matter. We find that, even among equally qualified students, selective institutions provide considerably more resources per student, lead to higher graduate rates than less selective colleges, allow greater access to graduate and professional degrees, leverage higher earnings, and provide access to managerial and professional elites that confer special access to earnings as well as personal and social power.

Part 4 shows the extraordinary number of students who are qualified for selective four-year colleges who either do not go on to college at all, or who attend colleges below their levels of tested ability. For example, we find that every year almost 600,000 students graduate from the top half of their high school class and do not get a two- or a four-year degree within eight years of their graduation. More than 400,000 of these students come from families who make less than $85,000 a year. More than 200,000 come from families who make less than $50,000 a year, and more than 80,000 come from families with incomes below $30,000.

The chapter culminates in Part 5, which provides an empirical analysis of one way in which admissions preferences might be structured so that social, economic, and racial characteristics are mixed among qualified applicants. This part of the chapter quantifies the predicted SAT scores of students from different socioeconomic and racial backgrounds, teasing out the relative weights of various economic and racial disadvantages so that colleges and universities can better identify "strivers"—those qualified students who exceed their expected scores.

Finally, the chapter concludes with a discussion of policy implications. We find that affirmative action and other policies that give broader access to selective education can reduce—but are unlikely to reverse—the stratification in access to the resources that are only available in selective institutions. In our view, the more likely strategy for improving access to quality education for a broader mass of Americans is to decide what outcomes define quality, and to match resources to their achievement irrespective of where institutions sit in the prestige hierarchy.

1. THE INCREASING STRATIFICATION OF AMERICAN POSTSECONDARY EDUCATION

America's current postsecondary system offers a fragmented institutional hierarchy, informally arrayed vertically by selectivity. From the bottom up, its offerings range from non-credit course clusters in community colleges, to industry certifications, to certificates, to associate of arts degrees, to baccalaureate degrees, and on to graduate and professional degrees. The choice comes down to price, quality, and prestige at one end of the continuum, and education on the cheap and narrow at the other. Affordable quality is rarely on the menu. Upward mobility through affirmative action and student transfer is positive, but affects very few students. There is a limited and hotly contested mandate for inclusion and affirmative action throughout the top tiers of selectivity. There are very few enforceable, system-wide outcome standards in place that reflect the diversity of applied and academic missions or program quality, especially in the least selective four-year colleges, community colleges, and proprietary colleges. There are few systemic pathways that link courses, certificates, certifications, and degrees horizontally within institutional tiers, or vertically between institutional tiers.

In the current U.S. postsecondary system, cost-effective quality and upward mobility—the core offerings natural to a mass education system in a democratic society—are increasingly unavailable. The current postsecondary system is becoming more and more polarized—the choices offered are the lavish, full-service degrees offered by the pricey brand-name colleges that come with a graduation, graduate school, and good jobs warranty, or the bargain-basement alternatives offered on the cheap with no guarantees of completion or long-term value in the labor market.

In the current system, both public and private expenditures per student increase with institutional selectivity and student test scores. Implicit in the current distribution of spending is the notion that we should spend the most on the students with the highest test scores, class rank, advanced placement (AP) courses, teacher recommendations, and ability to pay.

Defenders of the current highly stratified system argue a tough-minded realism that asserts that the current arrangement is both fair and efficient. They argue the current stratified system is fair because the students with the highest grades and test scores are most deserving of elite education. They argue that the current system is efficient because spending the most on students with the greatest ability to benefit from elite education gives us the most bang for our post-secondary bucks—if we measure returns as individual learning and earning.[37]

The notion that the current stratification is efficient and fair is widely assumed or asserted by policymakers and analysts, but is rarely subjected to analytic or political scrutiny. The trend toward large and growing disparities in spending per student is accompanied by a parallel trend in which the lowest spending institutions, especially the community colleges, serve not only the largest share of students, but also a growing concentration of African-American, Hispanic, and lower-income students. Consequently, the hierarchy of per-student spending doubles as a hierarchy by race, ethnicity, and socioeconomic status.

A closer analysis challenges both the efficiency and equity assumptions that commonly are offered in defense of the current post-secondary regime. Questions of fairness in the current arrangements are longstanding. It seems clear that ability to benefit from high-quality postsecondary programs as measured by the SAT and ACT is highly correlated with racial, ethnic, and socioeconomic disparities. As such, these traditional metrics are—at least in part—mechanisms for legitimizing illegitimate differences in opportunities to learn that begin long before the nation's youth take college entrance exams.[38] In addition, admissions tests and other traditional metrics for college admissions are relatively weak as predictors of performance in college and in careers, especially above the middle range of test scores. While tests are useful in college admissions, they are used well beyond their predictive validity. Moreover, legacy admissions and all the other exceptions to the meritocratic rule in college admissions suggest there is ample room for growth in affirmative action to improve racial, ethnic, and socioeconomic diversity, if such diversity were to become a higher priority.[39]

The current hierarchical regime in postsecondary resources and quality also suffers from serious efficiency problems. Allocating resources based on prestige and reputational value concentrates resources at the top of the postsecondary hierarchy and reduces system-wide returns, especially if we think of returns in terms of access, quality, completion, and upward mobility. In addition, it is not at all clear that prestige, as opposed to gross differences in spending, actually produces differences in individual learning and earning. Prestige is an intangible and insatiable target for postsecondary investments. It is hard to argue that increasing spending per student at selective four-year colleges relative to spending at community colleges, which is what we have been doing for a long time now, increases overall access, completion rates, or program quality in the postsecondary system.

The pursuit of selectivity by students and institutions can turn into a rat race for status with relatively low investment returns for individuals directly involved or the broader mass of postsecondary students. Economists have written on the failure of markets to maximize investment returns in the consumption of positional goods since Adam Smith wrote on class-based consumption in England. Later on, Keynes distinguished between investments in "absolute" and "relative" goods. Veblen called these investments "conspicuous consumption." They all argued that, once economies move beyond subsistence, there is a tendency to consume some goods and services for status-seeking. Education and housing are among the usual examples where consumer markets distort investments and reduce returns. These investments are valued precisely because increasing consumption at the top does not increase or decrease consumption of the good or service on average. Marginal returns in investments are small at the top and static in the rest of the distribution. In this manner, markets in positional goods are said to unleash "social limits to growth."[40]

Increasingly polarized postsecondary investments bring diminishing returns. If graduation rates are already over 85 percent in selective colleges, it seems logical that increases in funding might not improve them very much. By way of comparison, the fewest resources systematically are allocated to the institutions with the lowest graduation rates, where marginal increases in resources should have the largest effects on access, quality, completion, and equity. Prestige is largely intangible and not solely based on teaching and learning. Brand name has no intrinsic educational value. In addition, prestige is mostly attached to institutions, not curriculums, and has little relationship with the quality of teaching and learning. More systemic investments below the institutional level in teaching and learning tied to quantitative metrics such as completion and labor market outcomes, as well as qualitative outcomes like civic, cultural, and scientific awareness would seem a better investment.

It seems doubtful that the current polarization of resources maximizes outcomes system-wide, especially since the largest shares of students attend the least-funded colleges. Only 11 percent of students attend the top 193 colleges in the 2009 Barron's rankings, and almost half of students attend the nation's community colleges and other non-baccalaureate institutions. Only about 7 percent of students are enrolled in institutions that spend more than $25,000 per enrollee, and almost half enroll in institutions that spend less than $10,000 per enrollee.[41] The inequality in spending occurs along two dimensions: the differences in spending between more- and less-selective institutions and the differences in spending between public and private institutions. On average, differences in spending among public institutions run about $4,000 per student, per year. According to data from the Delta Project on Postsecondary Education Costs, Productivity, and Accountability, public spending ranges from $9,184 per student, per year for two-year colleges to $13,819 for public research universities. This difference in public spending, on average, adds up to about $8,000 over two years and $16,000 between those who get a two-year degree compared to those who get four-year degrees.

Private institutional spending is much higher per student, ranging from an average of $15,224 for private master's degree granting institutions to $33,234 for private research universities. As a result, there is a difference in public versus private spending that ranges between $6,000 and $20,000 per student, per year attended—a difference of $12,000 to $40,000 over two years and a difference of $24,000 to $80,000 over four years.

The differences in spending among the private two-year and four-year colleges and between the two-year and four-year publics are not only large, they also are growing. Spending per student, per year at two-year public colleges has declined, and spending at four-year public colleges has remained flat, but spending per student at private colleges has increased by 8 percent at schools giving only a baccalaureate, 10 percent at schools giving master's degrees, and 11 percent at private research universities.[42]

Many would argue that we should ignore private colleges in any discussion of spending inequality because they are privately funded. But we think public subsidies to private colleges are fair game in trying to ascertain future optimal levels and distribution of higher education investments.

PUBLIC AND PRIVATE COLLEGES: NOT GOVERNMENT, BUT CREATURES OF GOVERNMENTS

Government invests in both public and private institutions because they create high public returns that otherwise would not be funded by markets, owing to the idea that individual and institutional buyers cannot capture the full social economic benefits for themselves. Higher education creates high private returns, but it is also a public good because it creates high levels of both economic and social benefits that, if not for government subsidies, would go unfunded in traditional capital markets.[43]

Arguably, the lion's share of private college funding does come indirectly from public expenditures and tax policies. The legal standard for the invaluable not-for-profit status granted to all but a small share of private postsecondary institutions is that they serve public purposes that otherwise would fall to governments. While private colleges are more reliant on private money, the public subsidies they receive are substantial. Students at private institutions and proprietary schools receive grant aid and subsidized loans that go directly to their bottom line. The tax benefits that come with not-for-profit status encourage charitable contributions and reduce taxes on assets. Tax credits and deductions for college costs incurred by households and loan subsidies add more revenue into private coffers. Research and development grants from governments also carry indirect overhead funds for general support.[44]

Most would agree that, in theory, there is some optimal distribution of public investment across public and private institutions that maximizea both economic and social returns in our higher education investments. The current system bears only a passing resemblance to that theoretical ideal because we do not measure social and economic outcomes in postsecondary education. Selectivity is presently driven by the cost of inputs—faculty, facilities, equipment, prestige amenities, and student subsidies—necessary to attract students with high test scores from families that can afford high tuitions. The public goods produced that inspire public investments are cultural, economic, and civic outcomes. Insofar as we know, these derive from performances on institutional outcomes such as access, quality, completion, upward mobility, and overall contributions to human capital development. Currently, we rely on input measures of institutional performance, but they are very rough proxies for the desired outcomes that make postsecondary education a public good. More importantly, they drive selectivity, which operates as a disincentive to the achievement of diversity and upward mobility.

If we cannot specify publicly valued outcomes, we cannot allocate resources efficiently to achieve them. We know that the economic rate of return to a year of postsecondary education exceeds the rate of return for an equal investment in capital markets.[45] In general, we know that capital markets do not capture the full benefits of college investments, and that underinvestment is almost certain, especially when public subsidies are in decline. The price of college talent rises when it is undersupplied. Consequently, rising college wage premiums since the 1980s are the most obvious evidence of underinvestment.[46]

We also know that inequality exacerbates underinvestment in postsecondary education. Some students are qualified, but make sub-optimal decisions about college attendance.[47] They do not go to college because they cannot come up with the money and supportive social capital necessary to move them on to college when it is time to go. Others never get properly prepared because of longer-term investment inefficiencies and inequality in the K–12 system.[48]

Inequality in costs at selective colleges also results in individual underinvestment in college quality (as measured by per-student spending). Students who are prepared for college may have access, but costs limit their choices. Cost differentials between two- and four-year institutions have become so great that the decision to begin at a four-year college is too great a financial commitment for more and more students. The same is true for enrollment decisions among four-year colleges. Each level of selectivity changes the scope of the individual financial commitment considerably, encouraging students, especially lower-income students, to invest in lower-quality programs.[49]

THE CURRENT DYNAMIC OF SELECTIVITY

The postsecondary hierarchy that has emerged in the United States is increasingly out of touch with the majority of postsecondary students and the democratic goals of a mass postsecondary system.

The vertical hierarchy is itself governed by abstract one-dimensional measures of talent such as test results from the SAT and ACT that are only loosely correlated with postsecondary learning and even more loosely correlated with career success. As a result, the postsecondary hierarchy tends to be reflexive and self referential, wedded to narrow and ultimately mysterious metrics for measuring potential.

The dynamic of postsecondary growth encourages the development of the postsecondary system as a one-dimensional vertical hierarchy. The development and vertical integration of the postsecondary system since the California plan in the 1960s presumes complementarities between spending per student and SAT and ACT scores as measures of the ability of students to benefit from higher spending. The vertical differentiation and integration of the higher education system raises tough questions, especially in tough times when resources are scarce.

A degree from a selective college is valuable, in part, because of its reputational value. As more and more students go to college, a brand-name degree can distinguish a new graduate from the growing pack of graduates. Branding signals learning potential to employers and increases access to graduate and professional occupations—not because a brand-name degree necessarily embodies learning or the ability to learn. The real educational value of a degree or award lies in the quality of the teaching and learning, and the quality of the teaching and learning in any college reflects, for the most part, two interacting elements: (1) the cost-efficiency of cumulative investments in the students during their K–12 preparatory years and (2) the value added from postsecondary investments.

Prestige has reputational and positional value, but educational value depends on effective educational investments in students and institutions. Hence, what appears to be a hierarchy in institutional prestige is actually a hierarchy in cumulative human capital investments that reflects underlying racial, ethnic, and socioeconomic stratification. If our postsecondary institutions are the capstone in a system in which quality is driven by cumulative investments in advantaged students, it raises equal protection problems at the postsecondary level that have been a staple of the K–12 debate since *San Antonio v. Rodriguez* in the 1970s.[50]

versities that sat atop the middle tier of less-selective state colleges and junior colleges were intended to provide universal access to the most-selective public colleges. Second, statutory provisions encouraged transfer from two-year to four-year institutions as the primary function of "junior" colleges.

But in hindsight, we now can see that the original post–World War II architecture for the mass postsecondary system worked only as long as revenues and enrollments expanded during the postwar economic boom and baby boom. By the 1970s, the influx of baby boomers peaked, and the postwar economic boom soured with economic stagnation and inflation—"stagflation." When the baby boom petered out and the economic boom ended, budgetary stringency systematically undermined postsecondary funding and discouraged transfers from two-year to four-year colleges. Ever since the cycles of booms and busts in postsecondary budgets have been tied to the cycles of recession and recovery, and underneath the waves there has been a steady shift toward a funding hierarchy tied to selectivity, with a minimum of upward mobility between the selectivity tiers or transfers between the community colleges and the four-year colleges.

After little more than a decade of shared growth, win/win bargaining between the elite private colleges, flagship public colleges, state colleges, and community colleges began to unravel. By the 1980s, the component institutions in the California system and its progeny in the other forty-nine states had reasserted themselves into a fragmented set of resource-hungry and status-driven institutional silos and individual institutions in head-to-head competition for public and private resources.

Differences in per-student spending by selectivity have grown since California launched the American version of the modern mass postsecondary system. And the central thrust of the growth in spending per student has been vertical, based on one-dimensional test-based measures of selectivity that do not reflect student or community financial capacity or needs. Vertical differences in selectivity drive spending much more than horizontal differences in program cost or student need. In community colleges, for example, the instructional and equipment costs for providing academic associate degrees are less than the costs of many technical associate degree programs. As a result, cost structures drive the provision of academic associate degrees over high-cost technical programs, even if the earnings returns and labor market demand favors the technical programs.

The first round of efforts since the 1960s to build a comprehensive governance system for the burgeoning variety of postsecondary institutions has not lived up to the original efficiency and equity expectations. Initially, the rising demographic and economic tide that came with the post–World War II baby and economic booms raised all the postsecondary boats. Elite private colleges, public flagships, state colleges, and less-selective private and community colleges were able to cut win/win deals to share in the new revenues from baby boom expansion and the postwar economic boom. But the early consensus quickly returned to sharp-elbowed competition when the money and the students ran out.

The California Master Plan and its progeny gradually have evolved into a caricature of their original selves, emphasizing their hierarchical features and deemphasizing their allegiance to access and transfer.[54] Nationwide, differences in spending per student have skyrocketed by level of selectivity. Stratification and diversification have hardened institutional boundaries and reduced mobility within the higher education system. For example, while community colleges have evolved to serve many functions other than transfer and baccalaureate attainment, only 10 percent of students who start out at community colleges get a baccalaureate.[55]

The funding crunch and an increasing demand for training also have created a growing divide between more general forms of education and job training in the public and private postsecondary system. Our own analysis of available data shows that occupational certificates, most highly concentrated in community colleges, made up 23 percent of postsecondary degrees and awards in 2006 and are growing faster than two- and four-year degrees. Contract training for incumbent workers has become a crucial revenue source for community colleges.

The postsecondary hierarchy mimics and then reinforces the workforce hierarchy. The most selective institutions provide an on-ramp to the graduate professions, finance, and other elite private sector occupations. The state colleges provide seats for those in the middle ranges of socioeconomic status and test scores, and prepare students for careers in the rank and file professions, especially in the public sector—including school teachers, the uniformed services, accountants, health care professionals (except doctors), and public and private administrators. The mass of the remaining students are allocated to community colleges where they have access to associate degrees and certificates that prepare them for roles as technicians, state-licensed occupations, and support functions in both the public and private sectors.

The community colleges and proprietary colleges seem ideally suited to the democratic standards of a mass higher education system. They are inclusive, lower cost, and adaptive to changing economic and social demands. But the community colleges seem to have too many missions and not enough money; as they continue to spread revenue across a broader segment of the postsecondary population, spending per student appears to be so watered down and diffused that additional spending at the margin has minimal effects on outcomes.[56] Accessibility and lower prices are not substitutes for affordable quality based on measured outcomes.[57]

This growing divide between selective four-year colleges and the less selective four-year and two-year institutions where the other half of American students enroll reflects a deeper divide between more general and job-specific forms of education. One system prepares a select minority for leadership and the other prepares the mass of students for jobs. According to the National Leadership Council for Liberal Education, even as we "dismantle the inequitable systems of academic vs. vocational tracking in . . . American high schools . . . tracks of the same kind are multiplying in postsecondary education . . . and these tracks are stratified by income and race."[58]

Differences between public and private resources also have widened. The flagship publics have become de facto private institutions in the pursuit of revenue and prestige, selling off public assets and moving further away from public equity goals. The state flagships have less and less to do with the states in which they were founded as they cope with declining public support and compete for prestige in a national and global context. Out-of-state and international students usually pay three times as much as in-state residents for access to the elite public colleges. They make up half the students at the University of Iowa, for example, and 44 percent at Penn State.[59] The public flagships have less and less to do with public purposes, especially the public commitment to equity and upward mobility. For example, the share of Pell Grant students at the University of Virginia has declined below 10 percent, compared with an almost 50 percent shares of Pell Grant recipients at the University of New Mexico; and the share of Pell Grant students are declining at thirty of the fifty flagship institutions.[60]

As it currently operates, the American postsecondary model invests disproportionately in selectivity over access, persistence, and completion, and generally ignores its core function, which is to improve the craft of teaching and learning.[61] The self-defeating race for prestige makes a fetish of test scores and the other admissions metrics as a way of keeping score. Even the insiders complain that the competitive dynamic now focuses on prestige more than innovations in teaching and learning or student outcomes.[62]

MENDING NOT ENDING THE RACE FOR PRESTIGE

Mending the race for prestige in postsecondary education means shifting the balance in the basis of competition from inputs to outcomes. Funding outcomes based on student needs would shift competition for funds toward the things that matter in postsecondary education and in the broader society: things such as cost-effective teaching and learning, educational value added, and student success. A focus on outcomes would increase choices among educational and career pathways and begin to flatten the rapidly ascending growth in the postsecondary hierarchy, reducing the socially and politically charged "winner take all" competition for elite college seats.[63]

An outcomes-based system also would create a more even playing field and competition based more on measured performance and less on longevity. The most selective colleges are America's oldest institutions. They have been around long enough to become venerable brands and create dynastic advantages from generations of former students who become contributing alumni. Longevity brings reputational advantages, which become financial advantages because reputation leverages institutional fund-raising and higher tuitions. Students from the most-prestigious institutions do benefit from their association with these brand-name organizations, but the larger effects seem to be grounded in the differences in educational spending while they were in college.[64]

Hence, reputation and college rankings are a pretty good proxy for quality, because reputation leads to gross differences in spending. But reputation and quality are not the same things, and competition based on gross spending differences discourages efficiency. There are also apparent inefficiencies in the contest for admission to prestigious colleges. The extensive efforts of students to build competitive applications for enrollment at selective colleges does not seem to have increased educational achievement proportionately.[65] Furthermore, college preparation has become decidedly unequal. For example, according to a recent analysis, only 8.3 percent of lower-income students take test prep courses, compared with 78 percent of upper-income students.[66] More than a third of upper-income students visit more than six colleges, compared to a little over 4 percent of lower-income students.

The fixation on admitting students with the highest test scores either in the interest of prestige or to maximize the likelihood of graduation seems excessive. It seems to make selective colleges much too risk-averse in balancing equity and efficiency goals. For example, we find that Barron's "Most" selective and "Highly" selective colleges include the most prestigious 22 percent of college seats. The likelihood of graduating from one of these colleges for students with an SAT/ACT equivalent score of 1000 to 1200 is about 85 percent; but, according to Barron's, these colleges tend to require test scores above 1250 for admission. The 1250 SAT/ACT score does increase the likelihood of graduating from 85 percent to 96 percent, but it also excludes large numbers of students who scored between 1000 and 1250 and would have a very high (85 percent) likelihood of graduating. The 1250 test score requirement also excludes a large swath of less-advantaged students who would have an 85 percent chance of graduating. We find that roughly a third (32 percent) of those who achieve an SAT/ACT score between 1000 and 1100 and almost a quarter (23 percent) who scored between 1100 and 1200 come from the bottom-half of the SES distribution.[67]

A FLAWED SUCCESS

The increasing access to postsecondary education has been extraordinary over the post–World War II era. However, this American postsecondary educational success comes with a dilemma:

the undeniable benefits of growing access have been diluted by the tracking of students by race, ethnicity, gender, socioeconomic status. As a result, the benefits of increased access tend to come wrapped in the tensions inherent in increased racial, ethnic, and socioeconomic stratification by level of selectivity.

The connection between postsecondary expansion and stratification explains the puzzling fact that postsecondary degree production has not kept up with the growing economic demand for college talent. Understanding stratification in resources seems to be the key piece in solving one of the major puzzles that has confounded economists since the 1980s: the earnings returns to college have been rising rapidly since the 1980s because the rate of increase in the supply of college talent has not kept up with demand.[68] While an increasing share of Americans are going to college, graduation rates are low and declining, and the result has been an increasing wage inequality between college-haves and college-have-nots.

The economic question is: Why hasn't the lure of increasing earnings for college educated workers produced commensurate increases in college attendance and graduation rates?

At first blush, it looks like the lack of preparedness keeps young Americans from realizing the earnings returns that beckon from labor markets. But on closer examination, the evidence does not hold up. Readiness matters, but the role of relative preparedness in determining the ability to benefit from college is overstated. The "readiness" rationalization for low and declining graduation rates relies on aggregate and superficial correlations between graduation rates and test scores, grades, and other traditional metrics. While the average test scores in the least-selective colleges are lower than they are in selective institutions and have declined, test scores are only part of what determines college success.

At best, test scores and high school grades explain less than half the differences in college freshman grades, and are even weaker determinants of the likelihood of graduation. As we discuss below, the differences in college graduation rates are remarkably flat in the top half of the SAT and ACT test score distributions. Differences of one hundred points on SAT scores, for example, do not matter much as predictors of graduation above the mid-points of the SAT test score distribution, especially at selective colleges, even though the same differences matter much more in the competition for seats. And people

with the same test scores and grades graduate from college at remarkably different rates, especially when sorted by levels of selectivity. In
general, the full range of students in the upper half of the SAT/ACT
test score distribution see their chance of graduating with a baccalaureate increase with the selectivity of the college they enter.

THE RELATION BETWEEN STRATIFICATION AND COLLEGE PERFORMANCE

K–12 preparation deserves a healthy share of the blame for disap-
pointing college enrollments, persistence, and graduation rates, but the
evidence suggests that a substantial share of the blame for poor postsecondary performance also goes to the increasing stratification of resources
in postsecondary education itself. Using K–12 failure as the scapegoat for
poor college graduation rates does not hold up in the data. For example,
one 2009 study shows that student preparation accounts for no more
than 30 percent of the decline in graduation rates.[69] It finds that the shift
in resources as measured by student faculty ratios explains up to one-
quarter of the decline in completion. A 2000 study finds that the shift
in enrollments from more- to less-selective and less-well-funded institutions can account for up to 75 percent of the decline in completions.[70] In
addition, the commonly held view that college entrants are declining in
quality is overstated. For example, the influx of well-prepared females,
who were discouraged in the past from attending college, especially selective colleges, is a counterbalance to the increase in less-prepared students,
who tend to be males. In addition, the wide differential in admission
rates, persistence, and graduation rates among equally qualified students
suggests that there is more than preparation at work in explaining low
graduation rates. Hence, graduation rates are tied to spending per student
as well as institutional selectivity.

On balance, the evidence suggests that student quality matters,
but low and declining student graduation rates also are caused by the
increasing stratification in spending per student. Graduation rates are
increasing at selective private four-year colleges and the public flagships,
where resources and advantaged students are increasingly concentrated,
and declining in non-selective four-year and two-year colleges, where the
bulk of postsecondary students, especially less-advantaged students, are
concentrated.

On the whole, the ratio of per-student funding between public and private colleges declined from 70 percent in the mid-1970s to 58 percent in the mid-1990s.[71] The Delta Project finds an inverse relationship between spending per student, selectivity, and the numbers of students served.[72] One study reveals that resources per student at the selective colleges have increased to four times the resources at the non-selective public four-year colleges,[73] and a subsequent study by the same authors shows differences in student/faculty ratios of 19-to-1 in elite private colleges, 29-to-1 in public flagship colleges, and 56-to-1 in two-year public colleges.[74] One study finds a ratio of 8-to-1 in the difference in student subsidies provided by selective relative to non-selective colleges.[75]

Several studies by Stanford economist Caroline M. Hoxby show even greater disparities between the most selective and the less selective colleges.[76] Hoxby attributes these differences to the industrial organization of higher education. She shows the gradual integration of the higher education selection process through the adoption of a national testing regime based on the ACT and SAT. Hoxby argues that the polarization in resources is a natural outcome in a more integrated national system of testing and college attendance. She argues that the rising returns to college in general—and to selectivity in particular—combine with the growth in a national admissions testing regime, the nationwide reach of communications and information technologies, and lower transportation costs to create an integrated national market in higher education selectivity, with growing global reach.

Hoxby's observations are well-supported by data that show declining differences in admissions scores within colleges by selectivity, and increasing stratification among colleges by test scores. The result is a postsecondary system with increasing vertical stratification. According to Hoxby's data, in 1967 the least-selective colleges spent in (2007 dollars) about $3,900 per student and the most selective schools spent about $17,400, with other colleges fanning out in between—a difference of $13,500. By 2006, the low-selectivity colleges had resources of about $12,000 per student and the most selective colleges had about $92,000 per student—a difference of $80,000.

Hoxby documents the disparities in postsecondary spending, but then concludes, as many others do, that the disparities ultimately serve the public interest. In her view, the market structure of higher education produces optimal learning returns from our higher education investments. Hoxby argues that the current model of college access, the one that shapes our current postsecondary hierarchy, creates a direct ascending relationship between increasing expenditures and increasing test scores as most efficient in producing learning of benefit to the larger society.[77] In theory, the most expensive professors, combined with student bodies with the highest test scores, lower student/faculty ratios, and the best postsecondary facilities, equipment, and student services are required to mine the socially valuable abilities of students with high test scores.

The essential premise that justifies spending more on affluent students with high test scores and less on less-affluent students with lower test scores rests on the assumption that there are differences in the individual ability to benefit from high-quality education. From this perspective, more expensive learning environments are necessary to develop fully the high-testing students who have the ability to benefit from them. The corollary is that these high-quality and relatively expensive learning environments would be less effective and wasteful if made available to the vast majority of college students whose test scores demonstrate they are unable to benefit fully. Thus, the complementarities between increasing resources and student ability to benefit, as measured by SAT and ACT test scores, justify unequal spending in order to maximize the social and economic value of learning.

The Positive Effects of a Selective Education

Researchers tend to agree that there are robust and positive effects from going to elite colleges. On closer examination, the positive effects from selective college attendance seem due—as much or more so—to resource advantages rather than to peer effects or other factors tied to the increasing stratification in college access.

The current American model assumes that institutional quality and student quality are inseparable, and we cannot have more of one without more of the other. In this traditional view, there are learning gains that result from putting all the students with the highest test scores on the same college campuses. These "peer" effects assume that each student benefits from the high test scores of all the students on a particular campus because students learn from each other. In addition, generally it is assumed that the students with the highest test scores should go to the colleges with the greatest resources because the synergies between high-scoring student populations and institutional resources produce the highest learning returns to society.

Hoxby argues that the connection between peer relationships and resource advantages even extends across the generations.[78] In her model, the ongoing quality of education in each selective college benefits from a "dynasty" of financial support and connections provided by the historical accumulation of its contributing alumni.

Hoxby explains that, in the selective colleges, each generation pays a declining share of the full cost of their education but, as contributing alumni, they become part of the college dynasty by funding part of the next generation's education, just as previous generations funded their elite education. In order to ensure that this intergenerational funding mechanism continues, selective colleges need to do their best to see that students succeed in college and in their subsequent careers so that they can afford to join the dynasty if they are to replenish and grow endowments for the benefit of succeeding generations. The dynastic mechanism adds another dimension to the effects of differences in college quality and the tendency of those differences to reinforce intergenerational transmission of privilege.

It is in the consideration of peer effects that the consensus on the standard model for the current system of selectivity begins to unravel. Hoxby's explanation of the effects of affluent peers on spending in selective colleges does make intuitive sense. But the view that there are peer effects that improve individual learning, persistence, graduation rates, and subsequent career success are more muddled in the data. The notion of campus-wide peer effects on learning loses considerable authority when researchers look at actual students and their peer relationships on college campuses. The evidence of peer effects on persistence and learning shows up not in college class cohorts, but in more intimate relationships, such as those between roommates and friends. Peer effects are hard to find in the data. To the extent they are measurable, they do not tend to matter much, especially among the most-qualified students, but they do matter to some extent among less-qualified students.[79]

The finding that peers do not matter much among the more qualified students suggests that the increasing stratification in postsecondary test scores and preparation is suboptimal. As is commonly found in K–12 education research, there is probably some optimal mix of more- and less-prepared students in selective colleges that does not harm the educational performance of the better-prepared students and improves the performance of the less-prepared students.[80]

Researchers Stacy Berg Dale and Alan B. Krueger agree with Hoxby that earnings effects subsequent to graduation from selective colleges are strong and positive but they find this has little to do with peer effects.[81] They find that the average SAT scores of the students' peers while they were in college has no effect on the students' post-college earnings. They find that college selectivity produces robust earnings effects that are due primarily to the differences in resources at selective colleges.

In any event, even if the disproportionate investment in advantaged students is economically and educationally efficient, why do we allow policies that promote large differences in public investments among the nation's youth? Since the 1970s, these types of outsized differences have resulted in a spate of judicial rulings mandating greater equality and educational adequacy in K–12 education. At a time when access to postsecondary resources determines lifetime opportunity, how can we justify investing so much more in advantaged students over students from working families in the middle of test score distribution and low-income students in the bottom tiers of the test score distribution?

The disproportionate spending on affluent students in selective colleges seems indefensible on equity grounds. It seems all the more indefensible because the current extent of inequality in postsecondary education does not seem justified on economic efficiency and educational efficiency grounds either. Setting aside equity concerns, it appears that we have come to a point where the differences in spending per student in postsecondary education are inefficient.

LOSING GROUND: RACE, ETHNICITY, AND SOCIOECONOMIC STATUS

Americans are comfortable with inequality so long as there is upward mobility. Given this perspective, many take comfort in the view that postsecondary education is a hand-me-down system in which advantaged white and affluent students lead the charge on access and selectivity while African Americans, Hispanics, and lower-SES students follow closely. Eventually, in this view, once the demand for access and selectivity among advantaged whites and the affluent is saturated, then African Americans, Hispanics and low-SES students are supposed to move up the selectivity scale.[82] In recent years, the increasing demographic share of a high school class claimed by African Americans and Hispanics and the declining share of whites give added credence to the view that African Americans and Hispanics, if not low-income students, eventually would move into the postsecondary system and up the selective college hierarchy in good time. This view that progress is slow but inevitable is an article of faith in American culture.

Our data, however, cast doubt on the robustness of the hand-me-down dynamic in postsecondary education. What future projections there are say postsecondary inequality by race, ethnicity, and SES—as well as inequality in spending—will only increase.[83] Broadly gauged economic data show that upward mobility in the United States has slowed to European levels, in large part due to differences in postsecondary opportunity.[84] Our projections of future demand for college workers also suggest that the hand-me-down process is working too slowly to provide the skilled workforce America will need in the coming decades.[85]

In our postsecondary system, increasing access tends to benefit all groups; however, it also tends to sustain or even increase the distances between them. For example, data comparing postsecondary participation between 1982 and 2004 show a drop from 65 percent to 39 percent between 1983 and 2004 in the share of high school students from the bottom SES quintile who did not go on to postsecondary education.[86] Nonetheless, over the same period, the differences between the postsecondary access between the top and bottom SES quintiles actually increases from a little more than two-to-one to more than five-to-one.

Racial, ethnic, and socioeconomic isolation in postsecondary education is not just about preparedness. As we discuss and elaborate below, there has been ample evidence in the last several years that increased access at the K–12 level has created substantial numbers of highly qualified students from working class, minority, and low-income families who are ready for the most selective colleges but who never attend college or who attend colleges below their tested ability levels.[87] In particular, stratification and underachievement among highly qualified students in the postsecondary system is increasing because the growth in postsecondary education is occurring from the bottom-up in postsecondary education. African-American, Hispanic, and low-SES students are crowding in at the community colleges and the less-selective four-year colleges—and being crowded out by limited resources as these institutions try to serve more and more students with less and less money.[88]

Our dilemma is that, while the bottom-heavy expansion in post-secondary access has encouraged economic and social inclusion,[89] it has also tracked minorities and lower-income students into less selective colleges and ultimately into careers with lower earnings and status.[90] And as we show below, many qualified students from less-advantaged backgrounds get lost along the way from high school to selective colleges, resulting in significant levels of underachievement or undermatching between the most-able students and less-selective colleges.[91]

THE PURSUIT OF PRESTIGE

The engine of stratification in the college growth dynamic begins with the national and even international competition for prestige rankings among the selective colleges.[92] As the boundaries for selective competition grow from local to regional and national venues, selective college markets tighten and become more integrated. They also become more differentiated, and individual colleges become more internally homogenous by test scores, SES, race, and ethnicity. As a marker of the competition for prestige, it is telling to note that the Yale acceptance rate has fallen from 70 percent to 8 percent of its applicants since 1932.[93]

The pursuit of prestige is a self-propelled engine of stratification. Prestige is produced jointly through the interaction of institutional subsidies and student tuitions. Colleges raise revenues from a variety of sources and invest in prestige assets, including faculty, facilities, subsidies necessary to draw high SAT/ACT students, and student amenities. Students pay higher tuitions in order to gain access to prestige colleges. Affluent colleges are chasing high-performing students with institutional subsidies in hand. And affluent students are chasing affluent colleges with their SAT and ACT scores and parents' checkbook in hand. The result of this prestige-driven dynamic is increasing stratification in postsecondary expenditure per student

**Box 3.1 The Number of Competitive Colleges Is
Increasing in the Barron's Rankings since 1994, and the
Number of Less- and Non-Competitive Colleges
Has Declined**

CHANGES IN ENROLLMENT BY BARRON'S SELECTIVITY LEVELS

Our analysis relies on the levels of college selectivity defined by Barron's. We have combined several levels of their original groupings to condense selectivity from six levels to four. This was done to increase sample size of under-represented groups in the top colleges. We do not include "Special" colleges in our analyses.

MOST AND HIGHLY COMPETITIVE COLLEGES HAVE GROWN FROM 146 COLLEGES IN 1994 TO 193 IN 2006

Most Competitive—The Most Competitive colleges have highly competitive admissions, generally requiring high school rank in the top 10 percent to 20 percent and grade averages of a B+ and above. Median SAT scores are between 1310 and 1600 and 29+ on the ACT. Admissions are usually less than one-third of applications.

Highly Competitive—The Highly Competitive colleges look for students with B and better grade averages and a position in the top 20 percent to 35 percent of their high school class. Median SAT scores are between 1240 and 1310. Median ACT scores are 27 to 28. Admissions rates are between 33 percent and 50 percent.

Very Competitive Colleges Have Grown From 253 Colleges in 1994 to 279 in 2006

Very Competitive colleges admit students with GPAs of a B– and above and who rank between 35 percent and 50 percent of their high school class. Median scores are between 1150 and 1240 on the SAT and between 24 and 26 on the ACT. These colleges generally accept one-half to three-fourths of their applicants, but a significant number accept less than one-third.

Competitive Colleges Have Remained Constant; 578 Colleges in 1994 to 572 in 2006

Competitive is a broad category that generally admits students with median SAT scores between 1000 and 1140 and with ACT scores between 21 and 23. Some require high school GPAs of a B– or better, while others accept a minimum C GPA. Most of the competitive colleges admit 50 percent to 65 percent of applicants, while some admit between 75 percent and 85 percent. A small number of these colleges accept less than one-half of applicants.

Less- and Noncompetitive Colleges Have Shrunk Dramatically, Dropping from 429 in 1994 to 299 in 2006

Less Competitive—Median scores in this tier are generally below 1000 on the SAT or below 21 on the ACT, though some that require admissions tests do not report entry medians. Many of these colleges accept students with below C averages in high school and in the top 65 percent of their class. Acceptance rates are above 85 percent.

Noncompetitive—Noncompetitive colleges require only evidence of high school graduation. Entrance exams are sometimes used for placement purposes. Seating capacity can limit the acceptance rates in these colleges but those with acceptance rates of 98 percent and better are automatically included.

Source: Barron's Educational Series, College Division, 2009.

and college quality. Moreover, because the core metric for student quality is SAT or ACT scores, which break down along racial, ethnic, and socioeconomic lines, the resulting stratification in expenditure per student and college quality is closely aligned with racial, ethnic, and socioeconomic stratification.

STRATIFICATION AND PUBLIC INVESTMENT

As would be expected, college graduation rates increase with selectivity and resources. For example, baccalaureate graduation rates in the top tiers of what Barron's[94] refers to as the "Most" selective and "Highly" selective colleges are better than 85 percent on average, compared with 54 percent in the fourth tier, "Non-selective" four-year colleges, and only 36 percent in community colleges achieve a baccalaureate, associate degree, or certificate.[95] Much of the decline in college graduation rates can be accounted for by community colleges, and the overwhelming cause is the differences in resources available by level of selectivity.[96]

These relationships raise questions about the basic purposes of public investments in both public and private higher education: Where are the economic and social returns highest when it comes time to invest an additional public dollar in postsecondary education? Alternatively, do we invest in quantity improvements in persistence and graduation rates in the lower-cost and much more heavily populated public institutions and community colleges? This basic efficiency question can turn either way, but from an

equity perspective, when dollars are scarce, the downstream investment in the public institutions—especially the less-selective public
institutions—seems more sensible if we want to reduce both postsecondary stratification and the earnings differences it encourages.

These hard choices are complicated by the fact that the costs
of selectivity have no natural limits, except for those that arise
from limited public and family budgets. The pursuit of prestige
and the stratification it brings is like a race with no end in sight.[97]
One view that continues to gain support is the notion that we can
at least ameliorate the tendency toward increased stratification by
admitting more highly qualified students from working class and
low-income families into our most selective colleges by expanding racial, ethnic, and SES-based affirmative action. It seems clear
that selective colleges can choose among a broad group of qualified
students in the upper half of the admission test score distribution
with at least an 85 percent chance of graduating. There does not
seem to be much difference between people who score between
1000 and 1200 on the SAT; they all graduate at a rate of 85 percent. The same is true for those who score above 1200, who tend
to have a consistent likelihood of graduating well over 90 percent.
Admission tests matter in predicting grades and graduation rates,
but marginal differences in admissions test scores, especially above
the national average score, matter less than is usually supposed
and matters much less than the weight the SAT and ACT carry in
admissions decisions. Moreover, our own preliminary data analysis
on career effect differentials in the upper half of the admissions test
score distribution do not show much effect on earnings or occupational choice by one-hundred-point or even two-hundred-point
differences in SAT equivalent scores above 1000.[98]

Hence, it is unclear that the increasing marginal investments
in selectivity are as valuable as greater marginal investments in less
selective colleges if our goal is to increase access, quality, completion, and upward mobility. Higher investments in selectivity do
drive earnings differences among baccalaureates, but the effects
are marginal because they affect such a small share of students and
do not matter for the mass of students who do not attend the most
prestigious colleges. An alternative use of the funds for improving
resources at less-selective colleges could boost overall enrollment,

persistence, and graduation rates because smaller increments in spending can have larger effects on enrollments at less-selective and less-expensive institutions. Consequently, for example, the earnings and social returns to investing a marginal dollar in two-year colleges can have a higher economic and social payoff than using a marginal dollar for investing in the more selective four-year colleges.

2. RACIAL, ETHNIC, AND SOCIOECONOMIC STRATIFICATION

American postsecondary education has become bigger, better, and more inclusive, but more stratified at the same time. The rising tide of college enrollments has raised all the boats, but raised some more than others. White students from more-affluent families have moved up, concentrating in the top tiers of selectivity, while minorities and lower-income students have improved access but have become increasingly concentrated in the least selective four-year colleges and community colleges.

Four-year colleges have become increasingly top-heavy. The dynamic of colleges competing with each other by chasing students with the highest test scores and students chasing colleges with the most-selective admissions criteria appears to have resulted in an upward spiral of selectivity—and, arguably, an increasing stock of high-quality, four-year postsecondary institutions, and student quality. At the same time, annual enrollments in sub-baccalaureate institutions have increased to roughly half of all annual enrollments. While enrollment shares in Barron's "Less" and "Non-Selective" colleges have declined, the combined annual enrollments among sub-baccalaureate and "Less" and "Non-Selective" four-year colleges account for more than half of annual enrollments.

The American stock of selective colleges and students qualified to attend them has increased. Among four-year colleges, institutional capacity has shifted toward the more-competitive colleges and away from the less- and noncompetitive ones (see Figure 3.2).

- The number of four-year institutions that meet the Barron's standards for the first tier of "Most" and "Highly" competitive colleges has risen from 146 colleges to 193 colleges.

- The number of four-year colleges in the second tier of the "Very" competitive category has risen from 253 colleges to 279 colleges.

- The number of four-year colleges in the third tier, "Competitive" category has declined from 578 colleges to 572 colleges.

- The number of four-year colleges in the bottom tier of the "Less" and "Non-Competitive" category has actually declined from 429 colleges to 299 colleges. As will be discussed in more detail later, this change is married with a very significant increase in African-American enrollment share on these campuses.

Figure 3.2 Number of Four-Year Colleges, by Selectivity, 1994 and 2006

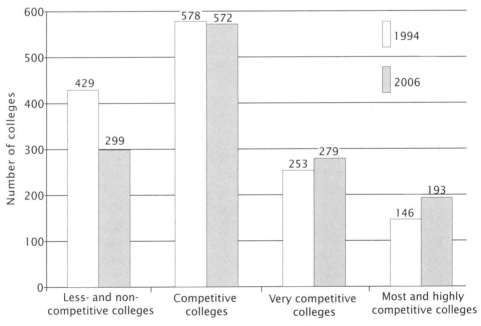

Source: Authors' calculations; Barron's Selectivity Rankings, various years.

The Barron's standards for the different levels of selectivity have not changed appreciably, but more colleges are meeting the higher standards set for them in the selective categories.

Enrollment follows the same pattern. Comparing the patterns of enrollment and college selectivity between 1994 and 2006 by examining enrollments in the National Education Longitudinal Survey (NELS) and the Education Longitudinal Survey (ELS). we can see that the share of four-year college enrollments in "Most" and "Highly Competitive" colleges grew from 16 percent to 22 percent, and the enrollment share of "Very Competitive" colleges grew from 21 percent to 27 percent (see Figure 3.3).

Figure 3.3 Percentage of Total Enrollments, by Selectivity, 1994 and 2006

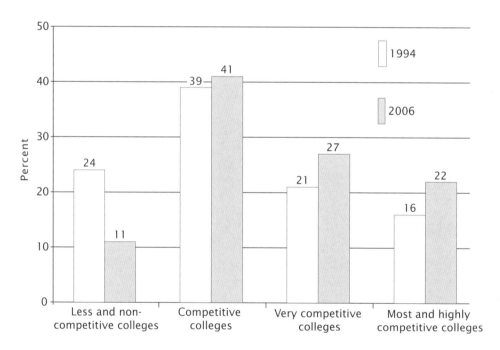

Source: Authors' calculations; Barron's Selectivity Rankings, various years; National Education Longitudinal Study: Base Year through Fourth Follow-Up, 1988–2000 (Washington, D.C.: UN.S. Dept. Of Education, National Center For Education Statistics, 2000); Educational Longitudinal Study: Base Year to Second Follow-Up, 2002–2006 (Washington, D.C.: U.S. Dept. of Education, National Center for Education Statistics, 2006).

Hence, the data suggest that the stock of selective college seats has increased and the stock of "Less" and "Non-Competitive" college seats has declined. In other words, the relative seating capacity in four-year selective colleges has increased and the relative seating capacity in "Non-Competitive" four-year colleges has declined. At the same time, we know that over the same period the stock of high school graduates with test scores high enough to meet the standards for selectivity in the three top tiers of selective institutions has increased.

THE GOOD NEWS AND THE BAD NEWS

This is both a good-news and a bad-news story. The good news is that we seem to be increasing the stock of quality institutions and producing enough highly qualified students to fill them. There is more good news in the fact that more high school students are going to college; this good news grows when we add community colleges into the mix. The community colleges allow us to keep the nation's promises of access and upward mobility by providing college on the cheap. Without them we could not afford an increased stock of selective colleges. Between 1994 and 2006, the share of two-year students increased from 22 percent to 36 percent of all college students, and more than half of annual freshman enrollments at public institutions.

The bad news begins with the fact that graduation rates have not kept up or improved with the growth in postsecondary education, and low graduation rates relate directly to the skewing of resources per student by selectivity. For example, one recent study finds that baccalaureate graduation rates among those who enter college have fallen from 45 percent to 40 percent since 1970.[99] Aggregate differences in graduation rates hide wide differences by selectivity. Graduation rates range from an average 86 percent in the top tiers of the almost 200 "Most" and "Highly" four-year selective colleges, to an average of 54 percent in the bottom tier of almost 300 "Less" and "Non-Selective" four-year colleges.

What is truly stunning is the variation in graduation rates within categories of four-year selectivity.[100] For example, within the bottom "Non-Selective" category, the graduation rate among the bottom ten colleges averages 13 percent, with Southern University dead last at 8 percent. Among the top ten colleges in the "Non-Selective" category, the average graduation rate is 66 percent, and two of these "Non-Selective" colleges, Arkansas Baptist College and Concordia College in Selma, clock in at 100 percent and 97 percent respectively, placing them among the top four graduation rates in the United States, along with Atlantic Union College and Harvard College in Massachusetts.

Graduation rates rise consistently by college selectivity but the range in every category suggests that, while higher graduation rates are one of the major benefits of selectivity, the benefit varies enormously. As illustrated in Table 3.1 the graduation rate in the top ten "Less Competitive" (72 percent) and "Non-Competitive" colleges (66 percent) exceeds the graduation rates in the bottom ten colleges in every more competitive category except the "Most Competitive" category (16 percent; 18 percent; 30 percent; 55 percent; and 77 percent). In an economy where graduation rates are tightly tied to earnings returns, choosing a college with a high graduation rate is just as important as choosing a level of selectivity.

Graduation rates at community colleges are not so easily characterized and compared with graduation rates at four-year colleges. People go to community colleges with a variety of aspirations and tend to be less ready for college than students who attend four-year colleges. Students at community colleges tend to be there for a variety of reasons, including job training, associate degrees, vocational certificates, transfer to four-year schools, and personal enrichment. (See Table 3.2, page 128.)

In general, the attainment rates for students who begin at two-year colleges are low relative to four-year schools. As you can see in Table 3.3 (page 130), 36 percent of community college students get a certificate (10 percent), an associate degree (16 percent), or transfer and get a baccalaureate (10 percent). Another 9 percent have transferred but are still enrolled.[101] Using the certificate, associate degree, and baccalaureate completion rate for the 36 percent of students who started at community colleges, the community college success rate is comparable to the graduation rates in the Barron's 429 "Less" and "Non-Competitive" colleges (39 percent), but below the graduation rates at the 572 "Competitive" colleges (49 percent), substantially below the graduation rates in the 253 "Very Competitive" colleges (62 percent), roughly half the graduation rate in the 111 "Highly" competitive colleges (75 percent), and 2.5 times less than graduation rates among the 82 "Most" competitive colleges (see Table 3.1).

Table 3.1 Graduation Rates, by Selectivity (percent)

	Most Competitive	Highly Competitive	Very Competitive	Competitive	Less Competitive	Non-Competitive
Mean graduation rate	88	75	62	49	40	35
Top ten colleges in graduation rates	95	87	82	75	72	66
Bottom ten colleges in graduation rates	77	55	30	18	16	13

Source: Authors' calculations from T. R. Bailey, D. Jenkins, and T. Leinbach, *Is Student Success Labeled Institutional Failure? Student Goals and Graduation Rates in the Accountability Debate at Community Colleges*, CCRC Working Paper 1 (New York: Community College Research Center, Teachers College, Columbia University, 2006). Columns do not sum to 100 percent due to rounding.

Table 3.2 Community College Attainment Rates, by Expectations upon Entry (percent)

Student Status	Expectations upon Entry					
	Do Not Know	No Credential	Certificate	Associate	Baccalaureate	Post-baccalaureate
Baccalaureate	6	—	—	3	10	18
Associate	11	11	11	24	17	16
Certificate	15	9	32	8	8	8
• Subtotal: degree attainment	32	20	43	35	35	42
No longer enrolled (no degree/no transfer)	52	74	58	54	41	29
Still enrolled (no degree/no transfer)	8	7	—	7	9	8
Transfer (no degree) still enrolled	7	—	—	1	10	14
Transfer (no degree) no longer enrolled	1	0	—	3	5	6
• Total	100	100	100	100	100	100

Source: Authors' calculations from T. R. Bailey, D. Jenkins, and T. Leinbach, *Is Student Success Labeled Institutional Failure? Student Goals and Graduation Rates in the Accountability Debate at Community Colleges,* CCRC Working Paper 1 (New York: Community College Research Center, Teachers College, Columbia University, 2006). Columns do not sum to 100 percent due to rounding.

Community college success rates follow the expected pattern by race and ethnicity and socioeconomic status (Table 3.3, page 130). For whites and the most-affluent students, degree completion (certificates, associate degrees, and baccalaureates) for students who start out in community colleges ranges between 40 percent and 46 percent. For nonwhites, certificate, baccalaureate, and associate degree completions do not rise above 30 percent. Community colleges do as well as the less-selective four-year colleges with low-income students. Their degree attainment rises to 39 percent among students from the bottom SES tier. This rate is comparable to that of whites as well as baccalaureate graduation rates with low-SES students in the least-selective four-year colleges, but below the graduation rates for the same SES cohort in the remaining more-selective four-year colleges. Attainment rates are relatively low for blacks and Hispanics, and relatively high for whites and students from families in the highest SES quartile.

Community college success rates do vary by the intentions of the students, but still tend to come in below 40 percent. The rate at which students say they want to transfer to a four-year college to get a baccalaureate and actually achieve one is 19 percent, with an additional 16 percent settling for an associate degree, and 5 percent settling for a certificate. Among those who say they want to achieve an associate degree or a certificate, 29 percent actually get one, and another 7 percent get baccalaureates. Among students who say they went to community college to get job skills, 17 percent get certificates and another 13 percent get associate degrees.[102]

RACIAL, ETHNIC, AND SOCIOECONOMIC STRATIFICATION IS PRONOUNCED AND INCREASING

The pattern of increasing stratification over time shows a growing concentration of students from white and affluent families in the top tiers of selectivity and an increasing concentration of African-American, Hispanic, and lower-income students left behind in the least-selective four-year colleges and community colleges. The trend toward racial and ethnic

Table 3.3 Community College Attainment Rates, by Race, Ethnicity, and SES (percent)

Student Status	All	White	Black	Hispanic	Lowest Income Quartile	Highest Income Quartile
Baccalaureate	10	12	2	5	5	18
Associate	16	18	8	15	19	14
Certificate	10	10	17	9	15	4
• Subtotal: degree attainment	36	40	27	29	39	46
No longer enrolled (no degree/no transfer)	43	40	54	49	44	33
Still enrolled (no degree/no transfer)	8	7	8	9	9	9
Transfer (no degree) still enrolled	9	9	5	9	6	16
Transfer (no degree) no longer enrolled	4	4	5	3	2	6
• Total	100	100	100	100	100	100

Source: Authors' calculations from T. R. Bailey, D. Jenkins, and T. Leinbach, *Is Student Success Labeled Institutional Failure? Student Goals and Graduation Rates in the Accountability Debate at Community Colleges,* CCRC Working Paper 1 (New York: Community College Research Center, Teachers College, Columbia University, 2006). Columns do not sum to 100 percent due to rounding.

Figure 3.4 Racial and Ethnic Distribution in Colleges, by Selectivity, 1994

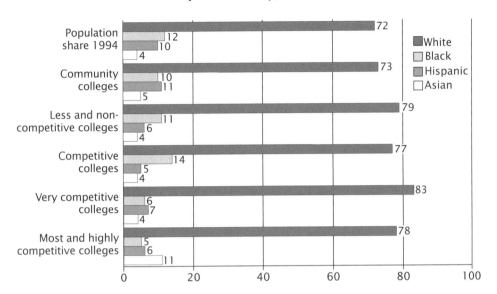

Source: Authors' calculations; Barron's Selectivity Rankings, various years; National Education Longitudinal Study: Base Year through Fourth Follow-Up, 1988–2000 (Washington, D.C.: U.S. Dept. of Education, National Center for Education Statistics, 2000).

stratification becomes apparent when we compare the freshmen enrollments in 1994 and 2006 with the population share of those groups among eighteen-year-olds in high school (see Figures 3.4 and 3.5).

The share of white students going on to college increased from 62 percent to 65 percent between 1994 and 2006. In spite of the increase in new college students, the white share of two-year college students and students in the "Less" and "Non-Competitive" colleges declined. White students moved out of the less-selective two- and four-year postsecondary tiers and concentrated in the more-selective four-year college tiers, even as the number of seats in the selective colleges increased and the share of white students among the high school class declined.

- Over the twelve-year period (1994–2006), the share of white students in the high school senior class declined from 72 percent to 60 percent, a single percentage point decline each year (see Figures 3.4 and 3.5).

Figure 3.5 Racial and Ethnic Distribution at Colleges, by Selectivity, 2006

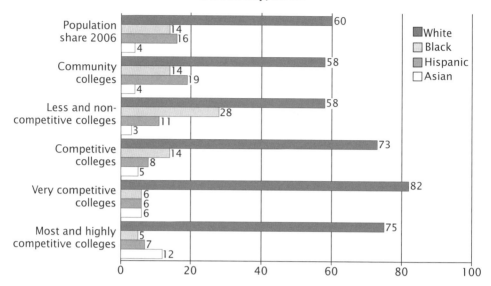

Source: Authors' calculations; Barron's Selectivity Rankings, various years; National Education Longitudinal Study: Base Year through Fourth Follow-Up, 1988–2000 (Washington, D.C.: U.S. Dept. of Education, National Center for Education Statistics, 2000).

- The decline of white students as a share of community college enrollments from 73 percent to 58 percent is roughly consistent with the decline in white students of the high school senior class over the twelve-year period.

- The white share in the "Less" and "Non-Competitive" institutions declined from 79 percent in 1994 to 58 percent in 2006.

- The disproportionate share of whites in selective colleges begins in the "Competitive" group of colleges. The white share of freshman enrollment in the "Competitive" colleges declined slightly from the 1994 level, from 77 percent to 73 percent. But the white share in these colleges relative to their share of the high school class increased from a five percentage point advantage in 1994 to a thirteen percentage point advantage in 2006.

- The disproportionate share of white students in the "Very" competitive colleges continued and strengthened the pattern. The absolute share remained essentially the same, but the relative advantage of whites given their declining share of the high school class doubled from 11 percent in 1994 to 22 percent in 2006.

- The relative advantage of whites continued to grow in the top tier of "Most" and "Highly" competitive colleges from a relative advantage of 6 percent in 1994 to 15 percent in 2006. Interestingly, the absolute share of whites drops between 1994 and 2006 due to the doubling of the share of Asians in the "Most" and "Highly" selective colleges.

Between 1994 and 2006, African Americans increased their share of the high school class from 12 percent to 14 percent and increased their postsecondary participation from 51 percent to 53 percent. In spite of their increasing postsecondary participation and their increasing share of the high school class, African Americans have become more concentrated in community colleges and in the "Less" and "Non-Competitive" colleges and are losing ground relative to their share of the high school class in the "Competitive," "Very" competitive, and "Most and Highly" competitive colleges.

- Over the twelve-year period, the share of African-American students participating in postsecondary education increased from 51 percent to 53 percent, and the African-American share of the high school class increased marginally, from 12 percent to 14 percent.

- African Americans increased their share of community college enrollments from 10 percent in 1994 to 14 percent in 2006, a level consistent with their share of the high school class.

- The African-American share of enrollment in the "Less" and "Non-Selective" colleges increased more than two and a half times, from 11 percent to 28 percent—a level twice their share of the high school class. The large increases in the African-American share in the "Less" and Non-Competitive" colleges is due in part to the concentration of African Americans in the Historically Black Colleges and Universities (HBCUs), many of which are in the "Less and Non-Comepteitve" category.

- There was no change in the absolute shares of African Americans in "Competitive," "Very" competitive, and "Most and Highly" competitive colleges at 14 percent, 6 percent, and 5 percent, respectively. But with their increasing share of the high school class, the flat performance in the most selective tiers represents a decline in relative shares.

The access of Hispanics to postsecondary education is increasing, but Hispanics actually are losing ground relative to their growing population shares. The share of Hispanics going on to college has increased from 46 percent in 1994 to 49 percent in 2006. But over the same period, the Hispanic share of the high school class has increased from 10 percent to 16 percent. In sum, Hispanics are losing ground, because their rate of college attendance has not kept up with the increasing share of Hispanics in the eighteen-to-twenty-four-year-old population. In addition, the increase in Hispanic participation has been very bottom heavy.

Hispanics are diminishing in their relative shares in four-year college enrollments, especially as selectivity increases. Hispanics increasingly are over-represented in community colleges and increasingly under-represented in four-year and selective colleges.

- The Hispanic share of community college enrollment increased from 11 percent to 19 percent and their share of enrollments at the "Less" and "Non-Selective" colleges from 6 percent to 8 percent. Even in the "Less" and "Non-Competitive" colleges, where African Americans are enrolled at twice their share of the high school class, Hispanics are enrolled only at 75 percent of their share of the high school class.

- Between 1994 and 2006, in the "Competitive" colleges, the ratio of Hispanic enrollees to the Hispanic share of the high school class remained steady at 50 percent.

- The ratio of the Hispanic eighteen-to-twenty-four-year-old population share to enrollments in the "Very" competitive and

"Most" and "Highly" competitive colleges has dropped from 70 percent and 60 percent to 38 percent and 44 percent.

STRATIFICATION BY SOCIOECONOMIC STATUS ECHOES THAT BY RACE AND ETHNICITY (1982–2006)

The pattern of increasing access and increasing stratification by race and ethnicity repeats itself when we examine enrollment trends by socioeconomic status (see Figures 3.6 and 3.7, pages 136–37). The analysis is drawn from data developed by Michael Bastedo and Ozan Jaquette of the University of Michigan School of Education. The Bastedo and Jaquette data track changes in SES over the twenty-four years between 1982 and 2006.

The top tier of "Most" competitive institutions remains remarkably stable in its SES distribution:

- The share of students from the highest SES quartile increased marginally from 69 percent in 1982 to 70 percent in 2006.

- The share of enrollments for the top half of the SES distribution also increased marginally, from 85 percent to 87 percent.

- The share of students from the lowest SES quartile also increased marginally, from 3 percent to 5 percent, but the share from the bottom half of the SES distribution remained unchanged at 14 percent.

The twenty-four-year history of socioeconomic status in the "Highly" competitive colleges mimics SES hierarchy in the "Most" selective colleges.

- The share of students from the top SES quartiles increased marginally from 62 percent to 63 percent and the share of the students from the top half of the SES hierarchy declined slightly from 87 percent in 1982 to 84 percent in 2006.

Figure 3.6 Socioeconomic Distribution at Colleges, by Selectivity, 1982

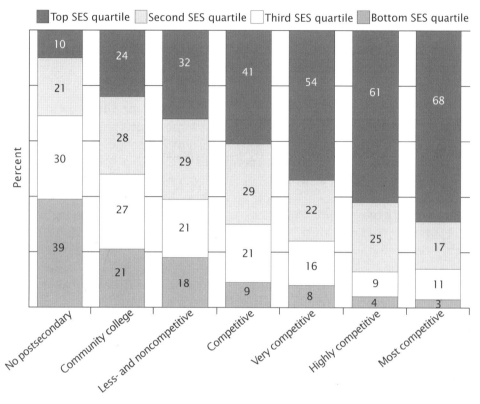

Note: Some columns do not total 100 due to rounding.

Source: Authors' calculations from M. N. Bastedo and O. Jaquette, "Institutional Stratification and the Fit Hypothesis: Longitudinal Shifts in Student Access," Paper presented at the Annual Meeting of the Association for the Study of Higher Education, Vancouver, British Columbia, November 4–7, 2009.

The share of students from the bottom half of the SES distribution increased marginally from 13 percent to 16 percent, due entirely to an increase in students from the bottom tier of SES from 4 percent to 7 percent.

Over the same twenty-four-year period, the SES distribution in "Very" competitive colleges improved slightly. There is some leavening in the SES distribution but the top half of the distribution dropped only from 76 percent of enrollment to 75 percent. The "Competitive" colleges seem to be a switching point in the SES distribution. There is a downward shift of ten percentage points between the top and bottom half of the SES distribution.

- The top half took 70 percent of the seats in 1982 and 66 percent in 2006.

The SES distribution in the "Less and Non-Competitive" colleges has been looking more like America since 1982. Since 1982, the share of seats

Figure 3.7 Socioeconomic Distribution at Colleges, by Selectivity, 2006

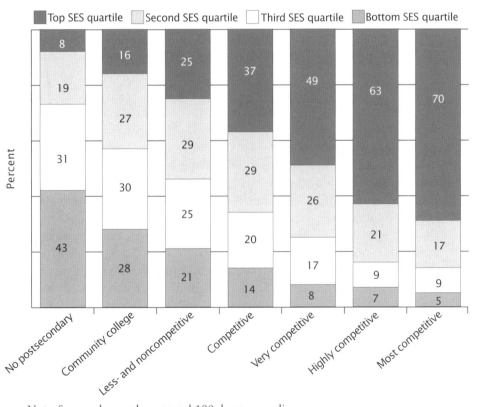

Note: Some columns do not total 100 due to rounding.

Source: Authors' calculations from M. N. Bastedo and O. Jaquette, "Institutional Stratification and the Fit Hypothesis: Longitudinal Shifts in Student Access," Paper presented at the Annual Meeting of the Association for the Study of Higher Education, Vancouver, British Columbia, November 4–7, 2009.

occupied by the top half of the SES distribution has declined from 61 percent to 54 percent. The SES quartiles are divided in roughly even fashion. The top SES quartile took 25 percent of the seats and the top half of SES distribution took only 54 percent of the seats.

The "Non-Competitive" four-year colleges and the two-year colleges have evolved similarly. The share of top quartile SES students at two-year colleges has declined from 24 percent to 16 percent since 1982, and the share of students from the top half of the income distribution has declined from 52 percent to 43 percent. As a result, the community colleges are the only selectivity tier in which the lower half of the SES distribution is dominant—except for those who do not go on to postsecondary education, where 74 percent come from the bottom half of the SES distribution, an increase from 69 percent since 1982.

Our findings on the increasing stratification by SES are corroborated by the work of others.[103]

THE IMPORTANCE OF SOCIOECONOMIC STATUS

When we look at access to selectivity, socioeconomic status has remained key. Top SES students were highly over-represented in 1982 and remained so in 2006. In light of the changing demographic distribution since 1994, increasing stratification becomes even more pronounced.

Bastedo and Jaquette's data show the dominance of SES in determining both access and selectivity in the twenty-four years between 1982 and 2006. Overall, this dominance is relatively stable among the more competitive colleges, as top SES overrepresentation, compared to population share, increased from 43 percent in 1982 to 45 percent in 2006. At the same time, low SES over-representation increased among non-college goers. (See Figures 3.8 and 3.9 page 140.)

On the other hand, stratification is increased more starkly when observed through a demographic lens. In 1994, in the "Most" and "Highly" competitive colleges, the overrepresentation of whites was 6 percent. By 2006, twelve years later, white overrepresentation increased 2.5 times, to 15 percent (see Figure 3.10, page 141). Over the same period, as the share of Hispanics and blacks in their high school class grew, they became more under-represented in their

Figure 3.8 Representation of College Students as Compared to Population Share, by Selectivity, 1982

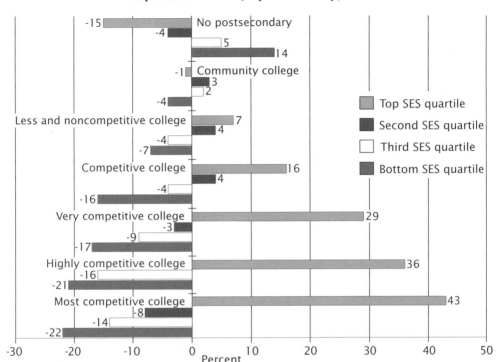

Source: Authors' calculations from M. N. Bastedo and O. Jaquette, "Institutional Stratification and the Fit Hypothesis: Longitudinal Shifts in Student Access," Paper presented at the Annual Meeting of the Association for the Study of Higher Education, Vancouver, British Columbia, November 4–7, 2009.

share of seats in the "Most" and "Highly" competitive colleges. Between 1994 and 2006, Hispanic underrepresentation increased from –5 percent to –9 percent, and black underrepresentation increased from –7 percent to –9 percent.

The same pattern emerges in the "Very" competitive colleges (see Figure 3.11, page 142). White overrepresentation doubles to 22 percent. Blacks became somewhat more underrepresented (declining to –8 percent) while the Hispanic population more than doubled their disadvantage to –10 percent.

White gains and minority losses continued in the "Competitive" schools. Hispanics increased their historic pattern of underrepresentation, while the black population moved from being slightly overrepresented (3 percent) to

Figure 3.9 Representation of College Students as Compared to Population Share, by Selectivity, 2006

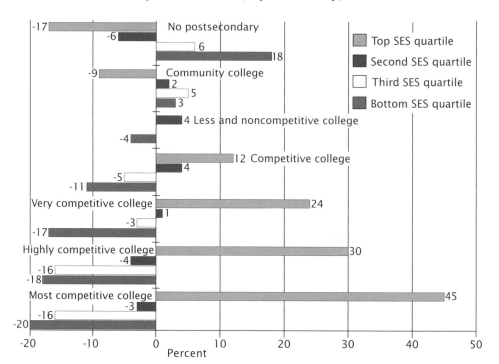

Source: Authors' calculations from M. N. Bastedo and O. Jaquette, "Institutional Stratification and the Fit Hypothesis: Longitudinal Shifts in Student Access," Paper presented at the Annual Meeting of the Association for the Study of Higher Education, Vancouver, British Columbia, November 4–7, 2009.

having an enrollment share roughly equal to their population share. While minority groups stalled or backslid, the white population nearly tripled their overrepresentation, going from 5 percent to 13 percent. (See Figure 3.12, page 143.)

The system shift toward more capacity in the competitive tiers appears to have left the black population behind in the "Less" and "Non-Competitive" schools. Black overrepresentation soared in the "Less" and "Non-Competitive" schools, growing from a slight underrepresentation to an overrepresentation of 14 percent. White overrepresentation (7 percent) disappeared as they moved up, and Hispanics continued to be underrepresented, slipping from –4 percent to –6 percent.

Figure 3.10 Representation of College Students as Compared to Population Share at "Most" and "Highly" Competitive Colleges, by Race and Ethnicity, 1994 and 2006

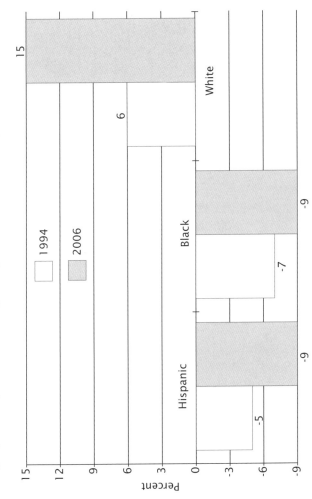

Source: Authors' calculations; Barron's Selectivity Rankings, various years; National Education Longitudinal Study: Base Year through Fourth Follow-Up, 1988–2000 (Washington, D.C.: U.S. Dept. Of Education, National Center For Education Statistics, 2000); Educational Longitudinal Study: Base Year to Second Follow-Up, 2002–2006 (Washingto, D.C.: U.S. Dept. of Education, National Center for Education Statistics, 2006).

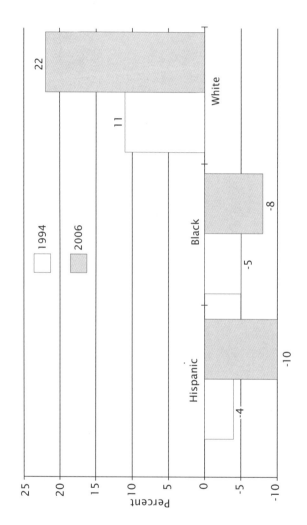

Figure 3.11 Representation of College Students as Compared to Population Share at "Very" Competitive Colleges, by Race and Ethnicity, 1994 and 2006

Source: Authors' calculations; Barron's Selectivity Rankings, various years; National Education Longitudinal Study: Base Year through Fourth Follow-Up, 1988–2000 (Washington, D.C.: U.S. Dept. Of Education, National Center For Education Statistics, 2000); Educational Longitudinal Study: Base Year to Second Follow-Up, 2002–2006 (Washington, D.C.: U.S. Dept. of Education, National Center for Education Statistics, 2006).

Figure 3.12 Representation of College Students as Compared to Population Share at "Competitive" Colleges, by Race and Ethnicity, 1994 and 2006

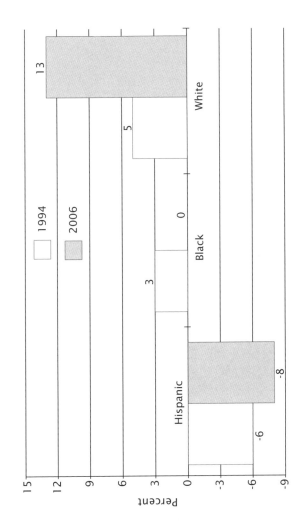

Source: Authors' calculations; Barron's Selectivity Rankings, various years; National Education Longitudinal Study: Base Year through Fourth Follow-Up, 1988–2000 (Washington, D.C.: U.S. Dept. Of Education, National Center For Education Statistics, 2000); Educational Longitudinal Study: Base Year to Second Follow-Up, 2002–2006 (Washington, D.C.: U.S. Dept of Education, National Center for Education Statistics, 2006).

Figure 3.13 Representation of College Students as Compared to Population Share at "Less" and "Non-Competitive" Colleges, by Race and Ethnicity, 1994 and 2006

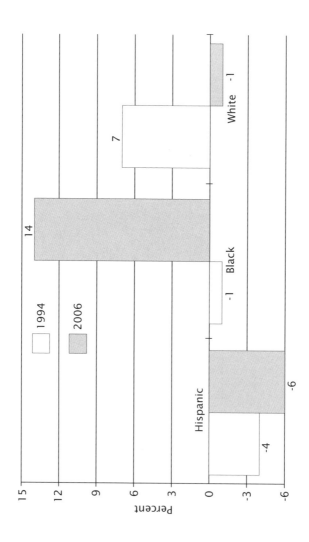

Source: Authors' calculations from Barron's Selectivity Rankings, various years; National Education Longitudinal Study: Base Year through Fourth Follow-Up, 1988–2000 (Washington, D.C.: U.S. Dept. of Education, National Center for Education Statistics, 2000), Educational Longitudinal Study: Base Year to Second Follow-Up, 2002–2006 (Washington, D.C.: U.S. Dept. of Education, National Center for Education Statistics, 2006).

3. Racial, Ethnic, and Socioeconomic Stratification Matters

Many argue that the public dialogue over admissions to selective four-year colleges has intensified far beyond its practical importance. They point out that a very small portion of college students attend theation's brd-name colleges. Is the selective college admissions debate worth all the trouble that comes with it? We think so, in part, because the limited level of racial and socioeconomic diversity on selective four-year college campuses directly challenges the commitment to upward economic and social mobility at the heart of the American creed. Access to selective colleges gives graduates a leg up in the competition for elite careers and leadership roles. Selective college graduation leads to higher earnings.[104] As you can see in Figure 3.14, graduation from selective colleges increases earnings in early careers, and these earnings accumulate and expand over a full career.

Figure 3.14 Entry-level Earnings of College Graduates, by Selectivity, 1999

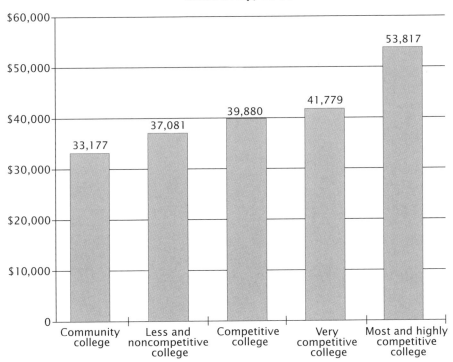

Note: Dollar amounts are in 2007 dollars.

Source: Authors' calculations from Barron's Selectivity Rankings, various years; National Education Longitudinal Study: Base Year through Fourth Follow-Up, 1988–2000 (Washington, D.C.: U.S. Dept. of Education, National Center for Education Statistics, 2000).

Spending per Student Increases with College Selectivity

Schools with higher selectivityinvest more in the education of their students. For example, in 2006, the average private research university spent $33,000 a year on each student, while the average community college spent $9,000 per student (see Figure 3.15). Moreover, the data show that the highest spending per student occurs in the colleges carrying the lightest enrollment burdens in the postsecondary education of American youth. For example, community colleges enroll more than six million students, but spend less than $10,000 on each of them. Private research universities enroll less than a million students, but spend almost $35,000 on each of them.

Students who go to more-selective colleges get higher subsidies from the institutions they attend. All colleges, except for-profit colleges, spend more per student than they charge in tuition. Colleges,

Figure 3.15 Spending per Student and Total Student Enrollments, by Type of College

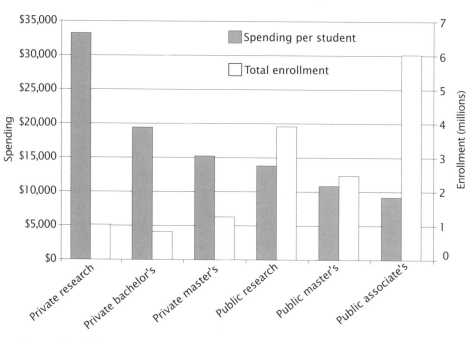

Source: The Delta Project on Postsecondary Education Costs, Productivity, and Accountability, Washington, D.C.

other than for-profit proprietary schools, do not make money on tuition and, in fact, spend substantial amounts of their own money for each full-time equivalent (FTE) student. The difference between tuition and fees and the total college spending per student is a student subsidy provided by the college. Colleges make up the difference between tuitions and their total spending per student in various ways, including public institutional aid, endowments, contributions/gifts, and other forms of public and private subsidy.

SELECTIVITY PAYS OFF

Selective colleges give bigger annual subsidies for each student's educational program. For example, in 2006 private research universities provided $15,000 in non-tuition subsidy compared with a subsidy of $6,500 by community colleges. In order to hold or increase their prestige rankings, colleges compete by using their financial and capital resources to bid for students with the highest test scores. For example, economist Gordon C. Winston at Williams College reports that Williams had offered a college education that cost about $65,000 for a net price to students of about $20,000.[105] The $45,000 subsidy for each student allows Williams to attract the student body with the highest test scores, thereby maintaining or increasing its prestige ranking and in turn maintaining or increasing ability to attract students with high test scores.

Looking at just how subsidies are distributed, Winston demonstrates that there is a wide variation in student subsidies between public and private institutions, a difference of almost eight-to-one (see Figure 3.16, page 148). In the top decile, the average private subsidy during the 1994–95 academic year was $31,000, compared with $4,000 in the bottom decile of institutions. In the lower half of the distribution of subsidies, the public subsidies are higher than the private subsidies. This means public colleges are a better deal than low-spending private colleges.

VALUE PER STUDENT DOLLAR

What is even more remarkable is that the students who go to the most-selective colleges contribute a smaller share of the total amount spent on them than students at the less-selective colleges. Colleges with high levels of endowments or favorable public funding can provide more student spending at lower relative prices (see Figure 3.17). So, as Winston points out, Williams College can sell a $65,000 per year education for $20,000, giving a net average subsidy to its students of $45,000 per year, or roughly $180,000 over a four-year degree period.[106] Winston calculates a cost, including educational spending, as well as the cost for maintaining infrastructure and capital. He finds that the average annual college cost in the United States is about $12,000. On average, student net cost is $3,800 for a $12,000 education. On average, students receive a subsidy of $8,200. Financial aid represents $2,150, or about 25 percent of the subsidy. The remaining $6,050 is the subsidy the average student receives below the sticker price of the college.

Figure 3.16 Student Subsidies, Public and Private Institutions, by Decile, 1995–96 Academic Year

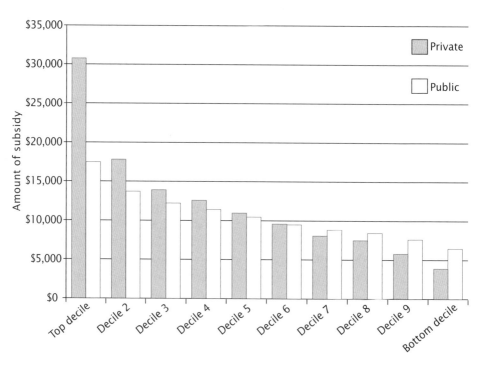

Source: Authors' calculations from G. C. Winston, *Economic Stratification and Hierarchy in U.S. Colleges and Universities,* Discussion Paper 58 (Williamstown, Mass.: Williams Project on the Economics of Higher Education, Williams College, 2000), http://www.williams.edu/wpehe/dps/dp-58.pdf, retrieved November 11, 2009.

Figure 3.17 Spending per Student and Percentage Paid by Student, by Decile

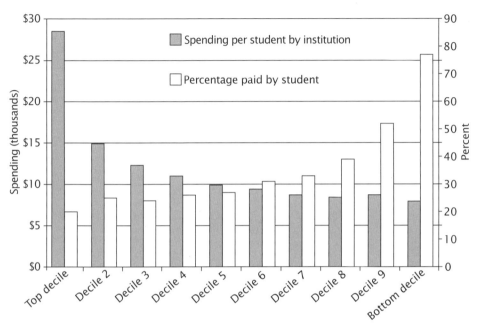

Source: Authors' calculations from G. C. Winston, *Economic Stratification and Hierarchy in U.S. Colleges and Universities,* Discussion Paper 58 (Williamstown, Mass.: Williams Project on the Economics of Higher Education, Williams College, 2000), http://www.williams.edu/wpehe/dps/dp-58.pdf, retrieved November 11, 2009.

In our system of stratified spending, the ratio of the student cost to the subsidy is also stratified. In Figure 3.17, the average school in the top decile charges each student $5,700 to provide a $28,500 education—a subsidy of $22,800 and a 20 percent price-to-cost ratio. The average college in the bottom decile charges each student $6,050 to pay for a $7,900 education—a subsidy of $1,850 and a 75 percent price-to-cost ratio.

SUCCEEDING AT SELECTIVE COLLEGES

Students at every SES level have higher graduation rates at selective colleges (see Table 3.4, page 150). Among students in the

Table 3.4 Graduation Rates, by Selectivity and Socioeconomic Quartile (percentage of initial attendees)

Selectivity	Bottom SES Quartile	Second SES Quartile	Third SES Quartile	Top SES Quartile
Tier 1 (highest)	76	85	80	90
Tier 2	61	63	71	79
Tier 3	60	58	59	66
Tier 4 (lowest)	40	63	55	58

Source: Authors' analysis of survey data from High School and Beyond (HS&B), U.S. Department of Education, National Center for Education Statistics, http://nces.ed.gov/surveys/hsb/.

bottom SES quartile, those who attend a bottom-tier "Least" or "Non-Selective" college in the Barron's ranking graduate at a rate of 40 percent, while those who attend a top-tier "Highly" competitive college graduate at almost double that rate, at 76 percent.

Among equally qualified students, who score above 900 (out of a possible 1600 SAT points), graduation rates at selective colleges are higher. For example, graduation rates at the "Most" and "Highly" competitive colleges for students who score between 1000 and 1300 on the SAT range from 85 percent to 96 percent compared with a range of 67 percent to 78 percent for similarly qualified students at Tier 4 "non-competitive" four-year institutions. (See Table 3.5.)

Graduation from selective colleges results in higher rates of acceptance at graduate and professional schools among equally qualified students. At top-tier colleges, students with SAT scores over 1200 are admitted into graduate school at a rate of 48 percent, compared with a 26 percent rate for similarly qualified students who attend a Tier 4 "non-competitive" four-year college.[107] (See Table 3.6.)

College selectivity also encourages access to elite roles that confer personal autonomy and power over others. Selective colleges give greater access to graduate and professional education and the jobs with the most economic, social, and personal power. In the postindustrial economy, everyone still has one vote, but the most selectively educated carry a new kind of personal empowerment that comes with esoteric knowledge, autonomy at work, and elite social positioning.[108]

Table 3.5 Graduation Rates, by Selectivity and SAT-Equivalent Score (percentage of initial attendees)

Selectivity	<900	900 to 1000	1000 to 1100	1100 to 1200	1200 to 1300	>1300
All	43	69	74	74	85	88
Tier 1 (highest)	30	61	86	85	96	96
Tier 2	44	71	83	70	85	90
Tier 3	45	74	71	68	78	78
Tier 4 (lowest)	39	61	67	*	78	*

*Data limitations.

Note: SAT-equivalent scores are based on SAT scores or an equi-percentile correspondence of ACT scores to SAT equivalence. The correspondence was developed by ETS and these data are presented in Appendix 2.

Source: Authors' analysis of survey data from High School and Beyond (HS&B), U.S. Department of Education, National Center for Education Statistics, http://nces.ed.gov/surveys/hsb/.

Table 3.6 Graduate School Attendance, by Selectivity and SAT-Equivalent Score (percentage of initial attendees)

Selectivity	All	<900	900–1000	1000–1200	>1200
All	21	10	13	21	38
Tier 1	35	19	15	25	48
Tier 2	25	15	14	22	43
Tier 3	18	10	15	20	28
Tier 4	15	8	9	22	26

Source: Authors' analysis of NELS 2000, U.S. Department of Education, Institute of Education Sciences.

An increasing share of workers is empowered on the job in the postindustrial service economy because service work inherently is more self-directed than, say, tending to inflexible machines. But the most educated, especially professionals, are the most self-directed, and direct others because of their position in the occupational and institutional hierarchy. Those with specific sub-baccalaureate certificates, certifications, and degrees do achieve middle-class wages, but they do not have access to the personal autonomy or institutional power of professionals, managers, and others with baccalaureates and graduate degrees. Collective rule, based on individual votes, remains in our political system, but it is accompanied by a new kind of self-rule and rule over others in a hierarchy of occupations tied to postsecondary selectivity.[109] Professional control over entry into occupations also creates labor market shelters and new spheres of power that are much less accessible to the sub-baccalaureate population.

Diversity in selective colleges is crucial to ensuring the legitimacy of the nation's institutional leadership. It is important that we measure and encourage racial, ethnic, and socioeconomic diversity in selective colleges, because the outcomes of the admissions process in the top colleges are the tip of the iceberg of a system of sorting the nation's human capital, economic opportunity, and social status. The outcome of the selective college admissions process is the distillation of all the social and economic sorting that occurs in PreK–12 education and foreshadows the differences in lifetime opportunities thereafter. To the extent the racial and economic sorting in the K–16 education system results in the intergenerational reproduction of elites, we risk cultural resentment and social instability.

Selective college admissions deserve our attention because they are the tail that wags the dog in both K–12 and postsecondary reforms and in their impact on equal opportunity. The round of education reform that followed the publication of *A Nation at Risk* in 1983 gradually has displaced the vocational, general, and college prep pathways typical of the comprehensive high school, replacing it with a single college prep pathway leading to two-year and four-year college enrollments.[110] Besides, the college admissions debate is not just about access to the top colleges. When Harvard sneezes, all of education catches cold. Or, as David Riesman wrote in 1956:

> In order to try to capture certain large trends in the movement
> and rhythm of American academic development, it may be

illuminating to see the avant-garde, both educational and more generally cultural, as the head of a snake-like procession—the head of which is often turning back upon itself, as at present, while the middle part seeks to catch up with where the head once was.[111]

4. A Mind Is a Terrible Thing to Waste

Perhaps the most striking finding in our analysis is the extent of wasted academic talent in the transition from high school to college and the workplace, especially among working class and low-income families.

Levels of readiness and SES explain a lot of the variances in college access and graduation rates, but they do not explain the striking differences in access and graduation rates in the top 25 percent or the top 50 percent of readiness or SES. Substantial shares of students who are college ready either do not go to college, or are going to two-year colleges when they are qualified for four-year colleges. This is true for students from the lowest SES quartile. But there are many students from the top 25 percent or top 50 percent of their high school class and from the top half of the SES distribution that do not attend a four-year college even though they appear to be academically prepared. We find, for example, that about 600,000 students in the top half of their high school class do not graduate from a two-year or four-year college.

These data clearly demonstrate that the transition from secondary to postsecondary education has both equity and efficiency problems. Qualified lower-SES students consistently transition to college and graduate at lower levels than their academic peers. The system demonstrates a clear pattern of unequal results for academic equals. On the whole, the postsecondary system favors students from the higher socioeconomic quartiles, even when the students from lower socioeconomic quartiles are equally qualified. In addition, the transition from secondary to postsecondary education, as it presently operates, wastes a substantial share of the nation's college-ready human capital. This is troubling, considering that the production of postsecondary human capital is crucial to international economic competitiveness, and that the United States has fallen behind the global leaders in college attainment.

The Mismatch between Talent and Attendance

The mismatch between college talent and college attendance is most startling in the top 25 percent of college-ready high school seniors. As illustrated in Figures 3.18 and 3.19 (pages 155–56), there are big differences in college attendance among high school seniors who scored in the top 25 percent of the test distribution in the National Education Longitudinal Survey (NELS). College attendance is highest for top-scoring students from the highest SES families, but degrades quickly thereafter as the data moves down the SES hierarchy. The extent of wasted human capital and under-achievement in the top 25 percent of the high school test distribution is phenomenal.

Among the most-affluent students in the top quartile of their class, 80 percent go on to a four-year school, compared with 66 percent, 51 percent, and 44 percent of students with the same stellar qualifications but who come from the second, third, and bottom SES quartiles respectively. It is disturbing that 20 percent of top students from the nation's most-affluent families do not go on to a four-year college, because they are qualified and one assumes their parents can afford to send them. They tend to come from families that make at least $85,000 per year. These data demonstrate that postsecondary underachievement is not just about readiness and affordability.

The fact that almost half the students from families in the second SES quartile who are ready for a four-year college do not attend one is more understandable as an affordability problem, but still wasteful of the nation's human capital. These families make roughly $50,000 to $85,000. They are probably not eligible for Pell Grants, although they can secure college loans. These students tend to fall through the cracks, as they are not wealthy enough to rely on their parents and yet they are not the target of federal grant aid. Nor are most of them the target of state or institutional merit aid, which tends to go to the very top few percent of the highest test scorers, or to minorities, or to those at the very bottom of SES distribution.

Another extraordinary finding is the extent to which these top students are diverted from four-year to two-year programs. Ostensibly, students in the top quartile of the test score distribution should be able to handle the work at a four-year college, yet, even among the most affluent of them, 14 percent go to a two-year college,

Figure 3.18 Postsecondary Destination of High–Scoring Students, by Socioeconomic Status

Top-scoring quartile of students

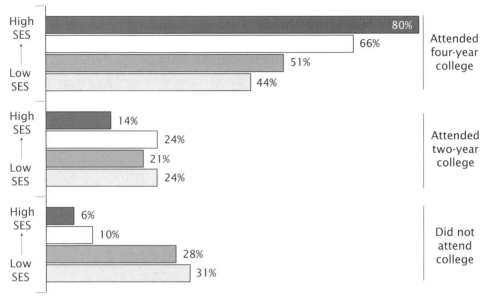

Second-highest-scoring quartile of students

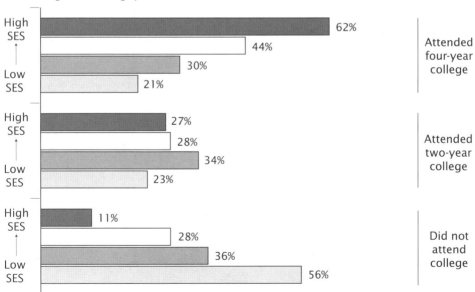

Source: Authors' Calculations of NELS data, U.S. Department of Education.

Figure 3.19 Postsecondary Destination of Low–Scoring Students, by Socioeconomic Status

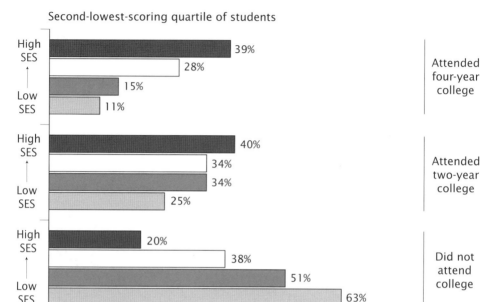

Second-lowest-scoring quartile of students

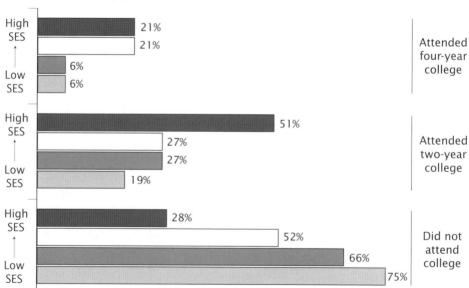

Bottom-scoring quartile of students

Source: Authors' Calculations of NELS data, U.S. Department of Education.

and the share of the top students in the bottom three socioeconomic quartiles who go to a two-year rather than a four-year college hovers between 20 percent and 24 percent.

The most striking fact about these top students with test scores in the upper 25 percent of their high school class is that a substantial share do not go to college at all. As would be expected, the share of these top performers who do not go on to either a two-year or four-year college is more concentrated in the bottom half of the distribution of socioeconomic status. This category increases from 6 percent of top performers in the top of the socioeconomic distribution to 28 percent and 31 percent of the top performers in the bottom two SES quartiles.

The pattern of wasted talent and underachievement is repeated in the second tier of high school talent. These students are all in the upper half of their high school classes, somewhere between the fiftieth and seventy-fifth percentile in test scores. In this second tier, a majority of the students from the lowest quartile of SES do not go to college at all, and the differences in college attendance by SES quartiles begin to gather momentum. For example, in the top SES quartile, 89 percent still go to a four-year (62 percent) or a two-year (27 percent) college. In this second group of test-scorers, a majority of student in the middle two quartiles do attend a two-year or four-year college, but a majority of the students in the bottom quartile do not go to any college at all.

In the bottom half of the test-scoring distribution, the differences in college attendance among equally qualified students continues to grow; the community colleges dominate college attendance among those who do go, and overall rates of college attendance fall below 50 percent for all but the highest SES category. Figures 3.18 and 3.19 also show a final irony: more than 70 percent of the highest SES students in the bottom half of test-scoring still go on to a two-year or four-year college, in spite of their low test scores. This level of college attendance is higher than the share of the top-performing students in the lowest SES quartile who go on to college. In other words, our lowest-performing affluent students go to college at a higher rate than the highest performing youth from the least-advantaged families.

In order to test our findings, we did further analysis focusing exclusively on baccalaureate completion rates using a combined measure that included test scores from the NELS test data as well as corresponding data from the SAT and ACT. The results are essentially the same: baccalaureate completion rates among equally qualified students also vary by income, so that students from affluent families are far more likely to complete their studies than equally qualified students from low-income families, as is shown in Figure 3.20.

- Among those with an SAT/ACT/NELS score between 1200 and 1600, the graduation rate for the top SES quartile is 82 percent, but 44 percent for those who score between 1200 and 1600 and come from the bottom SES quartile.

- For those who score between 1100 and 1199, the baccalaureate graduation rate for the top SES quartile is 67 percent, but the

Figure 3.20 Graduation Rates, by Socioeconomic Status and SAT–Equivalent Score (percentage of initial attendees)

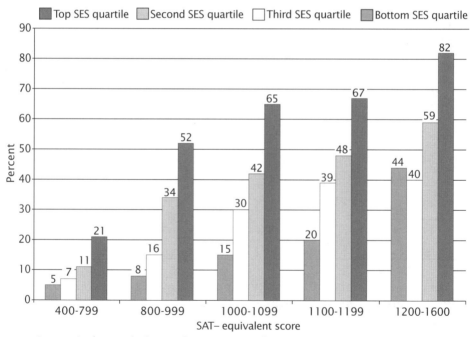

Source: Authors' calculations from Barron's Selectivity Rankings; National Education Longitudinal Study: Base Year through Fourth Follow-Up, 1988–2000 (Washington, D.C.: U.S. Dept. of Education, National Center for Education Statistics, 2000).

graduation rate for those from the bottom SES quartile is 20 percent.

- For those who score between 1000 and 1099, the baccalaureate graduation rate for the top SES quartile is 65 percent, but the graduation rate for those from the bottom SES quartile is 15 percent.

- For those who score between 800 and 999, the baccalaureate graduation rate for the top SES quartile is 52 percent, but the graduation rate for those from the bottom SES quartile is 8 percent.

- For those who score between 400 and 799, the baccalaureate graduation rate for the top SES quartile is 21 percent, but the graduation rate for those from the bottom SES quartile is 5 percent.

THE EFFECTS OF POSTSECONDARY EXPANSION

A key question in considering the equity effects of our expanding postsecondary system is the relative extent to which expansion has increased access and stratification. In general, expansion in the American postsecondary system has increased access drastically, but also has increased stratification, especially for minorities and students from low-income and working families. Relatively unrestrained by public regulation, our postsecondary apparatus grows dramatically in every direction. While the open-ended competition encourages quality and offers choice, it also has resulted in growing stratification, because the majority of growth in access for minorities as well as working families and low-income families has come from the least-selective four-year colleges and community colleges. The expansion also has taken on the characteristics of a de facto dual system, in which general preparation for the professions concentrates in the selective four-year colleges, and more narrow vocational preparation concentrates in a second tier of community colleges and exclusively vocational schools. Moreover, the institutional hierarchies that result seem frozen in place, with few opportunities for transitions between the upper tier of selective four-year colleges and the lower tier of non-selective four-year institutions and community colleges.

The solidification of the postsecondary hierarchy results in rigid inequalities and unequal treatment of equals. As you can see from our analysis of the National Education Longitudinal Survey (NELS), equally talented students, as measured by test scores, vary widely in attainment. (See Figure 3.21.) A decided minority of college students with SAT-equivalent scores below the average score of 1000 get four-year degrees; however, a growing majority of students with SAT-equivalent scores above 1000 do get degrees or certificates:

Figure 3.21 Degree Attainment, by SAT–Equivalent Score (percentage of initial attendees)

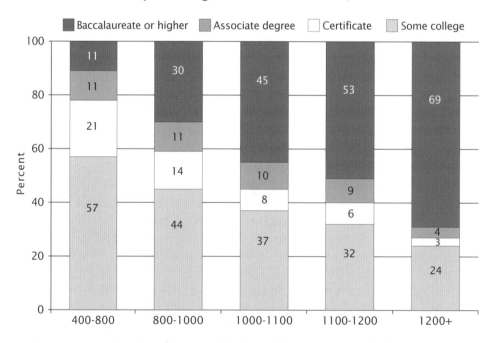

Source: Authors' calculations from National Education Longitudinal Study: Base Year through Fourth Follow-Up, 1988–2000 (Washington, D.C.: U.S. Dept. of Education, National Center for Education Statistics, 2000).

- 45 percent of students with an SAT equivalent score between 1000 and 1100 get baccalaureates, and all but 37 percent get a baccalaureate, an associate degree, or a vocational certificate;

- 53 percent of students with an SAT equivalent score between 1100 and 1200 get baccalaureates, and all but 32 percent get a baccalaureate, an associate degree, or a vocational certificate; and

- 69 percent of students with an SAT equivalent score of 1200 or above get baccalaureates, and all but 24 percent get a baccalaureate, an associate degree, or a vocational certificate.

It would seem likely that the students in this score range would be the most likely candidates to move from "some college," certificates, or associate degrees to four-year degrees.

In order to assess whether we could upgrade degree completion among those who currently go to college, we conducted a separate analysis of the High School and Beyond (HS&B) data, from which we can calculate graduation rates by a composite SAT/ACT score. As shown in Table 3.5, students with an SAT-equivalent score below 900 have only a 43 percent chance of graduating from a four-year college, and their chances of graduating do not improve much, irrespective of selectivity. At the same time, however, college students with SAT-equivalent scores above 1000 have a 74 percent to 88 percent chance of graduating from a four-year college, and their chances improve with selectivity to somewhere between 85 percent and 96 percent, depending on their actual test scores. Thus, it does seem realistic to suppose that there is substantial room for improvement in baccalaureate attainment in the current patterns of college attendance. These data also validate other analyses that suggest that increasing access needs to be balanced with some concern for the stratification that accompanies it.

ACADEMIC PREPARATION IS NOT ALL

As our data show, the conventional view that academic preparation is a monolithic barrier to access and choice among low-SES students is greatly overstated. There are large numbers of students from families with low income and low levels of parental education that are academically prepared for baccalaureate degree attainment, even in the most-selective colleges. These results were first reported by the Advisory Commission on Student Financial Assistance, a congressionally mandated commission led by Brian Fitzgerald. According to the commission, low-income students who graduate from high school and are at least minimally qualified for college enroll in four-year institutions at half the rate of their high-income peers.[112] Our own analysis of the NELS data in 2004 supported the Department of Education's finding.[113] Other researchers analyzing the SAT and ACT data for 2003 have shown substantial numbers of students from low-income families who can do the work at the most selective private four-year colleges.[114]

The most damning analysis comes from Dannette Gerald and Kati Haycock of the Education Trust.[115] They charge that the flagship public universities have been captured by the "relentless pursuit not of expanded opportunity, but of increased selectivity."[116] They argue that the flagship public universities are increasingly "rated less for what they accomplish with the students they let in than by how many students they keep out." As a result, they conclude that "these institutions are becoming disproportionately whiter and richer."

Gerald and Haycock find that large numbers of well-qualified, low-income students were ignored by the state flagship universities, and that in 2003 the flagship public universities spent $257 million on financial aid for students from families who earned over $100,000 and $171 million on families who earned less than $20,000. They also show that enrollments in flagship public universities include 22 percent of Pell Grant–eligible students, compared with 35 percent for all colleges and universities.

Most recently, a 2009 study by William G. Bowen, Matthew M. Chingos, and Michael S. McPherson reported similar findings using data for selected states and for the topmost tier of the selective public colleges.[117] Like Gerard and Haycock, they find disturbing levels of underutilization of high school talent, especially by SES. Bowen, Chingos, and McPherson refer to this phenomenon as *matching*, or "the extent to which the process of sorting students from high school to college aims high school students who are prepared to take advantage of especially promising educational opportunities to the colleges and universities best able to provide them."[118]

Bowen, Chingos, and McPherson go on to assert that "High schools have a dual role." They have the responsiblity to "provide their students with strong preparation . . . but also to provide the information and support that students and their families need if they are to translate 'preparedness' into enrollment at those college and universities that will allow them to take full advantage of their talents."[119] As presently constructed, American high schools are not up to the tasks that Bowen, Chingos, and McPherson set for them. The tripartite tracking into college prep, vocational education, and general education has become more muted, but academic tracking is growing stronger, both among and within K–12 institutions.

We agree with Bowen, Chingos, and McPherson that the information provided in high school influences students' expectations, especially minority, working class, and poor students who have little access to other information about going to college. But college counseling and supportive services are woefully lacking in American high schools. What counseling exists is focused on testing, scheduling, disciplinary actions, and crisis intervention. What little college counseling takes place often is tied to the most selective curriculum tracks, such as Advanced Placement (AP) or International Baccalaureate (IB). According to the National Association of College Admission Counseling, the ratio of students to counselors is 490 to 1.[120] In many states, including California, the ratio of students to counselors approaches or exceeds 1000 to 1.[121] Teachers are most often the counselors of last resort, and minority and low-SES students typically are taught by the least-qualified and least-effective teachers.[122]

The available evidence does suggest that the mismatch and underutilization among student talents in low-SES families can be substantially improved with appropriate counseling.[123] The best evidence of the effectiveness of counseling and social support is the effectiveness of high-SES families and communities in developing and matching the talents of their children with college selectivity as they move through the PreK–12 pipeline long before they arrive in high school. Even better evidence is the burgeoning private industry in college testing, test preparation, and college counseling.[124] Both ACT and the College Board along with ETS allow students to take admissions tests as often as they like, as long as they pay for each testing event, and choose which scores to report to colleges, even though they both claim that multiple test-taking does not influence the test score.

Counseling and outreach strategies for disadvantaged minorities and low-SES students essentially attempt to overcome the disadvantages of being born without a certain race or bank account. Advantaged students have their college-educated parents and the social and educational capital that comes with buying a house in a prosperous neighborhood. Children of working-class and low-income families essentially are on their own. As a result, the most substantial share of them leave K–12 education unprepared for college.[125] A surprising share does well in grade school, even though most disadvantaged high achievers eventually fall behind.[126] But as the data cited above show, those who make it through high school ready for college often attend colleges with levels of selectivity below their abilities, and remarkable numbers never get a two-year or four-year degree.

The large number of low-SES students who are qualified but do not attend or graduate from four-year colleges is striking, given consistent efforts by federal and state governments, colleges, and private philanthropy to encourage both minority and low-income college achievement. Upward Bound was the first such federal program, in 1964, followed by TRIO in 1965 and GEAR-UP in 1998. There are a wide variety of state programs as well, including California's Making It Happen, Minnesota's Get Ready program, and Rhode Island's Children's Crusade. There are a wide variety of private programs as well, including Eugene Lang's I Have a Dream program, the Mathematics, Engineering, and Science Achievement (MESA) program, and the Advancement Via Individual Determination (AVID) program. A substantial share of colleges participate in outreach and targeted recruitment programs.

External interventions and counseling programs work for those who come within their effective reach.[127] But despite positive evaluations, growth, and diversification of both public and private outreach programs, the above data suggest that they are not stemming the tide in the socioeconomic stratification of postsecondary education. They are not of sufficient scale. One estimate of the cost of full coverage has been placed at another $6 billion.[128] State programs are limited to roughly fifteen states, and only about a third of colleges have active outreach programs of their own. These programs represent a form of educational "triage" among those most adversely affected by powerful social, economic, and institutional forces beyond their control.

These programs focus on students instead of the core mechanisms that drive college expectations and success, many of which operate outside the context of the education system. Programs that celebrate individuals are useful, but the growing stratification of postsecondary opportunity is an institutional problem, not an individual problem. These interventions would work much better if they were used to leverage high-quality curriculums in a well integrated K–16 system that promoted high expectations for college among disadvantaged students.[129]

5. Can Affirmative Admissions Programs Be Colorblind, Yet Not Blind to the Effects of Race?

Many believe that race no longer matters, and that socioeconomic disadvantages, otherwise known as class, have become the universal barrier to equal opportunity. Our analysis of the NELS does not support the notion that we could use income or other socioeconomic characteristics as a substitute for race. Race and ethnicity have effects all their own, and we find that socioeconomic status is no substitute for race or ethnicity in selective college admissions. In particular, we tested the notion that wealth differences would explain away race-based differences in educational opportunity. Median household wealth for whites is ten times the median household wealth for African Americans.[130] As we discuss above, the differences in wealth between minorities and whites is even greater than the differences in other SES factors, but is rarely considered as an explanation because of data quality issues. Although it is possible that better information on wealth differences will produce substantial levels of racial diversity, our analysis relies on a limited wealth factor (college savings) that is self-reported by students and does not capture the full racial effects of a more robust wealth factor.[131]

In the final analysis, we find that there are good empirical reasons to increase the emphasis on income-based affirmative action in selective college admissions. Socioeconomic status has powerful negative effects on access to selective colleges among highly qualified students. Many of these SES effects work through identifiable channels that can be used as factors in judging merit among college applicants. SES-based affirmative action also deserves more attention, because the shares of low-income students are even smaller than the shares of blacks and Latinos at every level of college selectivity.

We find good reason to increase the emphasis on SES-based affirmative action, but we do not find good empirical reasons to abandon race-based or ethnically based affirmative action, either as a separate strategy or as a factor in class-based affirmative action. Race and ethnicity have negative effects on admission test scores all by themselves and, thus far, parsing all of the effects of race or ethnicity into their socioeconomic component pieces has been outside of our reach. We also find that the educational disadvantages of low socioeconomic status are more onerous for minorities, especially for African Americans. As a result, if we are going to use SES variables to gauge relative disadvantages, we will need to use race as an integral factor in determining affirmative action or preferences based on socioeconomic status.

For example, let us pretend that an admissions officer in a college that values class-based diversity receives two applications from equally qualified candidates. The two candidates have the same test scores, grades, and other qualifications. They come from the same low-income background and have overcome the same socioeconomic hurdles. One candidate is African American and one is white. Our findings suggest, as race-based affirmative action policies presume, that the African-American candidate is probably more deserving, because socioeconomic differences, when combined with race or ethnicity, have more powerful disadvantaging effects, and overcoming those effects is more difficult for the minority student.

With our data, we can explain many of the differences in admission test scores with colorblind social and economic variables such as income, parental education, school quality, and peer effects. We are able to parse the effects of family income into distinctive elements such as parental education, school quality, and neighborhood and peer effects. These variables alone reduce the independent effects of family income all by itself by more than 90 percent. Race and ethnicity prove more stubborn. For example, socioeconomic variables reduce the effects of race on test scores by more than half, but we are unable to eliminate race as a factor in driving down test scores, because race interacts with socioeconomic factors in uniquely powerful ways.

More importantly, we find that socioeconomic status itself is not race blind. The disadvantages of race persist even as African-American incomes rise. Improvements in socioeconomic status raise minority test scores, but in our data, they appear to do so at a lower rate than for whites with similar improvements. On average, African Americans still seem to suffer educational disadvantages from race even when they achieve middle-class or upper-middle-class economic status.

Racial isolation and socioeconomic status are inextricably bound and inseparable in any attempt to promote either race or socioeconomic diversity amidst the selective college admissions process. Affirmative action based solely on socioeconomic status ignores the very real disadvantages suffered by racial minorities at all income levels. If we attempted to introduce a system of affirmative action based solely on socioeconomic status, it would be unfair to minorities because low socioeconomic status is a greater burden for minorities than it is for whites. Minority status tends to increase the effects of low socioeconomic status on admissions test performance. While there is steady progress in test scores for minorities as their socioeconomic status improves, the progress is slower than it is for whites who make comparable improvements. The extra burden of minority status creates a lag in the positive effects of socioeconomic progress of minorities compared with white families who make similar socioeconomic progress.[132]

HOW WOULD A RACIAL, ETHNIC, AND CLASS-BASED APPROACH TO PREFERENCES WORK?

In order to envision what sort of approach may work in lessening stratification, in this section we use the NELS data to provide a systematic empirical accounting of the effects of racial and socioeconomic barriers on college admissions test scores. We provide college and university admissions officers with the conceptual tools to consider applicants' records in the context of obstacles overcome. Our findings are relevant only to the NELS data, and would have to be customized for qualified applicant pools in particular institutions.

Given the importance of SAT and ACT scores in selective college admissions, we assess the effects of barriers that are measured in terms of their effect on SAT/ACT scores as the most relevant and quantifiable indicator of the obstacles that students face. As such, they can be used as tools for assessing the effects of social circumstances on test scores and relative differences in deservedness among qualified applicants.

In order to measure the effects of class and demographic obstacles on admissions scores, we developed a composite SAT/ACT measure.[133] We created a composite SAT/ACT measure by converting ACT to SAT scores, which produced the ACT to SAT conversion table found in Appendix 1. For the sake of convenience, we will discuss our findings as they affect various socioeconomic and demographic variables on an SAT-equivalent score.

While the academic literature has long found that it is a disadvantage to grow up in a poor family, to live in racially segregated neighborhoods, or to attend a low-income school, for example, these realities give admissions officers only a vague idea of the scale of the obstacles that certain students face. This exercise seeks to give guidance by providing a relative weight to various disadvantages, measured in SAT/ACT-equivalent scores.

The SAT/ACT-equivalent score was used in a step-wise regression. Our goal was to sort through a wide array of student and peer, family, neighborhood, and school variables to identify what affects the SAT/ACT score. We grouped these factors as being environmental, or outside of a student's immediate choice set, and those where a student has had choice,[134] albeit loosely defined (for example, variables such as having children, taking AP courses or tests, not being arrested, and working status were included in the model but will not be discussed in detail).

This schema allows us to distinguish obstacles that clearly are outside of a student's control, which should, to a certain degree, be considered when comparing student performances. Of the variables that remained statistically significant in the final model:

- *Student factors* are African American and Hispanic race or ethnicity (compared to white). This was not statistically significant for other race/ethnic groups.

- *Family factors* are maximum parental education (compared to high school), family income quartiles,[135] having a sibling who dropped out of school, family wealth (based on savings for school), and occupational prestige (using the Duncan scale).

- *Neighborhood factors* are percent of households in residential zip codes headed by persons with less than a high school education or with a graduate degree (compared to those with a high school diploma), living in the South, or living in a rural area (compared to suburban).

- *School factors* are percent of enrolled population eligible for free and reduced price lunch, and school type (Catholic and public versus private).

- *Peer factors* are percent of school population that is Asian, concentration of Hispanic race/ethnicity at the school,[136] and having friends who plan to attend a four-year institution.

The above factors were found to have either a positive or negative relationship to SAT/ACT score. Students who suffer the full range of social, economic, and racial/ethnic disadvantages tend to lose several hundred points out of a possible 1600 points on their SAT/ACT-equivalent scores. Predicted scores would vary from 544 to 1328 if a student were to have every negative factor, having dropout parents with at least one sibling having dropped out of school, and no friends going to four-year schools, for instance, compared to a student with nothing but environmental advantage. The advantaged student would have easy access to one of the top 150 most selective colleges, a 96 percent chance of graduating, and a 60 percent likelihood of going to graduate or professional school. The disadvantaged student would go to a two-year or non-selective four-year school, with less than a 30 percent chance of getting a degree.

The summary data in Table 3.7 (page 170) show the relationship between the various factors and the SAT/ACT score. Of utmost importance are the values of the race and income factors. Part of this overall experiment has been trying to understand whether the effects of race can be replaced by the effects of other observable factors, most notably income. In an attempt to understand this, we ran Ordinary Least Squares (OLS) regressions of income and race on SAT score to

Table 3.7 The Cost of Disadvantage (in SAT points)

Factors outside Students' Control*	
• Lowest income quartile (compared to highest)	−13
• High school dropout parent (compared to most educated)	−43
• Father is a laborer (compared to being a physician)	−48
• Non-college-going peer group	−39
• Public high school (compared to private)	−28
• Majority of school enrollment eligible for free and reduced-price lunch (90 percent versus going to a school with no eligibles)	−38
• Neighborhood has few heads of household with graduate education (5 percent versus 90 percent)	−113
• Live in the South	−12
• No college savings (wealth) relative to having saved $40,000 (per $10,000)	−41**
• Black (compared to white)	−56
• Having a dropout sibling	−24
Subtotal	−455
Factors within Students' Constrained, or Environmental, Choice Set	
• Having a child	−34
• Having been arrested	−41
• Did not take an AP course	−81
• Working during high school	−13
• Not taking an honors course	−59
Subtotal	−228
Other	−101
Grand total	−784

* Previous literature has shown significant impact of single-parent households on academic outcomes, although not necessarily SAT scores. In our initial model single-parent households were statistically significant and negatively correlated with SAT scores. In our final model, we disaggregated SES into its component pieces as well as added additional explanatory variables, which added explanatory power, and in doing, single parent household was no longer statistically significant.

** We have produced these estimates as restricted by the range of wealth that is observed in the NELS data. Today's rising concerns about college costs among parents, as well as the introduction of new college saving programs, make it likely that the realistic maximum of this effect is much larger. For instance, if a wealthy family saves $175,000 for college, the gap between rich and poor would increase to -175 points.

demonstrate the relationship such a cursory glance would provide. In this context, we observed that, in stand-alone regressions, low income handicaps SAT score by roughly 180 points, compared to high income, while being African American leads to around 130 points lower than whites. When added to the same model, both race and income help explain differences in SAT performance; most interestingly, race and socioeconomic status (SES) have statistically significant interaction effects. This means increases in social status impact SAT scores differently for different race and ethnic groups; most importantly, as white youth move up the SES scale, their SAT scores increase more than for African-American youth.

In the full model, we have broken SES into its core components (family income, maximum parental education, and occupational prestige of father's occupation) to understand better how each piece is related to the SAT score. We also add the factors (student, family, neighborhood, school, and choice) discussed above. In this final iteration, low-income status accounts for only a thirteen-point lower score than high income, while African Americans score fifty-six points lower than whites.

THE SPECIAL CASE OF RACE

This result suggests that the disadvantages of class can be more easily decomposed to a set of observable, thus policy-malleable characteristics, while the disadvantages and advantages of race are more independent of other characteristics and not so easily separable. In other words, it is easier to find proxies for socioeconomic status than it is to find proxies for race in the admissions process. We have tried pursuing this in great detail and are left with the conclusion that socioeconomic status has different effects among different race and ethnic groups. Shifts in socioeconomic status affect the whole fabric of education disadvantages differently, and by different magnitudes, by race and ethnicity. The advantages and disadvantages of minority and majority applicants with the same socioeconomic profile are not comparable. Hence, when we use SES to determine admissions, it needs to be considered in the context of race and ethnicity.

Income, earnings, and even the more robust tripartite SES measure of class, do not fully measure the advantages and disadvantages of each race and each ethnic group, especially for African Americans. In addition, both majority and minority groups experience different levels of increased educational advantage with income or SES improvements. In particular, African Americans experience the smallest increases in educational advantage as their income or socioeconomic status rises, compared with other minority groups and whites.

To provide some more detail, we tried to measure the extent to which SES can be substituted for race or ethnicity in determining admission test scores. Neither factor completely disappears, although SES seems to be more easily parsed with other observable factors than race. A simple-minded regression shows a 132-point decline in admission test scores for being African American relative to being white, and a 109-point decline for being Hispanic relative to being white. A similar income regression demonstrates an even larger difference between the top and bottom income quartiles; students in the low-income quartile are predicted to score 182 points lower than students from high-income families. As observed in Table 3.7, income reduces to explaining 13 points of difference, while race and ethnicity (African-American, and Hispanic) still explain around 40 percent of what they did in the simple model. This is why we conclude that SES differences in test scores are more easily explained than race or ethnicity.

In our experiment, the effects of SES alone are fairly consistent, accounting for roughly 200 points of SAT variation. But when interacting with race, it appears that increases in SES among African Americans account for some 50 points in SAT variation, while similar increases in SES improve test scores quite a bit more for whites, Asians, and Hispanics. Admittedly, these regressions raise more questions than we have been able to answer;[137] questions about how income, ethnicity, and race need to be considered together and answered more fully before casting any aside in considering how admissions policy should evolve.

These factors can be grouped broadly as being either environmental (that is, outside of a student's immediate choice set) or being ones where the student has had choice, albeit loosely defined.[138] In order to make the findings more transparent we have grouped these variables as they would affect two students born with equal innate ability: one is raised under "highly advantaged" circumstances, and another is raised amidst "highly disadvantaged" circumstances.

- *The highly disadvantaged student.* The highly disadvantaged student (predicted to score 544 on the SAT) is created here to demonstrate the cumulative effects of disadvantaged circumstances and poor choices, at least poor choices in regard to predicted SAT scores. This student is African American (–56 points),[139] from a family with income in the lowest quartile (–13), with neither parent having a high school diploma (–43), who have not saved for their child's education (–41), and lives in a zip code where 88 percent[140] of the household heads also lack a diploma (–112). This student would have at least one child (–34), would have been arrested (–41 points), and works outside of school (–13). The student lives in the South (–12) and attends public school (–28). This student would never have taken an AP or honors course, let alone an AP test (all forfeited potential gains), and attended a school where virtually all students are eligible or free for reduced price lunch (–38).

- *The highly advantaged student.*[141] The highly advantaged student, predicted to score 1328 on the SAT, enjoys the benefits of circumstance, family environment, the best of schools and school resources, and other factors that support academic success. This white student is from a family of the highest socioeconomic status (avoiding the point handicap of lower SES); this highly advantaged student has at least one parent with a graduate degree and his or her family has saved $40,000 or more for his or her education; the student lives in the Northeast outside of a city. This student goes to a private school (reference group) where virtually none of the school population is eligible for free or reduced-price lunch. The highly advantaged student has not worked outside of school, has no siblings that dropped out of school, has never been arrested, and has friends who plan to attend a four-year institution. Academically this student has taken AP courses [142]and tests in addition to other honors courses.

In total, there is a 784-point gap between the predicted SAT score of the theoretical most advantaged (1328) and disadvantaged (544) students.

The student from the wrong side of the tracks would score 544—a loss of 510 points compared with the "average" student, who scores 1054. If that same student came from the right side of the tracks, he would have scored 1328 out of 1600 points—a gain of 274 points above average that would put our mythical student within reach of the vast majority of selective colleges. The total swing in our test scores for the same youth growing up on the wrong side or the right side of the tracks is 784 points on the SAT, but that does not mean that our applicant who scored 544 will perform the same as his or her alter ego on the right side of the tracks who scores 1328.

On average, students with the same test scores, grades, and other admissions markers will perform similarly. For example, a highly disadvantaged student with a score of 540 would have less than a 30 percent chance of graduating from one of the top 193 colleges, while the student's average alter ego with a score of 1054 would have an 86 percent chance of graduating, and the highly advantaged alter ego would have a 96 percent chance of graduating.

The environmental gaps between advantaged and disadvantaged students are real, but not monolithic. There are large numbers of youth who have overcome racial, ethnic, and socioeconomic status barriers to performance. For example, our student from the wrong side of the tracks who would have been predicted to score 544 on the SAT may actually score 1050. Having scored a hefty 506 points above what would have been expected, he or she would be a striver, and arguably more deserving than someone from a more privileged background who scored 1050. Of course, high-scoring, advantaged students can be strivers too. Advantaged youth work hard for their achievements. For example, if our advantaged student who was supposed to score 1328 actually scores a hefty 1500, he or she is a striver as well.

We recommend that universities employ the types of data included in this paper not in a mechanical fashion (adding or subtracting SAT points from candidates, depending on their socioeconomic status and race), but rather as a general guide for assessing the merits of an individual applicant. Universities and colleges should customize information about the various obstacles faced by applicants in the context of their own applicant pools and their own standards of readiness, based on past experience. We believe that assessing applicants' test scores, grades, and other qualifications based on the differences between expected and actual qualifications is a useful way to reward character and promote upward mobility.

CONCLUSION

Any discussion that touches on selective college access in postsecondary education quickly morphs into a brawl over race-based preferences. Race-based preferences have never been popular, although a strong majority of Americans favor affirmative action policies.[143] Preferences for African Americans came into being during a unique time of crisis in America, and have been orphaned ever since.[144]

While race-based affirmative action has been the model for all other minority and gender preferences, it is the most fragile of our affirmative action policies. In spite of its generative power as the model for securing the rights of immigrants, language minorities, the disabled, women, and gays and lesbians, it is the one set of preferences that is always most at risk in American politics. The reach of race-based preferences has been gradually whittled away by the courts and legislatures.[145] The U.S. Supreme Court has given race-based affirmative action a twenty-five-year lifeline, but that will not be near long enough to solve the African-American and Hispanic inequality problem.[146] Already, roughly a quarter of Americans live in states where racial preferences in higher education have been prohibited at public institutions.[147] Race-based affirmative action has declined significantly in selective higher education, especially in public institutions—and not because social progress in minority educational performance has obviated the need.[148]

Race-based affirmative action remains a hot-button issue in American politics, but it may not be as much a lightning rod in the future. Race-based affirmative action may become an early model for a more inclusive higher education system in the future. The decline of blue-collar jobs that paid well but required only a high school education or less creates a new demand for mass postsecondary education among the children of the lower middle class whose parents and grandparents were industrial workers. And, as is often stated, the U.S. population will be a majority-minority sometime after 2050. Increasing diversity and the growing population share of minorities will continue to add pressure for admissions policies that result in college campuses "that look like America." The tension between an aging white majority and a more diverse population of working families with school-age children may force a generational bargain to balance the public budgetary commitment to education, including postsecondary education, and programs for retirees.

In the future, the increasing economic interest in postsecondary education may legitimize race-based affirmative action in college admissions. Thus far, the affirmative action dialogue has been part of the culture wars in American politics. But increasingly, postsecondary access and choice are part of the more tangible politics of service provision where ideological fights mean less and pragmatic bargains over resources mean more. In that more grounded dialogue, issues of access and stratification will be the business of political executives and legislatures, not the courts.

The race-based affirmative action issue has proven too hot to handle for politicians in either party, and has been shipped off to the Supreme Court to be decided by judges who do not have to face the voters. And if the court shuts down affirmative action, and the issue bounces back into the legislatures, it may well merge with, and add scope to, the ongoing discussion of access and completion. To some extent, compared to the larger problems of stratification, affirmative action becomes a fig leaf to hide a larger system of inequalities.

The old school debate over affirmative action in name brand institutions still can get page one coverage, but probably cannot carry the political weight of the larger issue surrounding postsecondary stratification. Affirmative action carries too much of its own baggage already. And all by itself, it does not seem to have enough momentum to buck the tide of stratification. Financing is moving toward an ability to pay system. Merit aid is on the rise.[149] Inadequate financing and loan burdens discourage even the most qualified working-class and low-income students from enrolling and persisting.[150] Selective colleges can cut loans and increase grants for racial and ethnic minorities and students from working-class and low-SES backgrounds, but net cost is still high and aid does not make up the difference.[151] Moreover, there is a decided imbalance in affirmative action policies that creates inherent tensions over their expansion. If we cobble together a rough tip sheet on the value of preferences in SAT scores, based on the work of Princeton sociology professor Thomas Espenshade and his colleagues over the years (on a 1600 point scale), we get a picture of the preference values traditionally assigned to certain groups (see Table 3.8).[152]

Current affirmative action policies emphasize race-based affirmative action over socioeconomic status. This is due in part to the fact that affirmative admissions tend to emphasize low-SES students who are African American or Hispanic, and in part because low SES is a secondary priority in selective colleges.[153] In addition, there are tensions over race-based affirmative action policies that derive from the fact that many blacks at selective colleges are not descended from American slaves. Espenshade finds that two-thirds of black applicants to public universities and only one-third of applicants at private colleges are descendants of American slaves.[154] There is growing evidence that affirmative action at the most-selective colleges increasingly is focused on

Table 3.8 Value of Selected Preferences (in SAT points)

Category	Preference
Black	+310
Athlete	+200
Legacy	+160
Hispanic	+130
Lower class	+130
Working class	+70
Asian	−140

Source: T. J. Espenshade and A. W. Radford, *No Longer Separate, Not Yet Equal* (Princeton, N.J.: Princeton University Press, 2009). Table 3.5; T.J. Espenshade, C.Y. Chung, and J. Walling, "Admission Preferences for Minority Students, Athletes, and Legacies at Elite Universities," *Social Science Quarterly* 85, no. 5 (December 2004): 1431.

West Indian or African immigrants or their children—students of African descent from relatively more middle-class, affluent families raised outside the historical context of African-American history.[155] African Americans as well as Hispanics are more SES-diverse than whites at selective colleges, but still are largely drawn from middle-class and upper-class families.[156]

THE FUTURE OF INCOME-BASED AFFIRMATIVE ACTION

Income-based affirmative action has never fared well, but its momentum seems to be building. While income- and wealth-based policies and court decisions have been powerful in shaping the K–12 education system since the *San Antonio* v. *Rodriguez* case in 1973, remedies addressing spending inequality in postsecondary education have yet to take hold in the United States, in spite of the fact that spending differences in postsecondary education would be intolerable in a K–12 context. But momentum is growing in SES-based inequity in the American postsecondary system, and tight budgets and surging demand may force distributive questions to the fore—in distinctly more painful ways than the postwar economic and baby boom pushed access and choice to the fore after World War II.

To some extent, colleges already practice SES-based affirmative action, but it is the third wheel behind race and ethnically based affirmative action. Our own data show that African Americans and Hispanics represent roughly 12 percent of freshman enrollments in the most-selective colleges, compared with only 3 percent from the lowest SES quartile, and the low-SES preference is reserved largely for minority students.[157]

The most-selective colleges have made laudable attempts to increase SES diversity, but they are able to do so only because of their extraordinary wealth and because they have the fewest working-class and low-SES students. Moreover, most of these efforts do not result in any appreciable increase in working-class or lower-SES students, although they do treat the working-class and low-SES students who do attend selective colleges better. There are too many needy students and too little funds in the vast majority of postsecondary institutions to afford these kinds of generous SES-based policies without greater government support.[158]

As we have argued throughout the chapter, there is certainly a lot of low-hanging fruit for improving SES diversity at selective colleges. A shift to prospective graduation rates rather than the hyper-intensive ritual of testing and other entry metrics would add diversity and help refocus institutions from admissions to quality and completion. There are lots of working-class and low-SES students who are "undermatched" and could do the work at selective colleges, but do not go.[159] We could add even more SES diversity by seeking out these students and adding lots more would only lower graduation rates slightly.

There are no proven substitutes for race-based affirmative action, at least so far.[160] Much more can be done with SES-based affirmative action than is currently being done. An admissions system that moves undermatched students into the most selective colleges to achieve "socioeconomic neutrality" in need-blind admissions is within reach, if we want to go there.[161] We could do even more on SES diversity in selective institutions by relaxing overwrought and much too risk-averse admissions standards. But affirmative SES policies of these kinds are unaffordable or impolitic in the current public system, and they run against the tide in the drive for selectivity.

The alignment of race, ethnicity, and SES with educational opportunity has yet to finish its work. Ideally, socioeconomic neutrality would make the current system more fair and socioeconomically diverse in the short term. The student with the highest test scores would continue to go to the most-selective schools. But in the longer term, the sorting function implicit in the current test based admission process would only grow stronger and more efficient at aligning race, ethnicity, and SES with selectivity. The engines of stratification are still building momentum. In our own and other simulations of such an SES-neutral system, the race and ethnic diversity declines and SES diversity only increases at the margin.

WHERE TO BEGIN?

How do we get started on the goal of increasing racial, ethnic and socioeconomic mobility throughout the postsecondary system? First we need to continue to push for the information systems that track race, ethnicity, and socioeconomic status and tie them to transcript data throughout the K–16 education system. Systemic change is not possible as long as the process of K–16 education remains an opaque black box. Beyond better information, the basics have not changed. There is no substitute for high standards and coherence in teaching learning and assessment in the PreK–16 system.[162] And providing increased grant support to students from working-class and lower-income families is the indispensable policy of first resort in the transition from high school to college.[163]

Boutique programs to promote access in selective colleges can help, but they probably will not change the underlying systems trend toward greater postsecondary stratification. Boutique programs for minority or low-SES students tend to be most prominent at selective colleges with the lowest levels of minority or low-income access. New programs for low-SES tend to substitute one group of low-SES students already in attendance for new groups of slightly lower SES students, with no discernible change in the total shares of low-SES students on campus.

CHANGING THE METRICS OF ADMISSION

Reducing our reliance on the SAT and ACT would be a positive step in the right direction. The intensity of the competition between colleges and individuals for prestige and seats results in a reliance on the SAT and ACT exams that extends well beyond their scientific reach as predictors of college performance or labor market success. Marginal differences in admission test scores that determine access to selective colleges make relatively little difference in performance or graduation rates at selective colleges. The escalation of test score requirements for college admission inflates the effects of admissions tests beyond their actual utility. In the process, they exclude many students from working-class and lower-income families who have the academic ability to graduate from selective colleges.

More importantly, the inflation of ACT and SAT scores creates a moral hazard in selective college admissions. The available evidence suggests that the SAT and ACT probably measure race, ethnicity, sex, and socioeconomic characteristics directly, not simply as dimensions of academic readiness that happen to correlate with race, ethnicity, and sex. One study finds that race, sex, parental education, and income (as measured by eligibility for subsidized school lunch), and high school grade-point average (HSGPA) predict 45 percent of the variation in freshman grade-point average (FGPA). Adding the SAT score increases the ability to predict FGPA only to 48 percent—a relatively insignificant three additional points out of a possible one hundred points.[164]

A fundamental defect in using the SAT and ACT as tools for encouraging upward mobility is that they have no connection with teaching and learning in the K–12 system that prepares students for college. Nor do the SAT or ACT provide real diagnostic support for teaching and learning. Because of their weaknesses as spurs to achievement, the SAT and ACT seem to be on a collision course with the standards-based education reform movement that began with *A Nation at Risk* in 1983. In ideal form, the standards movement is based on the notion that all children can learn. The standards movement emphasizes the development of talent throughout the population, not finding innate aptitude among a select few, which is the essential premise of the SAT and ACT.

The standards reform movement should rely more on diagnostic achievement tests than tests of the ineffable "G." A stronger reliance on achievement tests than on tests of general aptitude would make the connection between college and K–12 standards-based teaching and learning and represent a step toward a comprehensive K–16 accountability system.

In our view, the immediate effects on college access and selectivity of shifting from the SAT and ACT toward more achievement-based testing would be marginal. In the final analysis, all education metrics are highly correlated with racial, ethnic, and SES differences to one degree or another. The justification for a shift toward achievement tests over the current ACT or SAT is that they send the right messages to all K–12 students, especially the least-advantaged students. The clear message that a switch to achievement tests would send is that studying in K–12 education matters in getting into college, especially getting into selective elite colleges. Hitting the books would be the best test prep because the material covered in the textbooks is covered in the test. College admissions testing would no longer be a high stakes game of tricky questions and beat the clock.

Reversing the Engine of Inequality

Better information, better tests, and more counseling will help, but deeper systemic changes ultimately will be required if we are to blunt the momentum toward increased stratification. The basic motivations and mechanisms that are the engine of inequality, including postsecondary selectivity, have been gathering renewed strength from economic change and political neglect for decades. Their power comes from the fact that they are a nested set of mutually reinforcing dynamics that can be overcome only by systemic changes in the way institutions are governed, financed, and held accountable.

A shift toward a more-equitable and productive postsecondary system would require a fundamental shift in the governing metrics for success in postsecondary education from quality measures that rely on differences in educational inputs—such as student test scores, rejection rates, and per-student spending—toward outcome measures such as the value added from learning, persistence, and graduation.

Ultimately, these are political questions. The public will decide. The public holds colleges—especially selective colleges—in the highest regard. But high costs and low graduation rates have already spurred demands for accountability. There is evidence that the long "honeymoon" between the public and the colleges may be coming to an end.[165] The federal bailout may hold off a reckoning, and a strong recovery may push it off even further, but even strong economic growth may not be enough to allow us to afford college for all without some major institutional changes.

The current fiscal trajectory in higher education is unsustainable. The change may come piecemeal or quickly after the stimulus money runs out. But we think the direction of the shift toward more postsecondary regulation based on outcomes is most likely: measures of completion need to be mindful that they do not result in unintended limitations on access for less-advantaged and non-traditional students. The current fragmentation and vertical hierarchy will need to be governed more and more as a state, regional, and national system in pursuit of collective efficiency and equity goals, and less as a free-for-all competition among individual institutions. Community colleges may well be the models for the next generation of reforms. The community colleges may provide the cheapest and most malleable institutional base for change. They are more amenable to change and can add programs at the least cost. For example, if we want three-year baccalaureates, it would be a lot easier to add a year of general education to two-year programs than to subtract a year at Harvard. It would be a lot easier to add student services, courses, and credits to associate degrees and certificates than it would be to subtract courses and credits in selective four-year institutions. Instead of continuing to struggle to move more students into selective colleges where the high-priced quality programs reside, we may be more successful moving money and quality programs to the community colleges where most of our students reside.

Appendix 3.1
Test Scores

ACT Composite Score	SAT V+M Equivalent Score
36	1560
35	1545
34	1490
33	1450
32	1400
31	1360
30	1345
29	1320
28	1300
27	1240
26	1230
25	1205
24	1190
23	1150
22	1100
21	1050
20	1000
19	940
18	880
17	830
16	770
15	700
14	650
13	600
12	530
11	490
10	450
1–9	400

Appendix 3.2

Racial Factors	
• Black	−56.2
• Hispanic	−47.9
• Hispanic, interacted with percent of enrolled students who are Hispanic (per percent enrolled)	0.41
Family Socioeconomic Factors	
• Low income	−13.3
• Parent maximum education:	
○ Dropout	−42.8
○ High school	−34.4
• Dropout sibling	−23.7
• Wealth (per $10,000)	10.2
• Occupational prestige (see Appendix 3.3 for example and discussion)	0.65
Neighborhood Factors	
• Percent of households headed by:	
○ High school dropout (per percent in neighborhood)	−1.28
○ Graduate (per percent in neighborhood)	1.33
• Living in:	
○ South	−12.0
○ Rural area	15.2
School Factors	
• Percent eligible for free and reduced price lunch (per percent in school)	−0.42
• Catholic	−22.7
• Public	−28.2

Peer Factors	
• Percent of enrolled students who are Asian (per percent)	1.10
• Having friends attending a four-year school.	38.9
Non-environmental Factors	
• Having children	−34.0
• Taking AP	81.3
• Taking AP test	69.1
• Taking honors courses	59.0
• Not being arrested	41.1
• Worked during school	−13.1

DISCUSSING REGRESSION ESTIMATES

The table below shows the regression estimates for the various factors observed to impact SAT scores. In the context of this discussion, they can be understood as the relative weights of advantage and disadvantage. The non-environment variables are also included for completeness.

EXPECTED SAT SCORES

These data in Appendix 3.2 are grouped by the various factors discussed earlier. For instance, the tables show that, controlling for all the other factors, being Hispanic is associated with a 48-point deficit on the SAT, compared to whites. On the other hand, Hispanic students benefit as the concentration of Hispanics increases.

Among family factors, low-income status is associated with a 13-point lower score, compared to high-income families, while lower parental education pulls SAT scores much lower, compared to having at least one parent with a graduate degree (–43 for dropout parent and –34 for high school graduate). On the other hand, increases in occupational prestige are associated with higher SAT scores.

Occupational prestige is a measure of how an occupation relates to class status, the likelihood of income growth, and the attainment of social power. The measure, and the idea of increases in prestige, is a little vague, so we have created a table of common occupations to show (relative to the top of the scale) the associated impact on SAT score.

Appendix 3.3
The Effects of Occupational Prestige on SAT-Equivalent Scores

Occupation	Status Index	SAT-Equivalent Score Effect
Physician	83	—
Professor	78	−3
Attorney	76	−5
Dentist	74	−6
Bank officer	72	−7
Engineer	71	−8
Architect	71	−8
Nurse	62	−14
Schoolteacher	60	−15
Accountant	57	−17
Computer programmer	51	−21
Bank teller	50	−21
Electrician	49	−22
Police officer	48	−23
Secretary	46	−24
Plumber	41	−27
Mechanic	37	−30
Bus driver	32	−33
Gas station attendant	22	−40
Garbage collector	17	−43
Janitor	16	−44
Laborer	9	−48

THE EFFECTS OF OCCUPATIONAL PRESTIGE ON SAT-EQUIVALENT SCORES

Socioeconomic status (SES) is the combination of parental education, family income, and occupational prestige. These equally weighted measures combine to create a robust predictor of lifetime earnings and status; this predictor is therefore a good measure as it shows how having the resources commonly thought of supports positive academic outcomes. We have broken SES into its component pieces to put each into the light of day, acknowledging that the interaction embodied in the composite measure might in fact be the better metric. And this is true of interpreting the "weights" in the table above. While it is possible to go through the above table line item by line item, it is better to think of the various factors working together to affect outcomes; thus, rather than go through the table, we have created three prototype individuals (discussed in the text) to illustrate the full range of interactions of the above factors.

Using the regression estimates in Appendix 3.2, the "average" student goes to a school where 24 percent of the population is eligible for free or reduced-price lunch (–10 points), a little more than 3 percent of the school population is Asian (+3), 36 percent is in the South (–12), 31 percent is rural (+15), 9 percent attend Catholic schools (–23), and 83 percent go to public schools (–28). These combined factors subtract roughly 40 points from the average[168] student's predicted SAT score.

This "average student" is 70 percent white (control group), 14 percent African American (–56 points relative to white), 4 percent Asian (0), and 11 percent Hispanic (–48). Race and ethnicity handicaps the average student by 13 points. Thirteen percent of these students have siblings who dropped out of school (–24 points), 4 percent have at least one child (–34), 36 percent took an AP course (+81), 15 percent took an AP test (+69), and 21 percent had at least one honors class (+59). Seventy percent of these "average" students have friends who plan to attend a four-year school (+41), 12 percent are working (–13), and 97 percent have not been arrested (+41). These factors contribute roughly 112 points to the predicted SAT score.

Eight percent of these students have parents who did not graduate from high school (–43 points), 22 percent have parents with high school diplomas (–34), 17 percent have parents with at least some college (no different from baccalaureate reference group), and 11 percent have parents with some type of graduate or professional degree (0), which decreases predicted SAT scores by 11 points.

The NELS "average" students' zip code areas have household heads with no high school diploma, 32 percent have diplomas, 24 percent have some college, 12 percent have a baccalaureate, and 7 percent have some type of graduate or professional degree. Only the concentration of non-diplomas (−28) and the concentration of graduate households (+15) appear to significantly impact predicted SAT scores.

NOTES

CHAPTER 1

1. Anthony P. Carnevale and Stephen J. Rose, "Socioeconomic Status, Race/Ethnicity, and Selective College Admissions," in *America's Untapped Resource: Low-Income Students in Higher Education,* Richard D. Kahlenberg, ed. (New York: Century Foundation Press, 2004), 106, Table 3.1.

2. Walter Benn Michaels, *The Trouble with Diversity: How We Learned to Love Identity and Ignore Inequality* (New York: Henry Holt, 2007), 108.

3. Lawrence H. Summers, "Higher Education and the American Dream," Address to the American Council on Education, February 29, 2004, http://ksghome.harvard.edu/~lsummer/speeches/2004/ace.html; and Mary Beth Marklein, "Harvard to Boost Aid to Needy Students," *USA Today*, March 1, 2004, 7D.

4. The lectures were later published in book form. See William G. Bowen, Martin A. Kurzweil, and Eugene M. Tobin, *Equity and Excellence in American Higher Education* (Charlottesville, Va.: University of Virginia Press, 2005).

5. See Richard D. Kahlenberg, "Class Action: Why Education Needs Quotas for Poor Kids," *Washington Monthly*, May 2005, 53–54.

6. Anthony Marx, Commencement Address, Amherst College, May 23, 2004, http://www.amherst.edu/commencement/2004/address.html; and Sara Rimer, "Elite Colleges Open New Door to Low-Income Youths," *New York Times*, May 27, 2007, 1.

7. Bowen, Kurzweil, and Tobin, *Equity and Excellence in American Higher Education*; Jerome Karabel, *The Chosen: The Hidden History of Exclusion at Harvard, Yale and Princeton* (New York: Houghton Mifflin Harcourt, 2005); Daniel Golden, *The Price of Admission: How America's Ruling Class Buys Its Way into Elite Colleges—and Who Gets Left Outside the Gates* (New York: Crown, 2006); Michaels, *The Trouble with Diversity*; *College Access: Opportunity or Privilege?* Michael S. McPherson and Morton Owen Schapiro, eds. (New York: College Board, 2006); Peter Schmidt, *Color and Money: How Rich White Kids Are Winning the War Over College Affirmative Action* (New York: Palgrave Macmillan, 2007); Peter Sacks, *Tearing Down the Gates: Confronting the Class Divide in American Education* (Berkeley: University of California Press, 2007); and William Bowen, Matthew Chingos, and Michael McPherson, *Crossing the Finish Line: Completing College at America's Public Universities* (Princeton, N.J.: Princeton University Press, 2009).

8. See Chapter 2, 17.

9. "The Politics of Inclusion: Higher Education at a Crossroads—Financial Aid Initiatives," Updated Conference Materials, University of North Carolina at Chapel Hill, September 2007.

10. See Chapter 2, 70.

11. See Karin Fischer, "Top Colleges Admit Fewer Low-Income Students: Pell Grant Data Show a Drop since 2004," *Chronicle of Higher Education*, May 2, 2008; Richard D. Kahlenberg, "Still Forgotten: Low-Income Students at Selective Colleges," *Minding the Campus*, May 8, 2008; and "Pell Grants: The Cornerstone of African-American Higher Education," special report, *Journal of Blacks in Higher Education* (Autumn 2009): 72, 74, 76.

12. Laura Fitzpatrick, "Colleges Face a Financial-Aid Crunch," *Time*, March 26, 2009.

13. Bowen, Chingos, and McPherson, *Crossing the Finish Line*, 24.

14. Ibid., 21, figure 2.2, and 30, figure 2.6.

15. See Kavita Kumar, "Anti-affirmative Action Initiative Tries for 2010 Ballot in Missouri," *St. Louis Post-Dispatch*, December 22, 2008; and Peter Schmidt, "Arizona to Vote on a Ban on Affirmative-Action Preferences in 2010," Color and Money Blog, July 8, 2009, http://colorandmoney.blogspot.com/2009/07/arizona-to-vote-on-ban-on-affirmative.html.

16. For a more complete discussion of the implications of PICS on the future of affirmative action in higher education, see Richard D. Kahlenberg, "Affirmative Action in Higher Education after the Seattle and Louisville

Decisions: Reexamining the Socioeconomic Alternative," Paper Prepared for the American Association for the Advancement of Science and National Action Council for Minorities in Engineering, January 15, 2008, http://php. aaas.org/programs/centers/capacity/documents/Kahlenburg_Post-Seattle. doc.

17. 127 S.Ct. 2738, at 2825 (Breyer, J., dissenting).

18. 539 U.S. 306, at 342.

19. 539 U.S. 306, at 343.

20. 539 U.S. 306, at 380.

21. 539 U.S. 306, at 394.

22. 127 S.Ct. 2738, at 2793.

23. 127 S.Ct. 2738, 2760.

24. 127 S.Ct. 2738, at 2827.

25. See Peter Schmidt, "Plaintiffs in Lawsuit Against U. of Texas Take Their Case to the Fifth Circuit," Color and Money Blog, September 22, 2009, http://colorandmoney.blogspot.com/2009/09/plaintiffs-in-lawsuit-against-u-of.html; Edward Blum, "Deciphering *Grutter* v. *Bollinger,*" American Enterprise Institute, September 27, 2009; and George LaNoue and Kenneth L. Marcus, "'Serious Consideration' of Race-Neutral Alternatives in Higher Education," *Catholic University Law Review* 57 (2008): 991–1044.

26. Michael A. Fletcher and Jon Cohen, "Far Fewer Consider Racism Big Problem," *Washington Post*, January 29, 2009, A6. See also *New York Times*/CBS News Poll, October 25–29, 2008, http://www.nytimes.com/ packages/pdf/politics/oct08e.trn.pdf (finding that the proportion of people who say blacks "have an equal chance of getting ahead" rose to 64 percent, up from 46 percent in 1997).

27. Jabari Asim, *What Obama Means* (New York: William Morrow, 2009), 210–11.

28. See Richard D. Kahlenberg, "What's Next for Affirmative Action?" *Atlantic Monthly Online*, November 6, 2008; Richard D. Kahlenberg, "Obama's RFK Moment: How He Could Win Over White Working-Class Voters," *Slate*, February 4, 2008; Richard D. Kahlenberg, "Barack Obama and Affirmative Action," *Inside Higher Education*, May 12, 2008; and Richard D. Kahlenberg, "Understanding King's View of Affirmative Action," *TPM Café*, March 31, 2009.

29. See, for example, Jennifer Delahunty Britz, "To All the Girls I've Rejected," *New York Times*, March 23, 2006, A25 ("the standards of admission to today's most selective colleges are stiffer for women than men"); and Nancy Gibbs, "Affirmative Action for Boys," *Time*, April 3, 2008.

30. See Chapter 2, 17.

31. See Chapter 2, 23.

32. See Chapter 2, 33–40.

33. See Chapter 2, 34.

34. See Chapter 2, 49–50.

35. See Chapter 2, 54–55.

36. See Chapter 2, 23.

37. See Chapter 2, 23.

38. Shirly Ort and LynnWilliford, "Carolina Covenant 2009 Program Update," University of North Carolina Powerpoint presentation, p.12, http://www.unc.edu/carolinacovenant/files/2009/Carolina%20Covenant%202009%20Update%20FINAL032509.pdf.

39. Ort and Williford, "Carolina Covenant 2009 Program Update," 17.

40. See Chapter 2, 61, Table 2.7.

41. See Chapter 2, 62, Table 2.8.

42. See Chapter 2, 67.

43. See Chapter 2, 22.

44. "Pell Grants," *Journal of Blacks in Higher Education,* 74.

45. Education Trust, *Opportunity Adrift: Our Flagship Universities Are Straying from Their Public Mission* (Washington, D.C.: Education Trust, January 2010), 20, Figure 19.

46. See Richard D. Kahlenberg, "The Colleges, the Poor, and the SATs," *Washington Post,* September 29, 1999.

47. Schmidt, *Color and Money,* 157.

48. Chapter 3, 132–33.

49. Chapter 3, 112.

50. Chapter 3, 112.

51. Chapter 3, 79.

52. Chapter 3, 151, Table 3.5; Bowen, Chingos, and McPherson, *Crossing the Finish Line,* 193–96.

53. Chapter 3, 106, 126.

54. Thomas Dye, *Who's Running America?* (Upper Saddle River, N.J.: Prentice Hall, 2002), 148.

55. Chapter 3, 173–74

56. Chapter 3, 174.

57. Sara Rimer, "Elite Colleges Open New Door to Low-Income Youths," *New York Times,* May 27, 2007, 1.

58. Chapter 3, 170, Table 3.7.

59. Carnevale and Rose, "Socioeconomic Status, Race/Ethnicity, and Selective College Admissions," 149.

60. Bowen, Chingos, and McPherson, *Crossing the Finish Line*, 102–6.

61. Joshua S. Wyner, John M. Bridgeland, and John J. DiIulio, Jr., *Achievement Trap: How America Is Failing Millions of High-Achieving Students from Lower-Income Families* (Lansdowne, Va.: Jack Kent Cooke Foundation and Civic Enterprises, 2007), 10 and 41–42, Appendix B.

62. Chapter 3, 157.

63. *University of California Regents* v. *Bakke*, 438 U.S. 265, at 310 (1978) ("Hence, the purpose of helping certain groups whom the faculty of the Davis Medical School perceived as victims of 'societal discrimination' does not justify a classification that imposes disadvantages upon persons like respondent, who bear no responsibility for whatever harm the beneficiaries of the special admissions program are thought to have suffered. To hold otherwise would be to convert a remedy heretofore reserved for violations of legal rights into a privilege that all institutions throughout the Nation could grant at their pleasure to whatever groups are perceived as victims of societal discrimination. That is a step we have never approved."); and *Grutter* v. *Bollinger*, 539 U.S. 306, at 323–24 (2003).

64. Dalton Conley, *Being Black, Living in the Red: Race, Wealth, and Social Policy in America* (Berkeley, Calif.: University of California Press, 1999) 2, 22, 58, 62, 64, and 134–35. See also Henry Louis Gates, Jr., "Forty Acres and a Gap in Wealth," *New York Times*, November 18, 2007.

65. Edward N. Wolff, *Top Heavy: The Increasing Inequality of Wealth in America and What Can Be Done About It* (New York: New Press, 2002), 20, table 4.1.

66. Conley, *Being Black*, 22, 57, and 133.

67. Chapter 3, 165, 170.

68. Peter Schmidt, *Color and Money*, 158. See also Peter Schmidt, "ETS Accused of Squelching New Approach on Racial Bias," *Chronicle of Higher Education*, November 10, 2006; and Chapter 3, 165.

69. See, for example, Richard D. Kahlenberg, *All Together Now: Creating Middle-Class Schools through Public School Choice* (Washington, D.C.: Brookings Institution Press, 2001), 32–34 (citing numerous studies).

70. See Darly Fears, "Disparity Marks Black Ethnic Groups, Report Says," *Washington Post*, March 9, 2003, A7.

71.   Dalton Conley, "The Cost of Slavery," *New York Times*, February 15, 2003; Conley, *Being Black, Living in the Red*, 22, 51.

72.   Carnevale and Rose, "Socioeconomic Status, Race/Ethnicity, and Selective College Admissions."

73.   Bowen, Kurzweil, and Tobin, *Equity and Excellence in American Higher Education*.

74.   Thomas J. Espenshade and Alexandria Walton, *No Longer Separate, Not Yet Equal* (Princeton, N.J.: Princeton University Press, 2009), 92, Table 3.5.

75.   Chapter 3, 170, Table 3.7.

76.   See Richard D. Kahlenberg, "The Next Step in Affirmative Action: Class-based Systems Can Skirt Court and Ballot Defeats—And Do a Better Job of Addressing Socioeconomic Diversity," *Washington Monthly* Online, September 30, 2009 (on correlation between bans on affirmative action and high rankings in the *Washington Monthly*'s social mobility index); and Richard D. Kahlenberg, "Still Forgotten: Low Income Students at Selective Colleges," *Minding the Campus,* May 8, 2008 (on the correlation between bans on affirmative action and high Pell grant percentages at colleges and universities).

CHAPTER 2

1. See "New Institutional Initiative to Improve Access for Low to Moderate Income Students," University of North Carolina at Chapel Hill, http://www.unc.edu/inclusion/initiatives.pdf.

2. Shirley Ort and Lynn Williford, "Carolina Covenant 2009 Program Update," University of North Carolina at Chapel Hill, http://www.unc.edu/carolinacovenant/files/2009/CarolinaCovenant2009updateFINAL032509.pdf.

3. All quotes in this chapter are from interviews conducted by the author, unless otherwise noted.

4. University of North Carolina Office of Institutional Research and Asssessment.

5. Letter from Chancellor James Moeser to UNC president Erskine Bowles, March 27, 2007.

6. "Low-Income Families Need More Information About Student Aid, Report Says," *The Sallie Mae Educator* 2, no. 12 (Spring 2002). See also

two reports, *Access Denied: Restoring the Nation's Commitment to Equal Educational Opportunity* (Washington, D.C.: Advisory Committee on Student Financial Assistance, February 2001) and *Empty Promises: The Myth of College Access in America* (Washington, D.C.: Advisory Committee on Student Financial Assistance, June 2002). See also publications of the College Is Possible Campaign of the American Council on Education, http://collegeispossible.org.

7. According to Ort, the argument for a work component is that it promotes student engagement with campus life, which has been shown elsewhere to correlate strongly with persistence and graduation rates. On-campus work has a higher correlation than off-campus jobs. Ort says that the tipping point—where working becomes counter-productive—previously was thought to be 19 hours, but that recent research suggests that it is in the range of 10 to 12 hours or so. For a recent discussion of this issue, see Jacqueline E. King, *Working Their Way through College: Student Employment and Its Impact on the College Experience* (Washington, D.C.: American Council on Education, 2006).

8. The reason for limiting the program to dependent students, Ort explained, is to avoid creating an incentive for students to wait until they are twenty-four years of age and then "come to college and go free regardless of family income." The program, she added, is "intended for the historically disadvantaged."

9. George Leef, "Do We Really Need the 'Carolina Covenant'?" Carolina Beat No. 707, John Locke Foundation, October 20, 2003.

10. See "New Institutional Initiative to Improve Access for Low to Moderate Income Students."

CHAPTER 3

1. A. P. Carnevale, N. Smith, and J. Strohl, *Ready or Not: The Jobless Recovery and Education Requirements (2008–2018)* (Washington, D.C.: Center on Education and the Workforce, Georgetown University, 2010), http://www.cew.geaorgetown.edu.

2. Current Population Survey, U.S. Census Bureau and the Bureau of Labor Statistics, Washington, D.C., http://www.census.gov/cps/.

3. R. Haskins and I. Sawhill, *Creating an Opportunity Society* (Washington, D.C.: Brookings Institution, 2009).

4. M. Handel, "Skills Mismatch in the Labor Market," *Annual Review of Sociology* 29, no. 135 (2003): 135–65; P. E. Barton, "How Many College Graduates Does the U.S. Labor Force Really Need?" *Change* 40, no. 1 (2008): 16–21; L. Mishel, "Future Jobs Much Like Current Jobs," Economic Policy Institute, December 19, 2007, http://www.epi.org/economic_snapshots/entry/webfeatures_snapshots_20071219/; W. N. Grubb and M. Lazerson, *The Education Gospel: The Economic Power of Schooling* (Cambridge, Mass.: Harvard University Press, 2007).

5. D. Yankelovich, "How Higher Education Is Breaking the Social Contract and What to Do About It," *Forum Futures 2009* (Cambridge, Mass.: Forum for the Future of Higher Education, 2009); J. Immerwahr, J. Johnson, P. Gasbarra, A. Ott, and J. Rochkind, *Squeeze Play 2009: The Public's View on College Costs Today* (San Jose, Calif.: Public Agenda for the National Center for Public Policy and Higher Education, 2009).

6. E. Beller and M. Hout, "Intergenerational Social Mobility: The United States in Comparative Perspective," *The Future of Children* 16, no. 2 (2006): 19–36; D. Leonhardt, "As Wealthy Fill Top Colleges, Concerns Grow Over Fairness," *New York Times,* April 22, 2004, A1; D. Viadero, "Rags to Riches in U.S. Largely a Myth, Scholars Write," *Education Week* 25, no. 41 (2006): 8.

7. Cheryl Russell, *Racial and Ethnic Diversity: Asians, Blacks, Hispanics, Native Americans, and Whites,* 5th ed. (Ithaca, N.Y.: New Strategist Publications, 2006).

8. J. Bound, M. Lovenheim, and S. Turner, "Why Have College Completion Rates Declined? An Analysis of Changing Student Preparation and Collegiate Resources," Working Paper, 2009, http://www.human.cornell.edu/che/PAM/People/upload/CR_Website.pdf.

9. T. J. Kane, P. R. Orszag, and D. L. Gunter, *State Fiscal Constraints and Higher Education Spending,* Urban-Brookings Tax Policy Center Discussion Paper 11 (Washington, D.C.: Brookings Institution, 2003).

10. Bound, Lovenheim, and Turner, "Why Have College Completion Rates Declined?"

11. D. Card and T. Lemieux, *Can Falling Supply Explain the Rising Return to College for Younger Men? A Cohort-Based Analysis,* NBER Working Paper 7655 (Cambridge, Mass.: National Bureau of Economic Research, 2000); P. Carneiro, J. Heckman, and E. Vytlacil, *Estimating the Rate of Return to Education When It Varies among Individuals,* Yale Department of Economics, Labor and Population Workshop, May 2001,

http://www.econ.yale.edu/seminars/labor/lap03/vytlacil-030418.pdf; C. Goldin and L. F. Katz, *The Race between Education and Technology* (Cambridge, Mass.: Belknap Press of Harvard University Press, 2009).

12. The increasing returns to college are among the more prominent reasons, but not the only reason for income dispersion (see T. Piketty and E. Saez, "Income Inequality in the United States, 1913–1998," *Quarterly Journal of Economics* 118, no. 1 (2003): 1–39; G. S. Becker and K. M. Murphy, "The Upside of Income Inequality," *The American* 4, no. 4 (2007): 20–23; and Goldin and Katz, *The Race between Education and Technology)*. Institutional factors like the composition of industry and occupations, declining bargaining power of unions, the declining value of the minimum wage, lower marginal tax rates for high earners and changing pay for performance are among the other prominent factors (see Mishel, "Future Jobs Much Like Current Jobs").

13. C. M. Hoxby, "The Changing Selectivity of American Colleges," *Journal of Economic Perspectives* 23, no. 4 (2009).

14. Robert J. Barro and Jong-Wha Lee, "Barro-Lee Dataset for a Panel of 138 Countries," Center for International Development, Harvard University, 2000, http://www.cid.harvard.edu/ciddata/ciddata.html.

15. C. Adelman, *The Spaces between Numbers: Getting International Data on Higher Education Straight* (Washington, D.C.: Institute for Higher Education Policy, 2009).

16. Carnevale, Smith, and Strohl, *Ready or Not*.

17. L. F. Katz, G. W. Loveman, and D. G. Blanchflower, "A Comparison of Changes in the Structure of Wages in Four OECD Countries," in *Differences and Changes in Wage Structures*, R. B. Freeman and L. F. Katz, eds. (Chicago: University of Chicago Press, 1995), 25–66; Card and Lemieux, *Can Falling Supply Explain the Rising Return to College for Younger Men?*; D. Acemoglu, "Cross-Country Inequality Trends," *The Economic Journal* 113 (2003): F121–F149; Goldin and Katz, *The Race between Education and Technology*; Carnevale, Smith, and Strohl, *Ready or Not*.

18. Barron's Educational Series, College Division, *2009 Barron's Profiles of American Colleges* (Hauppauge, N.Y.: Barron's Educational Series, 2009).

19. The idea that the postsecondary system in its entirety is driven by the logic of selectivity is often dismissed with the observation that only the top 20 percent to 30 percent of top colleges can choose their student

bodies. But even at the bottom of the four-year pecking order, colleges reject about 10 percent of their applicants. And the full range of colleges is organized by selectivity if we array them by student characteristics and spending levels. In addition, in a system where capacity no longer meets demand, selectivity becomes triaged in access and completion, especially in community colleges and the bottom tiers of selectivity and especially among nontraditional students (G. C. Winston, "Subsidies, Hierarchy and Peers: The Awkward Economics of Higher Education," *Journal of Economic Perspectives* 13, no. 1 (1999): 13–36).

20. Winston, "Subsidies, Hierarchy and Peers."

21. A. P. Carnevale and M. Desrochers, *Standards for What? The Economic Roots of K–16 Reform* (Princeton, N.J.: Educational Testing Service, 2003).

22. Carnevale, Smith, and Strohl, *Ready or Not.*

23. Alfred Marshall, cited in *Memorials of Alfred Marshall,* A. C. Pigou, ed. (London: Macmillan, 1925), 102.

24. Ibid., 105.

25. Neither Alfred Marshall nor T. H. Marshall was speaking in a vacuum. They were offering liberalism or democratic capitalism as an alternative to the collectivist ideas of their time. In Alfred Marshall's day the enemy was the feudal system as well as the budding new forms of utopian collectivism: the utopians, communists, socialists, and anarchists. In T. H. Marshall's time, just after World War II, democratic capitalism had survived fascism but faced new challenges from communism and socialism. Since the fall of the Berlin Wall in 1989, the historic argument has come full circle back to the debate between liberal capitalism and a revived onslaught from feudal theocracy and a new hybrid in the form of Chinese-style authoritarian capitalism.

26. T. H. Marshall, *Class, Citizenship, and Social Development* (Chicago: University of Chicago Press, 1964), 79.

27. T. H. Marshall, "Citizenship and Social Class," in *Contemporary Political Philosophy: An Anthology,* R. E. Goodin and P. Pettit, eds. (Oxford: Blackwell, 1997), 311.

28. U.S. Department of Education, *A Test of Leadership: Charting the Future of U.S. Higher Education: A Report of the Commission Appointed by Secretary of Education Margaret Spellings: Pre-Publication Report, September 2006* (Washington, D.C.: U.S. Department of Education, 2006).

29.   For a thorough review of these strategies, see *Economic Inequality and Higher Education: Access, Persistence, and Success*, S. Dickert-Conlin and R. Rubenstein, eds. (New York: Russell Sage Foundation, 2007).

30.   J. Oakes, M. Selvin, L. A. Karoly, and G. Guiton, *Educational Matchmaking: Academic and Vocational Tracking in Comprehensive High Schools* (Santa Monica, Calif.: RAND, 1992).

31.   *A Nation at Risk* (Washington, D.C.: National Commission on Excellence in Education, 1983).

32.   National Leadership Council for Liberal Education and America's Promise, *College Learning for the New Global Century* (Washington, D.C.: Association of American Colleges and Universities, 2007).

33.   J. P. Merisotis, "Proposal for A National Strategy to Rapidly Train Workers for High-Demand, High-Wage Jobs through Accelerated Postsecondary Degree and Credential Programs," Lumina Foundation, December 3, 2009, http://www.luminafoundation.org/newsroom/newsstories/topics/back_to_school_and_back_to_work.html, retrieved December 15, 2009.

34.   D. de Vise, "The Best and Brightest Take a Detour," *Washington Post*, November 30, 2009.

35.   J. V. Wellman, D. M. Desrochers, and C. M. Lenihan, *The Growing Imbalance: Recent Trends in U.S. Postsecondary Education Finance* (Washington, D.C.: Delta Cost Project, 2008).

36.   Winston, "Subsidies, Hierarchy and Peers"; Kane, Orszag, and Gunter, *State Fiscal Constraints and Higher Education Spending*.

37.   M. Rothschild and L. J. White, "The University in the Marketplace: Some Insights and Some Puzzles," in *Studies of Supply and Demand in Higher Education*, M. Rothschild and C. T. Clotfelter, eds. (Chicago: University of Chicago Press, 1993); M. Rothschild and L. J. White, "The Analytics of the Pricing of Higher Education and Other Services in Which the Customers Are Inputs," *Journal of Political Economy* 103, no. 3 (1995): 573–86; Hoxby, "The Changing Selectivity of American Colleges"; M. N. Bastedo, "Convergent Institutional Logics in Public Higher Education: State Policymakers and Governing Board Activism," *Review of Higher Education* 32, no. 2 (2009), 209–34; M. N. Bastedo, "Cascading in Higher Education: Examining Longitudinal Evidence on Institutional Stratification," Seminar Presentation at the University of Illinois, February 13, 2009.

38.   R. Rothstein, "College Performance Predictions and the SAT," *Journal of Econometrics* 121, nos. 1–2 (2004): 297–317.

39. P. Schmidt, *Color and Money: How Rich White Kids Are Winning the War over College Affirmative Action* (New York: Palgrave Macmillan, 2007).

40. F. Hirsch, *Social Limits to Growth: A Twentieth Century Fund Study* (Cambridge, Mass.: Harvard University Press, 1977).

41. J. V. Wellman, "The Higher Education Funding Disconnect: Spending More, Getting Less," *Change: The Magazine of Higher Learning* 40, no. 6 (2009): 18–25.

42. Ibid.

43. For an excellent review and commentary, see P. N. Courant, M. McPherson, and A. M. Resch, "The Public Role in Higher Education," *National Tax Journal* 59, no. 2 (2006): 291–318.

44. E. Brody and J. Cordes, "Tax Treatment of Nonprofit Organizations: A Two-Edged Sword?" in *Nonprofits and Government: Collaboration and Conflict*, E. Boris and C. Steuerle, eds. (Washington, D.C.: Center on Nonprofits and Philanthrophy, Urban Institute Press, 2006).

45. A. B. Krueger and M. Lindahl, "Education for Growth: Why and for Whom?" *Journal of Economic Literature* 39, no. 4 (2001): 1101–36.

46. Goldin and Katz, *The Race between Education and Technology*.

47. T. J. Kane and C. E. Rouse, "Labor Market Returns to Two- and Four-Year College," *American Economic Review* 85, no. 3 (1995): 600–14; D. Card, "Estimating the Return to Schooling: Progress on Some Persistent Econometric Problems," *Econometrica* 69, no. 5 (2001): 1127–60.

48. Carneiro, Heckman, and Vytlacil, *Estimating the Rate of Return to Education When It Varies among Individuals*.

49. S. Peltzman, "The Effect of Government Subsidies-in-Kind on Private Expenditures: The Case of Higher Education," *Journal of Political Economy* 81, no. 5 (1973): 1049–91; Courant, McPherson, and Resch, "The Public Role in Higher Education."

50. A. P. Carnevale, J. S. Berke, D. C. Morgan, and R. D.White, "The Texas School Finance Case: A Wrong in Search of a Remedy," *Journal of Law and Education* 1, no. 4 (1972): 659–86.

51. Hoxby, "The Changing Selectivity of American Colleges,"13.

52. C. E. Rouse and T. J. Kane, "The Community College: Educating Students at the Margin between College and Work," *Journal of Economic Perspectives* 13, no. 1 (1999): 63–84.

53. H. Holzer and D. Neumark, "Assessing Affirmative Action," *Journal of Economic Literature* 38, no. 3 (2000): 483–568; H. Holzer and

D. Neumark, "Affirmative Action: What Do We Know?" *Journal of Policy Analysis and Management* 25, no. 2 (2006): 463–90.

54.   P. M. Callan, *California Higher Education, the Master Plan, and the Erosion of College Opportunity*, National Center Report #09-1 (San Jose, Calif.: National Center for Public Policy and Higher Education, 2009).

55.   T. R. Bailey, D. Jenkins, and T. Leinbach, *Is Student Success Labeled Institutional Failure? Student Goals and Graduation Rates in the Accountability Debate at Community Colleges*, CCRC Working Paper 1 (New York: Community College Research Center, Teachers College, Columbia University, 2006); E. M. Bradburn, D. G. Hurst, and S. Peng, *Community College Transfer Rates to 4-Year Institutions Using Alternative Definitions of Transfer*, NCES Report 2001-197 (Washington, D.C.: National Center for Education Statistics, Institute of Education Sciences, U.S. Department of Education, 2001); J. V. Wellman, *State Policy and Community College-Baccalaureate Transfer*, National Center Report #02-6 (San Jose, Calif.: National Center for Public Policy and Higher Education, 2002); Bound, Lovenheim, and Turner, "Why Have College Completion Rates Declined?"

56.   K. Stange, "Ability Sorting and the Importance of College Quality to Student Achievement: Evidence from Community Colleges," Working Paper, University of Michigan, Ann Arbor, 2009.

57.   P. M. Callan, "Stewards of Opportunity: America's Public Community Colleges," *Daedalus* 126, no. 4 (1997): 95–112.

58.   National Leadership Council for Liberal Education and America's Promise, *College Learning for the New Global Century*, 8; S. G. Brint, M. Riddle, L. Turk-Bicakci, and C. Levy, "From the Liberal Arts to the Practical Arts in American Colleges and Universities: Organizational Analysis and the Curricular Change," *The Journal of Higher Education* 76, no. 2 (2005): 151–80.

59.   D. de Vise, "In-State Students Admissions Obstacle: Their Home Address," *Washington Post*, November 14, 2009.

60.   T. G. Mortenson, "Pell Grant Enrollment at State Flagship Universities 1992–93 and 2001–02," *Postsecondary Education Opportunity* 140 (2004); D. Gerald and K. Haycock, *Engines of Inequality: Diminishing Equity in the Nation's Premier Public Universities* (Washington, D.C.: Education Trust, 2006).

61.   W. F. Massy, *Honoring the Trust: Quality and Cost Containment in Higher Education* (San Francisco: Jossey-Bass, 2003); D. Bok, *Our Underachieving Colleges: A Candid Look at How Much Students Learn*

and Why They Should Be Learning More (Princeton: Princeton University Press, 2005); R. Zemsky, *Making Reform Work: The Case for Transforming American Higher Education* (New Brunswick, N.J.: Rutgers University Press, 2009).

62. Massy, *Honoring the Trust: Quality and Cost Containment in Higher Education;* Bok, *Our Underachieving Colleges;* Zemsky, *Making Reform Work.*

63. R. H. Frank, *Higher Education: The Ultimate Winner-Take-All Market?* CHERI Working Paper no. 2, Cornell University ILR School, 1999, http://digitalcommons.ilr.cornell.edu/cheri/2, retrieved November 11, 2009.

64. S. B. Dale and A. B. Krueger, *Estimating the Payoff to Attending a More Selective College: An Application of Selection on Observables and Unobservables,* NBER Working Paper 7322 (Cambridge, Mass.: National Bureau of Economic Research, 1999).

65. Bound, Lovenheim, and Turner, "Why Have College Completion Rates Declined?"

66. T. J. Espenshade and A. W. Radford, *No Longer Separate, Not Yet Equal* (Princeton, N.J.: Princeton University Press, 2009).

67. Barron's Educational Series, *2009 Barron's Profiles of American Colleges.*

68. Card and Lemieux, *Can Falling Supply Explain the Rising Return to College for Younger Men?;* Goldin and Katz, *The Race between Education and Technology.*

69. Bound, Lovenheim, and Turner, "Why Have College Completion Rates Declined?"

70. A. Light and W. Strayer, "Determinants of College Completion: School Quality or Student Ability?" *Journal of Human Resources* 35, no. 2 (2000): 299–332.

71. Kane, Orszag, and Gunter, *State Fiscal Constraints and Higher Education Spending.*

72. Wellman, Desrochers, and Lenihan, *The Growing Imbalance.*

73. J. Bound, M. Lovenheim, and S. Turner, *Understanding the Decrease in College Completion Rates and the Increased Time to the Baccalaureate Degree,* Population Studies Center Research Report no. 07-626 (Ann Arbor, Mich.: Population Studies Center, University of Michigan, Insitute for Social Research, 2007).

74. Bound, Lovenheim, and Turner, "Why Have College Completion Rates Declined?"

75. Winston, "Subsidies, Hierarchy and Peers"; G. C. Winston, *Economic Stratification and Hierarchy in U.S. Colleges and Universities,* Discussion Paper 58 (Williamstown, Mass.: Williams Project on the Economics of Higher Education, Williams College, 2000), http://www.williams.edu/wpehe/dps/dp-58.pdf.

76. C. M. Hoxby, *How the Changing Market Structure of U.S. Higher Education Explains College Tuition,* NBER Working Paper 6323 (Cambridge, Mass.: National Bureau of Economic Research, 1997); Hoxby, "The Changing Selectivity of American Colleges"; C. M. Hoxby and B. T. Long, *Explaining Rising Income and Wage Inequality among the College Educated,* NBER Working Paper 6873 (Cambridge, Mass.: National Bureau of Economic Research, 1999).

77. Rothschild and White, "The University in the Marketplace"; Rothschild and White, "The Analytics of the Pricing of Higher Education and Other Services in Which the Customers Are Inputs"; C. T. Clotfelter, *Buying the Best: Cost Escalation in Elite Higher Education,* NBER Monograph (Princeton, N.J.: Princeton University Press, 1996); D. A. Black and J. A. Smith, *How Robust Is the Evidence on the Effects of College Quality? Evidence from Matching,* CIBC Human Capital and Productivity Project Working Paper no. 20033 (London, Ontario: University of Western Ontario, CIBC Human Capital and Productivity Project, 2006).

78. Hoxby, "The Changing Selectivity of American Colleges."

79. Dale and Krueger, *Estimating the Payoff to Attending a More Selective College;* Winston, *Economic Stratification and Hierarchy in U.S. Colleges and Universities.*

80. R. D. Kahlenberg, *All Together Now: Creating Middle-Class Schools through Public School Choice* (Washington, D.C.: Brookings Institution Press, 2001); P. A. Noguera, "Racial Politics and the Elusive Quest for Excellence and Equity in Education," *Education and Urban Society* 34, no. 1 (2001): 18–41; J. Oakes, "What Educational Indicators? The Case for Assessing the School Context," *Educational Evaluation and Policy Analysis* 11, no. 2 (1989): 181–99; E. A. Hanushek, J. F. Kain, J. M. Markman, and S. G. Rivkin, *Does Peer Ability Affect Student Achievement?* NBER Working Paper 8502 (Cambridge, Mass.: National Bureau of Economic Research, 2001); C. M. Hoxby, *Peer Effects in the Classroom: Learning From Gender and Race Variation,* NBER Working Paper 7867 (Cambridge, Mass.: National Bureau of Economic Research, 2000).

81. Dale and Krueger, *Estimating the Payoff to Attending a More Selective College.*

82. Y. Shavit, R. Arum, A. Gamoran, and G. Menahem, eds., *Stratification in Higher Education: A Comparative Study* (Stanford, Calif.: Stanford University Press, 2007).

83. A. Gamoran, "American Schooling and Educational Inequality: A Forecast for the 21st Century," *Sociology of Education* 74, Extra Issue (2001): 135–53; Winston, *Economic Stratification and Hierarchy in U.S. Colleges and Universities.*

84. Haskins and Sawhill, *Creating an Opportunity Society.*

85. Carnevale, Smith, and Strohl, *The College Economy.*

86. M. N. Bastedo and O. Jaquette, "Institutional Stratification and the Fit Hypothesis: Longitudinal Shifts in Student Access," Paper presented at the Annual Meeting of the Association for the Study of Higher Education, Vancouver, British Columbia, November 4–7, 2009.

87. D. T. Ellwood and T. J. Kane, "Who Is Getting a College Education? Family Background and the Growing Gap in Enrollment," Paper Written for the Macalester Forum on Higher Education Conference, Macalester College, St. Paul, Minnesota, June 1999; B. K. Fitzgerald and J. A. Delaney, "Educational Opportunity in America," in *Condition of Access: Higher Education for Lower Income Students,* D. Heller, ed. (Westport, Conn.: American Council on Education, Praeger Series on Higher Education, 2003); Mortenson, "Pell Grant Enrollment at State Flagship Universities 1992–93 and 2001–02"; A. P. Carnevale and S. J. Rose, "Socioeconomic Status, Race/Ethnicity, and Selective College Admissions," in *America's Untapped Resource: Low-Income Students in Higher Education,* R. D. Kahlenberg, ed. (New York: Century Foundation, 2004); G. C. Winston and C. B. Hill, *Access to the Most Selective Private Colleges by High-Ability, Low-Income Students: Are They Out There?* Discussion Paper 69 (Williamstown, Mass.: Williams Project on the Economics of Higher Education, Williams College, 2005), http://www.williams.edu/wpehe/dps/dp-58.pdf, retrieved November 11, 2009; Gerald and Haycock, *Engines of Inequality;* W. G. Bowen, M. A. Kurzweil, and E. M. Tobin, *Equity and Excellence in American Higher Education* (Charlottesville, Va.: University of Virginia Press, 2006); W. G. Bowen, M. M. Chingos, and M. S. McPherson, *Crossing the Finish Line: Completing College at America's Public Universities* (Princeton, N.J.: Princeton University Press, 2009).

88.   J. Bound and S. Turner, "Cohort Crowding: How Resources Affect Collegiate Attainment," NBER Working Paper 12424, *Journal of Public Economics* 91, nos. 5–6 (2007): 877–99.

89.   K. J. Dougherty, *The Contradictory College: The Conflicting Origins, Impacts, and Futures of the Community College* (Albany, N.Y.: State University of New York Press, 1994).

90.   S. G. Brint and J. Karabel, *The Diverted Dream: Community Colleges and the Promise of Educational Opportunity in America, 1900–1985* (Oxford: Oxford University Press, 1989); Shavit, Arum, Gamoran, and Menaham, eds., *Stratification in Higher Education.*

91.   Bowen, Chingos, and McPherson, *Crossing the Finish Line.*

92.   Hoxby and Long, *Explaining Rising Income and Wage Inequality among the College Educated;* M. McPherson and M. Schapiro, *Reinforcing Stratification in American Higher Education: Some Disturbing Trends* (Stanford, Calif.: National Center for Postsecondary Improvement, Stanford University, 1999); Winston, "Subsidies, Hierarchy and Peers"; Winston, *Economic Stratification and Hierarchy in U.S. Colleges and Universities;* Winston and Hill, *Access to the Most Selective Private Colleges by High-Ability, Low-Income Students;* Hoxby, "The Changing Selectivity of American Colleges."

93.   A. Finder, "Yale Plans to Increase Spending from Its Endowment, with Financial Aid to Benefit," *New York Times,* January 8, 2008, A12.

94.   Barron's Educational Series, College Division, *2009 Barron's Profiles of American Colleges.*

95.   Bailey, Jenkins, and Leinbach, *Is Student Success Labeled Institutional Failure?*

96.   Bound, Lovenheim, and Turner, "Why Have College Completion Rates Declined?"

97.   G. C. Winston, *The Positional Arms Race in Higher Education,* Discussion Paper 54 (Williamstown, Mass.: Williams Project on the Economics of Higher Education, Willliams College, 2000), http://www.williams.edu/wpehe/dps/dp-54.pdf, retrieved November 11, 2009. See also Gamoran, "American Schooling and Educational Inequality."

98.   Carnevale and Rose, "Socioeconomic Status, Race/Ethnicity, and Selective College Admissions."

99.   Bound and Turner, "Cohort Crowding."

100. F. M. Hess, M. Schneider, K. Carey, and A. P. Kelly, *Diplomas and Dropouts: Which Colleges Actually Graduate Their Students (and Which Don't)* (Washington, D.C.: American Enterprise Institute, 2009).

101. Bailey, Jenkins, and Leinbach, *Is Student Success Labeled Institutional Failure?*

102. Ibid.

103. M. Hout, "Educational Progress for African Americans and Latinos in the United States from the 1950s to the 1990s: The Interaction of Ancestry and Class," Paper presented at the U.S./U.K. Ethnic Minority and Social Mobility Conference, Bath, England, 1999; Gamoran, "American Schooling and Educational Inequality"; D. Karen, "Changes in Access to Higher Education in the United States, 1980–1992," *Sociology of Education* 75, no. 3 (2002): 191–210; Carnevale and Rose, "Socioeconomic Status, Race/Ethnicity, and Selective College Admissions"; Leonhardt, "As Wealthy Fill Top Colleges, Concerns Grow Over Fairness"; A. W. Astin and L. Oseguera, "The Declining 'equity' of American Higher Education," *Review of Higher Education* 27, no. 3 (2004): 321–41; J. Selingo and J. Brainard, "The Rich-Poor Gap Widens for Colleges and Students," *Chronicle of Higher Education* 52 (April 7, 2006): A1; K. Fischer, "Mass. Merit Aid Fails to Increase Access," *Chronicle of Higher Education* 52, no. 29 (March 24, 2006): A29; K. Fischer, "Elite Colleges Lag in Serving the Needy," *Chronicle of Higher Education* 52, no. 36 (May 12, 2006): A1; L. Smith, "Four Decades of Survey Data on American Freshmen Reveal Widening Socioeconomic Gap," *Chronicle of Higher Education: Today's News* (April 9, 2007); P. Sacks, "How Colleges Perpetuate Inequality," *Chronicle Review, Chronicle of Higher Education* 53, no. 19 (January 12, 2007): B9; P. Sacks, *Tearing Down the Gates: Confronting the Class Divide in American Education* (Berkeley: University of California Press, 2007); J. Roksa, E. Grodsky, R. Arum, and A. Gamoran, "Changes in Higher Education and Social Stratification in the United States," in *Stratification In Higher Education: A Comparative Study,* Y. Shavit, R. Arum, A. Gamoran, and G. Menahem, eds. (Stanford, Calif.: Stanford University Press, 2007); Bastedo and Jaquette, "Institutional Stratification and the Fit Hypothesis."

104. Hoxby and Long, *Explaining Rising Income and Wage Inequality among the College Educated*; Dale and Krueger, *Estimating the Payoff to Attending a More Selective College.*

105. Winston, "Subsidies, Hierarchy and Peers."

106. Ibid.

107. National Center for Education Statistics, National Educational Longitudinal Study of 1988, Updated for 2000 (NELS 2000).

108. A. P. Carnevale, *Graduate Education in 2020: What Does the Future Hold?* (Washington, D.C.: Council of Graduate Schools, 2009).

109. R. H. Wiebe, *Self-Rule: A Cultural History of American Democracy* (New York: University of Chicago, 1996).

110. Oakes, Selvin, Karoly, and Guiton, *Educational Matchmaking.*

111. D. Riesman, *Constraint and Variety in American Education* (Lincoln: University of Nebraska Press, 1956), 35.

112. Fitzgerald and Delaney, "Educational Opportunity in America."

113. Carnevale and Rose, "Socioeconomic Status, Race/Ethnicity, and Selective College Admissions."

114. Winston and Hill, *Access to the Most Selective Private Colleges by High-Ability, Low-Income Students.*

115. Gerald and Haycock, *Engines of Inequality.*

116. Ibid., 3.

117. Bowen, Chingos, and McPherson, *Crossing the Finish Line.*

118. Ibid., 99.

119. Ibid., 99.

120. D. Hawkins, *The State of College Admissions* (Alexandria, Va.: National Association for College Admission Counseling, 2003).

121. P. M. McDonough, *The School-to-College Transition: Challenges and Prospects* (Washington, D.C.: American Council on Education, Center for Policy Analysis, 2004).

122. K. Haycock, "Closing the Achievement Gap," *Educational Leadership* 58, no. 6 (2001): 6–11; K. Haycock, "The Opportunity Gap: No Matter How You Look at It, Low-Income and Minority Students Get Fewer Good Teachers," *Thinking K–16* 8, no. 1 (2004): 36–42.

123. P. Gandara and D. Bial, *Paving the Way to Higher Education: K–12 Intervention Programs for Underrepresented Youth* (Washington, D.C.: National Postsecondary Education Cooperative, 2001); S. B. Plank and W. A. Jordan, "Effects of Information, Guidance, and Actions on Postsecondary Destinations: A Study of Talent Loss," *American Educational Research Journal* 38, no. 4 (2001): 947–79.

124. P. M. McDonough, *Choosing Colleges: How Social Class and Schools Structure Opportunity* (Albany: State University of New York Press, 1997); P. M. McDonough, A. L. Antonio, M. Walpole, and L. X. Perez, "College Rankings: Democratized Knowledge for

Whom?" *Research in Higher Education* 39, no. 5 (1998): 513–37; Bound, Lovenheim, and Turner, "Why Have College Completion Rates Declined?"

125. C. Adelman, "The Relationship between Urbanicity and Educational Outcomes," in *Increasing Access to College: Extending Possibilities for All Students,* W. G. Tierney and L. S. Hagedorn, eds. (Albany: State University of New York Press, 2002), 15–34.

126. J. S. Wyner, J. M. Bridgeland, and J. J. DiIulio, *Achievement Trap: How America Is Failing Millions of High-Achieving Students from Lower-Income Families* (Landsdowne, Va.: Jack Kent Cooke Foundation, 2007).

127. L. J. Horn, *Confronting the Odds: Students at Risk and the Pipeline to Higher Education,* NCES Report 98-094 (Washington, D.C.: U.S. Department of Education, Office of Educational Research and Improvement, 1997); P. Gandara, "Meeting Common Goals: Linking K–12 and College Interventions," in *Increasing Access to College: Extending Possibilities for All Students*, W. G. Tierney and L. S. Hagedorn, eds. (Albany: State University of New York Press, 2002), 81–104.

128. McDonough, *Choosing Colleges.*

129. Gandara and Bial, *Paving the Way to Higher Education;* M. W. Kirst and A. Venezia, eds., *From High School to College: Improving Opportunities for Success in Postsecondary Education* (San Francisco: Jossey-Bass, 2004); L. Perna and W. S. Swail, "Pre-College Outreach and Early Intervention Programs," in *Conditions of Access: Higher Education for Lower-Income Students,* D. Heller, ed. (Westport, Conn.: Praeger, 2002); L. Perna, "The Key to College Access: Rigorous Academic Preparation," in *Preparing for College: Nine Elements of Effective Outreach*, W. G. Tierney, Z. B. Corwin, and J. E. Colyar, eds. (Albany: State University of New York Press, 2005), 13–28.

130. E. N. Wolff, *Recent Trends in Household Wealth In the United States: Rising Debt and the Middle-Class Squeeze,* Working Paper 502 (Annandale-On-Hudson, N.Y.: Levy Economics Institute of Bard College, 2007).

131. P. Schmidt, "ETS Accused of Squelching New Approach on Racial Bias," *Chronicle of Higher Education* 53, no. 10 (2006): A1.

132. These lagged effects on social improvements are quite common. White ethnics made more money, especially in the blue collar economy, long before their children and grandchildren moved on to elite colleges. Much the same story holds for improvements in mathematics and general educational attainment for white females.

133. Missing composite scores were imputed using the composite NELS test scores.

134. We strongly argue that choice is constrained or endogenous.

135. Family income is grouped in the NELS data. Quartiles were assigned to individuals where quartile boundaries fell in a group by using a logistic regression, built on the full sample, to predict income among those limited individuals who did not clearly land in one quartile or another.

136. This measure was inspired by Hoxby's study of the Texas Classroom Longitudinal Study that demonstrated Hispanic students benefit when they are a small part of the school or when the school is largely Hispanic. See Hoxby, *Peer Effects in the Classroom.*

137. We attempted to included a fully specified interactive regression but found the sample size to not support this.

138. Knowing that poverty and likelihood of arrest are highly correlated makes it difficult to assert that poverty describes an environmental variable without also asserting that likelihood of arrest (as a proxy for criminal behavior) is endogenously determined.

139. The values in parentheses are the SAT equivalent point disadvantage associated with each statistically significant characteristic. Variables, like African American, are simply the regression coefficient compared to the omitted or reference group. Values, like those associated with not having saved for college are relative to the highest observed value in the data. In all cases, the disadvantaged compared to the advantaged status are presented.

140. Maximum regional advantage observed in the geo-coded census data.

141. Many of the factors discussed in this section have negative weights attached; thus by not doing the particular activity (for example, having kids) the highly advantaged students avoid a point handicap. For this reason, many of the discussed factors are not attached with a parenthetic point value as seen in the other sections.

142. Research conducted by Westat with the ELS data demonstrates that about 70 percent of schools offer AP courses.

143. *Trends in Political Values and Core Attitudes, 1987–2007: Political Landscape More Favorable to Democrats* (Washington, D.C.: Pew Research Center for the People and the Press, 2007).

144. J. D. Skrentny, *The Ironies of Affirmative Action: Politics, Culture, and Justice in America* (Chicago: University of Chicago Press, 1996); J.

D. Skrentny, *The Minority Rights Revolution* (Cambridge: Belknap Press, 2004).

145. E. Grodsky and D. Kalogrides, "The Declining Significance of Race in College Admissions Decisions," *American Journal of Education* 115, no. 1 (2008): 1–33.

146. A. B. Krueger, J. Rothstein, and S. Turner, "Race, Income, and College in 25 Years: Evaluating Justice O'Connor's Conjecture," *American Law and Economics Review* 8, no. 2 (2006): 282–311.

147. Schmidt, *Color and Money.*

148. Grodsky and Kalogrides, "The Declining Significance of Race in College Admissions Decisions."

149. B. T. Long and E. Riley, "Financial Aid: A Broken Bridge to College Access?" *Harvard Educational Review* 77, no. 1 (2007): 39–63.

150. C. Avery and C. M. Hoxby, "Do and Should Financial Aid Packages Affect Students' College Choices?" in *College Choices: The Economics of Where to Go, When to Go, and How to Pay for It*, C. M. Hoxby, ed. (Chicago: University of Chicago Press, 2004), 239–99; D. M. Linsenmeier, H. S. Rosen, and C. E. Rouse, "Financial Aid Packages and College Enrollment Decisions: An Econometric Case Study," *Review of Economics and Statistics* 52, no. 28 (2006): 126–45; T. R. Stinebrickner and R. Stinebrickner, *The Effect of Credit Constraints on the College Drop-Out Decision: A Direct Approach Using a New Panel Study*, NBER Working Paper 13340 (Cambridge, Mass.: National Bureau of Economic Research, 2007).

151. J. A. Karikari and H. Dezhbakhsh, *Are Selective Private and Public Colleges Affordable?* Social Science Research Network, July 2009, http://papers.ssrn.com/sol3/papers.cfm?abstract_id=1440281, retrieved December 15, 2009; S. M. Tilghman, "Expanding Equal Opportunity: The Princeton Experiencce with Financial Aid," *Harvard Educational Review* 77, no. 4 (2007): 435–41.

152. Espenshade and Radford, *No Longer Separate, Not Yet Equal.*

153. Ibid.

154. Ibid.

155. P. R. Bennett and A. Lutz, "How African American Is the Net Black Advantage? Differences in College Attendance between Whites, Immigrant and Native Blacks," *Sociology of Education* 82 (2009): 70–100.

156. T. J. Espenshade, C. Y. Chung, and J. L. Walling, "Admission Preferences at Elite Universities," *Social Science Quarterly* 85, no. 5 (2004): 1422–46; Espenshade and Radford, *No Longer Separate, Not Yet Equal.*

157. Espenshade and Radford, *No Longer Separate, Not Yet Equal.*

158. M. McPherson and M. Schapiro, *Reinforcing Stratification in American Higher Education: Some Disturbing Trends* (Stanford, Calif.: National Center for Postsecondary Improvement, Stanford University, 1999).

159. Ellwood and Kane, "Who Is Getting a College Education?"; Fitzgerald and Delaney, "Educational Opportunity in America"; Mortenson, "Pell Grant Enrollment at State Flagship Universities 1992–93 and 2001–02"; Carnevale and Rose, "Socioeconomic Status, Race/Ethnicity, and Selective College Admissions"; Winston and Hill, *Access to the Most Selective Private Colleges by High-Ability, Low-Income Students;* Gerald and Haycock, *Engines of Inequality;* Bowen, Kurzweil, and Tobin, *Equity and Excellence in American Higher Education;* Bowen, Chingos, and McPherson, *Crossing the Finish Line.*

160. Carnevale and Rose, "Socioeconomic Status, Race/Ethnicity, and Selective College Admissions"; Espenshade and Radford, *No Longer Separate, Not Yet Equal.*

161. C. B. Hill and G. C. Winston, "How Scarce Are High-Ability, Low-Income Students?" in *College Access: Opportunity Or Privilege?* M. S. Mcpherson and M. O. Schapiro, eds. (New York: College Board, 2006), 75–102; Espenshade and Radford, *No Longer Separate, Not Yet Equal.*

162. Kirst and Venezia, eds., *From High School to College;* M. Martinez and S. Klopott, *Improving College Access for Minority, Low-Income, and First Generation Students* (Boston: Pathways to College Network, 2003).

163. D. E. Heller, "The Effects of Tuition and State Financial Aid on Public College Enrollment," *Review of Higher Education* 23, no. 1 (1999): 65–90; Fitzgerald and Delaney, "Educational Opportunity in America"; M. B. Paulsen and E. St. John, "Social Class and College Costs: Examining the Financial Nexus between College Choice and Persistence," *Journal of Higher Education* 73, no. 2 (2002): 189–236; McDonough, *The School-to-College Transition.*

164. Rothstein, "College Performance Predictions and the SAT."

165. P. Callan and J. Immerwahr, "What Colleges Must Do to Keep the Public's Good Will," *Chronicle of Higher Education* 54, no. 18 (2008): A56.

INDEX

Note: page numbers followed by *f* and *t* refer to figures and tables, respectively.

About the Contributors

Anthony P. Carnevale currently serves as research professor and director of the Georgetown University Center on Education and the Workforce, and is an internationally recognized authority on education, training, and employment. Between 1996 and 2006, he served as vice president for assessments, equity, and careers at Educational Testing Service. He was appointed by President Bill Clinton as a commissioner to the White House Advisory Committee on Technology and Adult Education and Training, and reappointed by President George Bush. He was appointed by President Clinton to chair the National Commission for Employment Policy, while serving as vice president and director of human resource studies at the Committee for Economic Development. Earlier, he had been president of the Institute for Workplace Learning, an applied research center affiliated with the American Society for Training and Development. He has held senior staff positions in the U.S. Senate and House of Representatives and the U.S. Department of Health, Education, and Welfare. He was director of legislative affairs for the American Federation of State, County, and Municipal Employees (AFSCME). He coauthored the principal affidavit in *Rodriguez v. San Antonio*, a landmark U.S. Supreme Court action to remedy unequal tax burdens and educational benefits; this landmark case sparked significant educational equity reforms in a majority of states. Among his many publications, he is the coauthor (with Stephen J. Rose) of "Socioeconomic Status, Race/Ethnicity, and Selective College Admissions," which appeared in *America's Untapped Resource: Low-Income Students in Higher Education,* edited by Richard D. Kahlenberg (The Century Foundation Press, 2004).

Edward B. Fiske, formerly the education editor of the *New York Times*, has written extensively on school reform in the United States and other countries. He is the author of *The Fiske Guide to Colleges* (Sourcebooks), an annual publication that is a standard part of college admissions literature, as well as numerous other books on undergraduate admissions. *Smart Schools, Smart Kids* (Simon and Schuster, 1991), a study of systemic school reform in the United States. In 1993–94 he lived in Cambodia, where he worked on a UNICEF cluster school project and authored a study of the situation of Khmer women in education for the Asian Development Bank entitled *Using Both Hands*. He has traveled on assignment to more than sixty countries and written about international education for the Academy for Educational Development, UNESCO, the World Bank, the Aga Khan Foundation, the Asia Society and other organizations. He is coauthor with Helen F. Ladd of *When Schools Compete: A Cautionary Tale*, a study of New Zealand's experiment with market-based school reform (Brookings, 2000), and *Elusive Equity: Education Reform in Post-Apartheid South Africa,* based on research carried out while living in Cape Town in 2002 (Brookings, 2004). He also is co-editor with Ladd of the *Handbook of Research in Education Policy and Research* (Routledge, 2008). A resident of Durham, North Carolina, he serves as chair of the advisory board of the North Carolina Center for International Understanding, a public service project of the University of North Carolina. He is also vice-chair of College for Every Student, a nonprofit organization that promotes access to higher education for disadvantaged students in urban and rural areas. He was founding member of the board of the Central Park School for Children, a public charter school in Durham.

Richard D. Kahlenberg is a senior fellow at The Century Foundation and writes about education, equal opportunity, and civil rights. Previously, he was a fellow at the Center for National Policy, a visiting associate professor of constitutional law at George Washington University, and a legislative assistant to Senator Charles S. Robb (D-VA). He also is a nonresident senior fellow at Education Sector. He is the author of four books: *Tough Liberal: Albert Shanker and the Battles Over Schools, Unions, Race, and Democracy* (Columbia University Press, 2007); *All Together Now: Creating Middle-Class Schools through Public School Choice* (Brookings Institution Press, 2001); *The Remedy: Class, Race, and Affirmative Action* (Basic Books, 1996); and *Broken Contract: A Memoir of Harvard Law School* (Hill & Wang/Farrar, Straus & Giroux, 1992). In addition, he is the editor of five Century Foundation books: *Improving on No Child Left Behind: Getting Education Reform Back on Track* (2008); *America's Untapped Resource: Low-Income Students in Higher Education* (2004); *Public School Choice vs. Private School Vouchers* (2003); *Divided We Fail: Coming Together Through Public School Choice: The Report of The Century Foundation Task Force on the Common School* (2002); and *A Notion at Risk: Preserving Public Education as an Engine for Social Mobility* (2000).

Jeff Strohl is director of research at the Georgetown University Center on Education and the Workforce, where he continues his long involvement in the analysis of education and labor market outcomes and policy, leading the center's research investigating the supply and demand of education and how education enhances career opportunities for today's workforce. His research also focuses on how to quantify skills and how better to understand competencies given the evolving nature of the U.S. workplace. Before moving to the center, he was a senior analyst and project director at Westat, Inc., where he was involved in program evaluation and analysis of education outcomes. He helped design and direct several projects that investigated socioeconomic diversity in American education and sought to affect postsecondary admissions policies, and also helped design a model that predicts occupational risks to offshoring as a function of workplace competencies. While at Westat, he used economic modeling to evaluate the Federal GEAR UP program, the Federal Youth Opportunity Grant Initiative, the Pre-Elementary Education Longitudinal Study, the Office of Federal Contract Compliance programs, and the Occupational Safety and Health Administration's National and Local Emphasis programs.